To John:
A fellow "Breakfast
Clubber." Best Wishes
always, Enjoy the
read.
John J Schulz

WHAT READERS ARE SAYING ABOUT THIS BOOK...

I'm not a pilot, but now I've flown the "Hun," I've lived in the Bien Hoa hootches and flown as a warrior in places I still can't find on a map. John Schulz writes that well. His poetry and devotion to his wife and the pilots with whom he flew make for a compelling read. It's a fun read, an informative read and a fast read. He makes it real, very real....
– John Bennitt, former wire service senior executive

o-0-o

This is not just another "I did this" book; it is a reflection of the core values of the officers who flew the missions assigned with dedication and élan, oblivious to the risk of life and limb. As a long-time fighter pilot who flew frequently in Vietnam with incredibly talented then-Captain John Schulz, who shared his combat flying poetry with us as it was written, I strongly endorse this wonderful book! The "songs" from his (still vibrant for me) "distant cockpit" come from his heart and show the passion and intellect of "fighter jocks" that are often buried in the macho ethic we showed the outside world. Read and savor this tome of personal and song-filled reflection.
– Gary Tompkins, Col., USAF (ret.) fellow Diceman, "Misty 4"

o-0-o

Fasten your seat belts, as you prepare to take one of the most exciting rides of your life...from the varsity athletic fields and stadiums of Montana, to supersonic, high altitude and high-G dives and turns. In training and in combat and around the world... to the shadows, set-backs and losses common in everyone's life, John Schulz has masterfully painted in prose and poetry an honest portrait of an American fighter pilot. As you read his book, you'll be proud, you'll be concerned, you'll be reflective, and when done, you'll be better and you'll find it easier to set your sights on what you may want to do in your life! Enjoy...and grow! – Gregory S. Martin, General, USAF (Ret), former Commander US Forces Europe

o-0-o

Once I started it I could not put it down.; A fascinating and personally compelling story; It is also unique in that the story is told in both prose and poetry. I think it took an act of courage to tell a story of this subject matter by combining both these styles. A job well done!
–Dave Baker, former USAF Captain, U.MT AFROTC grad. Denver, CO

Someone once described flying as hours of boredom punctuated by moments of stark terror. Flying the F-100 Super Sabre, as John Schulz so aptly describes, was never boring and it gave you more than your fair share of moments of stark terror. John has done a great job of conveying the feel and emotion of being a fighter pilot. His poetry adds a very special and unique component to his well-told story.
– Bill Gorton, Maj. Gen., USAF (Ret.),
President, Super Sabre Society

o-0-o

In the epic movie Braveheart, *the "warrior-poet" was defined as "baddest of the bad." To me, a warrior poet has the heart of a lion, the guts of a pirate and a soft, creative passion. John Schulz is such a man. At the National War College I knew him as a guy with a 40-pound brain who could discuss just about anything... then I learned of his creative skills. Much later I learned he and I shared a common bond: fighter pilot. He has written an amazing book. If you've never been there, this will take you there, down a path only a warrior poet could lead you. You'll enjoy a great read!* – Hal M. Hornburg, General, USAF (Ret.)

o-0-o

Even if you know nothing of flying, you will love this book. John Schulz's amazing gift of poetry adds so much. I was a "Hun Driver" during the Cold War, and sat many boring hours "On Alert" with a nuclear weapon strapped to the belly of an F100 waiting for the Red Phone to ring. We expected it to be a one way trip if we ever had to go. I have often wondered what it would have been like to be flying missions with the enemy firing back at me. Through John Schulz's vivid descriptions, I now know. I could almost feel the "G" forces as he maneuvered his F100. His amazing gift of poetry adds a very enjoyable dimension to his stories. Songs from a Distant Cockpit *is like a movie that you like to watch over and over. Enjoy!*
– Ray Kelley, Capt. 67th Tactical fighter Squadron,
Kadena AB, Okinawa 1957-1960.

o-0-o

This book is a remarkable. It arrived yesterday; I've not yet read it all, but every time I open it and begin reading, I am hooked. And the poems, oh, the poems! I can't wait to read it from cover to cover. I'm buying another copy; another lucky person will receive it as a Christmas gift this year! –Margaret O'Rourke, Senior Executive, Treasury Dept.

"Songs" is a remarkable account, a wonderful read...the excitement of flying Air Force jets as in Vietnam, punctuated by the horror of war and made memorable by the lessons learned. And then, John Schulz's poetry gives us a poignant contrast to the risk, the challenge, the adrenalin that all pilots feel when they "scramble" and push the envelope to get the job done, and the sadness when they remember all those who "bought the farm." You can't miss his letters to lovely Linda. They are a treasure. Songs From a Distant Cockpit *follows in the footsteps of Antoine de Saint-Exupery, one of my favorite authors, the famed French aviator who flew the mails across to North Africa and wrote with such insight in his 1932 trilogy,* Airman's Odyssey. *This book, too, makes you feel what it was like. It will stand the test of time.*

– Chris Komisarjevsky,
Army helicopter pilot, RVN, and CEO (ret.)

o-0-o

"Songs" is a fantastic book. I couldn't put it down! – Susan Groark, San Francisco; (Australian Surgical Team, Bien Hoa City, '68)

o-0-o

There were times when I was reading it that I could smell the rubber on my oxygen mask. Now that is writing!!!! – Michael McShane, Charlottesville, VA, former Vice Pres., TRW (flew B-52s over RVN '67-8)

o-0-o

John Schulz is a man of great heart and soul, and I grew to admire and respect him when we were National War College students (1986-7) because he was the "real deal"–extremely bright, thoughtful, focused and articulate. These qualities combined with his openness and cheerful nature, made him both approachable and a valued team player. His book reflects his strength of character, his extraordinary leadership, and his Vietnam experience as a combat pilot, a war hero and patriot. His book is inspirational. Indeed, it is one-of-a-kind, filled with many lessons learned that we would be wise to follow.

– Frank Libutti, Lt. Gen, USMC (Ret.)

o-0-o

Songs From a Distant Cockpit *gives readers a unique, fascinating picture of the challenges and dangers fighter pilots experienced in Vietnam. The love poems to Linda match the beauty and intensity of poems created to paint vivid pictures of combat flying. The book is utterly engaging. And the man writes beautifully, as you'd expect from a pro.* –Dr. Norman Moyes, Boston Univ. Journalism Prof., (ret.)

For those of us fortunate enough to have earned the Navy Wings of Gold or the Silver Air Force Wings, this is a compelling piece of work. From the Flight Training experience, Instructor duty on through to flying at the "Tip Of The Spear" in combat to support our troops on the ground. The memories Schulz brings home! This book is small in size but huge in content. He has "nailed" Vietnam from an Attack/Fighter Pilot's perspective, be Air Force, Marines or Navy. BRAVO ZULU!
(Well done, Zoomie!).   –"WARACE," USN.

o-0-o

I really enjoyed this wonderful book. I was struck by the author's insightful nexus between our (shared) football experience and our warrior aptitude. It never occurred to me but he is so right on. Playing QB at our level was the perfect proving ground for doing what we did as well as we did it in combat. We were able to "just do it!!" Watching game films, counting 5 Utah linemen get up off of you, we could smile knowing that we completed the pass. Truly the work of a fellow warrior.
–Tim Grattan, U.MT QB and former Major, US Army, Whitefish, MT

o-0-o

In 2007, when I learned of John Schulz's fascinating life in the Air Force and his civilian experiences and achievements, I recruited him as an Assistant to the Editor (me) of The Intake, *the Journal of the Super Sabre Society . We both flew "Huns" at Bien Hoa during 1967-8, and he brings memories of that time to life. I learned early on that John was a gifted poet, as well as an insightful reporter and keen analyst of military and international geopolitics. But he has the heart of a poet, and his book is a jewel! It combines the best of his poetry and his "no holds barred" analysis of war in general with the inner feelings of a warrior in the midst of an unpopular war. The combination is powerful! A synergistic and authoritative read unlike any other I know of.*
– R. Medley Gatewood, Lt. Col. USAF (Ret.),
Editor & Publisher, The Intake

o-0-o

As a former AF flight instructor I enjoyed Schulz's description of USAF flight school and what it was like to be a flight instructor for new AF officers. But his book has something for everyone: AF flying; close-air support flying in Viet Nam; wives of fighter pilots both during Viet Nam and currently; non-combat flying; Vietnam correspondents, and a broad selection of poetry on each of these topics. The whole thing is great, even if you do not like poetry.   –K. Webster, Newbury Park, CA

I have ordered this book of prose and poetry for each of my kids. It is the best book I have read about our F-100 flying in Viet Nam. Hopefully, they will enjoy it as much as I did. The author's experiences mirror mine.... – Don Schmenk, former F-100 pilot, VN; Ottowa, OH

o-0-o

One of the favorite aviation writers of pilots everywhere is Antoine de Saint-Exupéry. "Saint X" was able to write prose that bordered on poetry without the reader ever realizing that he had slipped unknowingly into this world of near-poetry. John Schulz has the opposite and probably more difficult task of writing poetry that slips, almost unnoticed into image-laden prose. I admit to being apprehensive when I opened the book to find poetry and prose mixed as if there were really no distinction. That might be OK for academics, but what about all of us he-man fighter pilots? We are not generally known for our ability to grasp the nuances of emotion-sustained verse.

My advice is: read on–you'll get the message and you'll find it all the more meaningful. I at first resented the intrusions of poetic phrases into a page-turning narrative; -later I found myself looking forward to the intrusions and even cheating a bit to find the next one.

John Schulz has written a book that will be discussed in our aviators' world for many years. It is a tale of courage, loneliness and sacrifice, and some of the stories are not for the faint of heart. For those of us who read it having long ago been in those "distant cockpits," it expresses many thoughts that may have been buried too deep to have ever otherwise found expression. For all who never had the privilege of flying from those distant cockpits, this is how it was!"
–Al deGroote, Author, *A Flight Through Life*, "Dice" Asst. Ops., RVN '67

o-0-o

My tour ended in the "Dice" Squadron ended not long after JJ arrived. It was not hard to tell he was special, one who believed that the way home was to hunt and kill all the enemy. I no longer hunt either. He has captured the emotions I felt so well that perhaps the title should be "Tears From a Distant Cockpit" His book is a masterpiece, conveying all the emotions of combat flying. I am proud of my time in the Hun and prouder to call him my friend. He is truly a warrior poet, He continues to amaze me..– Frank Loftus, 90th TAC fighter squadron mate at Bien Hoa

o-0-o

I've read "Songs" twice now, and really like it. Schulz did a great job!. I'll probably want more copies to give as gifts to special friends His

war stories were most exciting. Some of the poems must have sparked a special interest in me .... (Note: He sent the author a poem he wrote.)
–Alan Jones, NWC '86, Col. USA, (Ret.), combat helicopter pilot, RVN

o-0-o

I just finished reading "Songs." It was enthralling! Schulz certainly a has a way of putting a pilot's emotions into poetry – bitter, sweet, humorous – happy and sad. I very much enjoyed the read, as will anyone, male or female, aviator or civilian, the minute they pick it up.
–Col. Bob Swedenburg, USAF Ret.

o-0-o

Never in my life have I had the pleasure of reading a book with a story that I was even remotely connected to. Reading your wonderful book, I found myself smiling, teary eyed and wondering if there was something that I didn't do, but could have done more, while I was a Crew Chief. I'm glad he mentioned his wife; I have always said it takes a special woman to contend with the rigors of a military career. Many kudos for an exceptional inside view to the workings of a Fighter Pilot. With warmest regards and a whole lot of respect,
– Bob Ingram, former Senior Master Sergeant, USAF Aircraft Crew Chief, "Dice" Squadron, RVN 1967-8

o-0-o

What a great read!! So many memories brought back to life. Schulz tells a story that I was living with him as I read. Once I got started, I couldn't put it down. This is not just another "been there done that book." We were classmates, but I got to know John Schulz a lot better, and got the idea he enjoyed his time in the Hun..
–John Heslin (Classmate, 64-E, Williams AFB, '63-4), Temecula, CA

o-0-o

I read "Songs" in 3 sittings–until 5 a.m.–because it was hard to put down. I came away with a greater appreciation for the pilots flying the F-100 Super Sabre and other high performance aircraft....I often felt I was right there in the cockpit flying those missions Although I am not a strong lover of poetry, as I read along through the book I started to enjoy them even more. Former U.MT classmate John Schulz, certainly had a gift then as he does now to "put it all down on paper."
–Col. "Butch" Hendricks, U.MT Class of '62; USA (Ret.)
Jacksonville, FL (Two RVN "tours," one with "Dice" air cover (1967)

After reading John Schulz's book, I confess to honest admiration and a wee bit of jealousy. It is remarkably powerful and yet concise and precise about the subject at hand: the warrior and his weapons. (The jealousy comes from his ability to recite poetry we all learned at Loyola High 50 years ago.) The personal touch of dedication to his wife and his commitment to perfecting his craft is honest, sincere and genuine. It is remarkable that his "talents" were honed to skill levels that allowed him fly, to think and to write... and to "reach out and touch the face of God," yet also succeed in eluding death in the HUN!
– Henry Buescher, Loyola '58 Valedictorian and later, US Navy pilot

o-0-o

I flew fighters for 28 years, including combat tours in Korea in F84's and Viet Nam in F100's and this is the best description of what a fighter pilot is and what makes him that way that I have ever read. I am not an avid reader, but enjoy reading books about flying and this is absolutely great!   –Ira T. Holt

o-0-o

After reading "Songs from a Distant Cockpit," I realized John Schulz managed to do what all writers hope for, but few achieve. There are passages about his combat engagements that are so far past "what, where, when and how" that the reader is compelled to feel he is in the cockpit with him. I read–a lot–and very rarely have such a feeling. His wanted to convey combat and fighter flying in a vivid, gripping manner, and he did just that. He wrote of his motivations and related actions during the attacks so clearly, with such depth of feeling and understanding that his reader is obliged to be completely there with him, even if he has never been on an aircraft in his life. This is not a story of our shared time in Vietnam, but of a man facing the end of his world..and a minute or so later, doing it again.
–James Nelson CMSgt USAF (Ret.)
Line Chief, 90th TAC Ftr Squadron, Pair-O-Dice, (1967)

o-0-o

As a former AF flight instructor I enjoyed Schulz's description of USAF flight school and what it was like to be a flight instructor for new AF officers. But his book has something for everyone: AF flying; close-air support flying in Viet Nam; wives of fighter pilots both during Viet Nam and currently; non-combat flying; Vietnam correspondents, and a broad selection of poetry on each of these topics. The whole thing is great, even if you do not like poetry.   –K. Webster, Newbury Park, CA

Songs From a Distant Cockpit *is* <u>*Magnificent!*</u> *Like others have said, I could not put it down once I started it. Ferling's book, The Ascent of George Washington, was set aside once I began reading "Songs." –* Charles "Rich" Armstrong, Col., USMC (Ret.), NWC '86

o-0-o

I am not qualified as a literary critic but I know "good" when I see it and I know "excellent" when I read it. "Songs" is a breathtaking story about what it was like to fly combat in Vietnam. I thoroughly enjoyed it and will recommend it to all. The poetry gave the book a special added dimension, enriching a truly excellent story that is also a bit of a biography about a man who is interesting, well-traveled, sophisticated, thoughtful and informed...perhaps even wise...and most certainly brave! Bravo! – Jim Oestreich, Carlsbad, CA (Loyola HS Classmate, '58.)

o-0-o

Readers, beware! When you start reading Songs From A Distant Cockpit it is virtually impossible to put aside. My initial reaction, was: "fascinating." Now, after finishing the chapter on flight training, my reaction is "amazing." In scrupulous and engrossing detail Schulz describes the demands of AF Pilot Training, That rigor stands in stark contrast to the training for my Uncle Richard, a Spitfire pilot during the Battle of Britain. He had only 8 hours in a "Spit" before his first combat sortie.

The balance of humor and serious thoughts in "Songs" is so well done that any officer, but particularly fighter pilots and senior NCOs, need to experience Schulz's words. This book should be on the USAF "professional reading list," and the Navy and Marine professional reading lists could equally benefit from this book. In the language a Marine rifleman would use, amid the humor, there is a lot of serious "stuff"* that today's pilots need to reflect on. With all their missions in Iraq and Afghanistan they never experienced some of the sophisticated air defenses Vietnam air crews encountered so much of the time.
– Dr. Paul Godwin, National War College
Professor of China and East Asian Studies (Ret.)

* (I know officers say "stuff." As Marines in Korea we were more vulgar.)

SONGS FROM A DISTANT COCKPIT

SECOND EDITION

by

JOHN J. SCHULZ

Library of Congress Control Number:

2013920581
N. Charleston, SC

TABLE OF CONTENTS

ACKNOWLEDGEMENTS

The author would like to thank John Bennitt, Orest Pelech, Norm Moyes and Melinda Kelash for their sharp-eyed copyediting, and Gary Tompkins and Medley Gatewood, a masterful magazine editor, for their editorial and technical suggestions; both were Hun drivers at Bien Hoa during the period reported in this book. *Collectively, any mistakes in this book are, of course, their fault.*

Send comments or book orders to
jjschulz@bu.edu

SONGS FROM A DISTANT COCKPIT

By

John J. Schulz

FOR LINDA, WHO LOVED,
NEVER VOICED HER FEARS BUT GOT NO MEDALS

FOR THOSE ONCE AMONG US WHO MADE ONE LANDING TOO FEW
AND FOR THE MANY WHO KNOW
AND EVERY DAY, STILL LIVE WITH,
THESE SONGS FROM A DISTANT COCKPIT:
THANK YOU FOR KNOWING, CARING,
AND SO OFTEN SHARING AND ENJOYING
THAT WHICH WE NOW
SHARE WITH OTHERS.

An Irish Airman Foresees His Death
(an extract known to many U.S. pilots in Vietnam)

"I know that I shall meet my fate
Somewhere among the clouds above.
Those that I fight, I do not hate;
Those that I guard, I do not love.

No law nor duty bade me fight,
Nor public man, nor cheering crowds.
A lonely impulse of delight
Drove me to this tumult in the clouds.
           -- William Butler Yeats

CHAPTER I
(August, 1959)
IN THE BEGINNING WAS THE JET...

It was nearing sunset, and the first hints of deep gold and purple were beginning to etch the hills and mountains that surround the city of Missoula, Montana. I'd been in the vacant lot next to our house in my football cleats, throwing passes at a swinging tire for nearly two hours.

It was August now, and more and more of the passes found their mark no matter how I threw them: running left, right or backwards, tumbling toward the ground, or from a classic "dropback" stance. I was hot, sticky and grimy from rolling in the dust, but not nearly as sore and sweaty as I would be in a month, across town at the University practice field where I was the resident passer.

As I stood catching my breath, my ears began to ring with a strange sound that filled, not just my ears, but the whole wide valley floor on which Missoula sprawls.

The source of the sound was a sleek tactical fighter jet, flying low and fast beside nearby Mount Sentinel. I stood transfixed as the pilot suddenly nosed his plane up, avoiding another oncoming mountain, and watched, agape, as he continued up and up, then paused, fell off on one wing, and nosed down to the same low altitude and raced back the way he came. The pilot reversed the process several times and did a number of acrobatic maneuvers for which I knew no names. Then, with a series of "victory rolls," he disappeared down the valley, headed north.

For several minutes after he had gone, I stood in the growing dusk lost in thought. It was the first fighter jet I'd ever seen airborne, and my sense of wonder was only exceeded by an envy I had never known for any man alive. I had just seen a man demonstrate complete maneuverability through 360 degrees, diving, soaring, rolling–free from the shackles of earth and even from the laws of gravity.

Most of all, there was a man experiencing something few humans ever could, in the cockpit of a vehicle that only a handful of men could ever qualify to fill. It was then I knew: some day, I must be a fighter pilot.

o-0-o

The next day, I learned much more about the pilot of the evening before. The front page of our daily paper said he had been a basketball star at the local county high school 10 years before. In his Marine fighter jet, he had flown over the city to say hello to his sister and brother-in-law, who still lived in our town.

The rest of the story was continued in the obituary section. Fifteen minutes later and north of Missoula about 90 miles, his jet had blown up a few feet above Flathead Lake as he performed similar flying stunts for relatives on shore, killing in an instant all that joy he tried to share with relatives and friends.

But it was too late for me.

He had already taken me on my first step toward a love affair that lasted nearly nine years with those "sleek mistresses"–the trainers and fighter jets of the U.S. Air Force.

o-0-o

After eight years of flying, many football games, a wife, a child and a war later, I relaxed inside in comfort on a late November night while outside the cold English fog enveloped the alert compound where I sat. Long lines of camouflaged supersonic fighter jets were parked a bit further from the nearby runway. The insidious fingers of fog slipped past several bolted gates also to enshroud the special hangars that housed the "cocked and armed" jets in the RAF Lakenheath Alert compound. Within one hangar sat an F-100 Super

2

Sabre with my name and that of my crew chief painted on either side of the cockpit. My helmet and parachute were inside the cockpit to help speed the time to a rapid takeoff based on orders we hoped would never come.

But I couldn't go anywhere near my airplane alone. Locked gates and sturdy armed guards prevented me from doing so. This was as it should be, because fastened to the belly of my fighter was a nuclear bomb—to be delivered in the event of WWIII.

The corridor of time into which I stepped on a cloudless evening in August in Missoula over a decade before had many unexpected twists and turns. It had as well the hopes and joys common to any other young man. But my journey in the years that followed also took me to many uncommon experiences, travel to distant lands, conversations with men and women who were of nearly every color, creed and nationality--adventures not even vaguely imagined that long-ago evening in Missoula.

And, in those early flying years, to the collection of innumerable calling cards left by Death, as well.

In those eight-and-a-half years, I saw the Temple of the Dawn in old Siam, and the snow-silenced vastness of the Alaskan mountains. I wiped perspiration from my eyes as I flew just 10 feet above the North African desert, and gained far more respect for Hannibal as I retraced his wintry path across the Alps from 40,000 feet above.

I saw far more than one dead man and the angry glow of lead fireflies as they searched the sky for human flesh. I saw, up very close, the places men hid to shoot at me and "returned the ingredients of that poisoned chalice to their own lips," as Shakespeare put it. And I've called more than four dozen men "my friend," who—during my five years of flying the "Hun" (the nickname comes from "hundred," part of the F-100's full name)—were not so lucky in the passing of that cup.

So many of the feelings and experiences that follow on these pages are shared by other men; they are a very special breed. They are few in number, because they are all F-100 Super Sabre pilots. Many were the sights they saw, the things they felt, the terrors that visited so suddenly, when Death came calling—but left again as suddenly, without a "customer." What we have most in common to this day is

3

that they, and I, enjoyed our "Songs" in distant cockpits, high above, or down so low, so fast, so far away, that only God could find us.

o-0-o

Even now, occasionally, after moving on to other challenges a long time ago, some friend or acquaintance or cocktail party stranger who has learned that I was once a fighter pilot will ask, as you might wonder as well, "What's it like, flying fighters?" You are likely to find the longer answers here.

Saying that these pages get closer to "a much fuller answer" may sound presumptuous, but I made a habit to check what I wrote with other F-100 pilots, because I wanted to capture accurately what they thought, felt and experienced in that highly dangerous profession and that plane nicknamed "the Widow Maker." Thus, much of the prose and poetry that follows is based on many very highly enthusiastic responses from them.

I should stress that while it is perhaps underplayed in this book, there is a constant and very evident atmosphere around a fighter flying squadron building, and that is laughter, a universal and omnipresent *joie de vivre*. The humor comes out at any moment, even at the most tense and dangerous times. I have been at many squadron farewell banquets where the humor at the expense of the departing guest of honor would rival the best "banquet roasts" done by professional comedians.

Another key to better understanding should also be stressed. There is a huge difference between fear, which lurks and lingers, and terror, which comes and goes in unexpected moments. F-100 pilots in Vietnam and throughout the world, and those who flew the F-84s, F-86s and all the other Air Force, Navy and Marine fighters in the Korean War, loved to fly and were addicted to the planes that transported them to moments of ecstasy—and yes, to moments of stark terror. That meant maintaining a "healthy respect" for the ability of those early jet fighters to kill us in an instant, just as it had killed so many of our "brother men who fly." And I well recall that many of us, when asked about what it was like to "fly the Hun" would smile and say, "You can't get a ride like that in any circus," and leave it at that, because no truer words were ever spoken. And I would guess that

4

same "healthy respect," and the joyful anticipation of the next "circus ride," are still very much evident in the hearts and minds of the men and women who fly the "fast movers" in our armed forces today.

So if it be only fair to say that not all fighter pilots write poetry, and that some from my era have urged me to write what follows as much on their behalf as mine, it should also be said those songs are now, for us, from long ago, and from a distant cockpit. And for me, the songs are only sporadic, a small part of what became a far larger, richer symphony, which blended 40 more years of challenges, adventures, unexpected honors and a wide variety of "job titles" completely unrelated to flying. Some of each were very much part of a life plan first conceived in my college years, and some were totally unplanned course-changes that took me down paths, and up mountains, that in earlier days, were not on the road map I charted, or on my list of "things to do."

Songs From A Distant Cockpit

I walk with different sorrows now.
Ideas all get weighed,
   and different, safer smiles are worn
                 by different, safer men.
But I've sung songs in cockpits far away,
Bent the wings and done it all.
And I've known a strange and special breed of men,
and lived with facts
   that would appall me
           now—but didn't then.
And those songs and lessons give me pause to heed:
 I long ago learned
Death is just a wingman,
      waiting
           his inevitably perfect chance
                  to lead.

5

My new "associates" do not believe
that he will come at all,
or not, at least,
in times foreseeable....

II

I forget for many hours
or for days and even years
how the snarling of the cannons
and precision
and such speed
ran at headlong, crazy angles
just remotely within grasp.
And how all that awesome Power
roared and rumbled....
How the Vision
and the Creed
always blurred the awesome threats...
and the sorrows...
and the deaths.

Ah yes,
how rough cut
were you all--
Men and planes
and all.
Sons of Icarus,
Men of Steel,
fly and fight and laugh!
But please,
forget to feel.

6

III

For me, now Earthbound,
          "flying" is all paid for,
flannel-suited, stewardessed and ferried
     when e're I travel cross the lands
     to different challenges,
which all now have
     a different smell,
   and taste and sound...
               and speed.

But I'm told there is the Hawk--
          or more--about me
that at times comes out in fun
                    or out of need.
"Look out for that guy over there...
          a dangerous gentleman.
Used to fly, you know...
               yep, fighters....
Back in 'Nam
     he flew the 'Hun.'"

IV

But I walk with different sorrows now
               and "run-up" doesn't thrill me.
And though I've sung it all in distant cockpits,
   Now, some other thing
               will
                    kill

                         me.

-- Tokyo, 1979

7

CHAPTER II

"HEADIN' ACROSS THE BLUE PACIFIC"
Within a Fighter Pilot's Letters (From Vietnam)
Part One

(April 12 - 26, 1967)

As anyone who has sat in on a bar, campfire, or fraternity "bull session" knows, it is sometimes necessary to begin a story somewhere in the middle to whet the listeners' appetite for what follows, or the story teller may not have the floor for long....

LET'S START THEN, IN THE MIDDLE...in the middle of the vast Pacific Ocean in a huge cargo plane carrying a half-a-dozen newly trained fighter pilots to their F-100 base in South Vietnam. Soon, the plane will land us at Clark Air Base, in the Philippines, where we will go through a week of Jungle Survival School.

From now on, the tensions will begin to build until we are actually flying combat missions. From now on we must discipline ourselves not to think too much about "fear" or "death," or the "Wife and Family" who are a long, long year away. And from now on, all my letters will begin, "Dear Linda."

DEAR LINDA:

En route to Clark Air Base: 10 April 1967—Left Travis AFB, California on a C-141 "Starlifter" at 10 a.m. your (San Francisco) time, and landed in Hawaii five and a half hours later. Reached Wake Island about 4 a.m. and we arrived at Clark AB about 8 a.m., (your time). During the 22 hours we were aboard that monster, the seats got very uncomfortable for everyone, especially those with long legs, like mine. Wake Island was dark, small and the loneliest spot on the earth. The biggest form of entertainment was watching the very colorful tropical fish in the huge tank in the Base Operations check-in room.

Wednesday, April 12—2 a.m. (my time)—Arrived at a motel outside Clark AB here in the Philippines; really a sleazy place in many ways. I never saw such a barren set of accommodations before; $4.50 a night gets you the room and a whole herd of long-haired, rather hoody-looking "boys" who chase you everywhere you go looking for tips for every little favor (not at all typical of most Filipinos). One of them showed us directions to the rooms—"Spence" (Doug Spenser) and I are rooming together—and then the guy followed us all the way over the two blocks to where he had pointed for us to go, just hoping for a tip.

9

I'm beginning to comprehend, slowly, just what life in the "Third World" means: wrenching, grinding poverty for the vast majority, including that guy.

I sat around in our room with "Stu" and "Mick" for a couple of hours having beers before rolling into bed. It seemed like a million years since I've slept on anything but an airliner seat.

Wednesday, April 12th–(noon to Night) Went to the Officer's Club and rolled dice for Mai Tai drinks at 75 cents a glass, after checking in to "tent city." Got a "crew cut" haircut after I had drunk enough courage. It will be cooler and a lot less trouble to keep, but it sure feels funny. I haven't had a crew cut since my senior year in high school. I got kidded pretty badly by the other five guys, but in the next 45 minutes they all got one too, (except Mick, who already had one!)

Ran into John G., who was with us at Vance Air Base, and "Tip" Clark from dear old U. of Montana days.

(*Added note: Tip was a college senior and the AFROTC Wing Commander when I was appointed to be his "Wing Sergeant Major" my sophomore year. Because neither of us knew what someone of that exalted enlisted rank should do, exactly, he made up some quick duties on the spot:: I was to call out "in that big quarterback voice of yours" for the Wing to "fall in." After reporting to him that the wing had, indeed, fallen in. I was to do some smart, square-cornered steps that put me behind him as he began issuing orders, and I was to then continue my march over to the Student Lodge, where several hundred coeds sat with few if any men around on ROTC drill days. (I was ever-grateful to my Cadet Wing C.O.)*

Much later, Tip retired as a Brigadier General with 30 years of service, and was proud to say he had never served a day in the Pentagon– a rare feat for anyone promoted to flag rank.)

Tip and John were in the checkout class ahead of me in F-100 training at Cannon AFB. John apparently goofed somehow over here and is leaving his F-100 squadron to be a duty officer somewhere else at a headquarters in South Vietnam for the rest of his tour. Tip is here for a short rest–guess he took a bad hit in the fuel tank the other day that rattled him pretty good. But he makes it sound hilarious when he tells of it.

Thursday morning, April 13—We are all laughing this morning at Stu's expense. He came in about 3:30 in the morning, plowed out of his mind. We were all asleep in "tent city" in the far corner of Clark AFB, which is filled with "hooches" that have sloped tin roofs, screen sides and doors, and small cots and lockers.

He first tried to get the Monsoon-rain-warped door to close just right, and ended up slamming it about five times to make it fit, thus waking all of us. His next project was to pick up the heavy, green G.I. wool blankets that Fred Thompson and Major Fred F. had discarded in the heat.

Gently, he laid the unwanted covers on the two drowsy forms, and as he tucked them in for what was left of the night, he stage-whispered "You dropped your blanket...." Then, staggering to his own cot, he noticed that the huge fan wasn't aimed just right, and nearly lost an arm while trying to turn it a little so he'd get more air, all the while thinking he is being sooo quiet. Unsuccessful with the fan, he began straightening his big foot-locker, sorting and folding each already sorted and folded item.

When I informed him that "your locker is fine—*go to bed!*" he decided to drape his own extra wool blanket outside the screen by his bed to keep out the soon-arriving sun. Up went the blanket, rattle, rattle" went the sloped tin roof he tried to hang it on, "fallump" would go the blanket as it hit the ground after sliding off the roof.

The legendary spider in Robert Bruce's Scottish cave needed six futile tries before success was hers as she spun her web. The inebriated Stuart B. easily doubled that number, in far noisier attempts, before the growing roar from the large and unappreciative audience made him realize the wisdom of the aphorism: "Better bed, than dead." (*Before his year was done, Stu, who was assigned to a sister squadron at Bien Hoa, would become one of only four recipients of the Silver Star "for gallantry in action" during our year there. That was hard to imagine on this night, as he finally gave up and crashed for what was left of the night.*)

April 14–We just finished our morning classes on jungle survival (which began at 6:30 a.m.). We had eight hours of free time yesterday and saw a little of this huge Base, went to the BX (Base Exchange, a military mini-department store), and spent most of the time at the beautiful Officer's Club staying cool, drinking and talking with combat pilots who were here for "Rest and Relaxation" (R&R).

Tonight at 5 the classroom lectures end and we will be eating at the club and sleeping and then out to bivouac for three days in the jungle. The guys who've been through it say it's a gentlemen's outing compared to what we endured at the Survival School last November in the Bob Marshall Wilderness Area (located 100 miles northwest of Missoula).

April 18–We finished Survival School today after spending three days and nights in the jungles of the Philippines with the Negritos. They are the mountain and jungle dwelling "aborigines." They are very dark-skinned and very small, and often wear loincloths and nothing more. They are superb trackers and hunters. In WWII they did astounding things against the Japanese invaders. For their heroism, they have been awarded free medical privileges at Clark Air Base, and are hired as guards and sentries at the installation.

This does not sit well with some Filipinos, who look upon them as primitive savages, but they are the best guards and jungle people in the world, I am told. It was they who pursued us on our escape and evasion exercise in the jungle. It was a most interesting and rather rewarding experience in many ways. We all learned a lot, I think, about how to live and evade in the jungle. Most of all, most of us got over any fear of being in a jungle, especially at night. It was actually a lot of fun, and because we were in the mountains, the heat wasn't too bad.

One of my prior impressions of "the jungle" was completely wrong; six months of the year in this region it is hot, steamy and wet, and there is rain almost every day of the Monsoon Season. But the other six months, the jungle is dry as a bone, even dusty as you walk through it; not at all what I ever expected.

An incident occurred while we were in the jungle that I would never believe if I hadn't seen it. Part of the jungle training exercise was to pair up with another guy and head for the hills to hide. We were given three "capture chits" and a one-hour head start. Then the Negritos set forth to track us. We were to give a capture chit to the first three of them to find us, and they could turn these in for two pounds of rice, thus providing them with a strong incentive for finding all the air crews in hiding.

We took off an hour before sunset, moving as far as fast and as quietly as we could. Out almost a mile, we ran across two of the other guys, who were headed for the same hiding thicket we had spotted. So, the four of us joined up and headed up the hill to the hiding place to bed down for the night.

We hadn't been inside the thicket of trees and bushes five minutes when one of the guys quietly signaled, "Shh," and pointed down the hill. There, a small, loincloth-clad figure was picking his way through jungle, obviously reading signs to pick up traces of our passage. We could see his face puckered in a frown as he stopped in the growing dusk not 10 feet from our hiding place, looked around a moment, took a couple of steps in our direction, then went, "Ho," in both surprise and triumph as he spotted us hiding there. We laughed a bit, like kids caught with our hands in a cookie jar, and the tracker joined us in laughter.

Then came the most extraordinary part of this incident: one of the guys had lost his khaki green flashlight somewhere in the jungle en route to our hiding place. Through a combination of sign language and "pidgin" English we asked our intrepid tracker to go try to find the flashlight and promised him a U.S. dollar for his trouble.

Off he went down the hill, looking to and fro in the gray of gathering night.

Less than three quarters of an hour later, a figure appeared at our "doorway" from the almost total darkness—with the missing flashlight in his hand. No clever substitution had been made, because the flashlight had the guy's name tag on it. As we all agreed later, never was a dollar more gladly spent, nor was one ever earned in such a remarkable manner.

Oh, by the way, we were not even two hours out in hiding before we had lost all our "capture chits." I guess word travels fast in the jungle.

I have several impressions of Clark AB, and of the Philippines and its people, and about the scenes at the Officer's Club.

For one thing, you know there is a war near Clark AB because there is a constant stream of R&R types–especially the Air Force pilots–everywhere you look in the huge Officer's Club. Yet, these men are very different from the ones I've read about in all the WWII books about fighter pilots at war, and at relaxing at a "nearby" bar at night. These men, in *this* war, don't talk about flying over there, or about the war, even if they are flying "North." You can spot the fighter jocks here for a break (either temporary duty or actual R&R) by their deep tans, and by the rather hungry look they give the many bikinied and suntanned school teachers, nurses and dependents who are at the club's beautiful pool, in club bars, etc.

A page in flying history seems to have turned forever in America, because a generation ago this club was filled with suntanned younger men, mostly in their early 20s, excitedly talking in close-knit groups around the bar. These pilots today are older, more mature, often over 30 years old. They look bored, a bit lonely, and yet seem to prefer their solitude to mixing with the "uninitiated."

Also in contrast to yesteryear, you seldom, if ever, see any of these men talking with their hands about flying or about their missions. When they do talk with friends who are "on the way over," they talk instead about conditions at their particular bases, how many missions they have (The guys flying F-105s and F-4s out of Thailand say, "Ya only count the ones North--I've got 24 now...") and where the best R&R places are. They are here for a rest between missions. But one thing I've noticed: their hands, their eyes...never, somehow relax....

The Filipinos are an interesting study, too, at least the ones on or near the base. They are all over the base, in the club, driving cabs, working at the BX (Base Exchange) etc.

They are, first, very beautiful people in my opinion, both male and female. But many of the men and boys look a bit "scruffy." These same people, and most all others I've seen, are very musically inclined

14

and very talented singers. They have a marvelous orchestra here at the Officer's Club—like the 1940s "Big Bands" of WWII—with about 16 pieces; the male and female vocalists are just outstanding. All the Filipinos I've heard, the professionals and even the shoeshine boys, sing American tunes nine out of 10 times.

Just off base there are about six or eight "Aero-Hotels" that are like one-level college dorms but with each room furnished like a motel room in the States (sans TV). Few of the motels could get AAA "very good" ratings, but the one I'm in now is excellent for here, and at least "good" by U.S. standards. We have to stay here because there is no room on base.

For two nights we stayed in "tent city" (during jungle survival classes), which was very nice, and a lot better than it sounds.

But the first night we arrived, we were shipped to another aero-hotel off base, run the same way this one is, only it was very poorly kept and depressing, and we had dozens of Filipinos running in front of us every time we went to do something, all of them trying to get another tip. They worked for the motel and ranged in age from about 18 to about 35 or so. After that first night we got wise and quit tipping, except for extreme cases, and then only a quarter.

We moved out of that place and we came back to the Aero-hotel" after our jungle "visit." This is much better--not least because there is the added bonus that it's used by the commercial airliner crews for layovers, and the swimming pool is decorated from dawn to dusk with sunbathing stewardesses.

April 19—En route to Saigon—The Pacific below is a deep, deep blue and studded with small puffs of clouds. Far in the distance a larger formation of clouds is trying to build and gather for a storm no one will ever see out in this almost endless expanse of sky and sea. Occasionally, a somehow different substance passes just beneath us: long flat wispy clouds--a "scud deck" that you could seemingly stand on, or maybe land this plane on.

The flight to Saigon will take a bit over two hours, and perhaps by tonight we'll be in Bien Hoa. Our Boeing 727 is owned by Southern Air Transport and has four Japanese stewardesses aboard, all wearing white blouse jackets and grey skirts. Japanese women usually aren't very "stacked." But one of the four has the 80 odd men from all the armed services slightly agog as she passes to and fro; she is definitely an exception to the above statement and apparently has had to customize her blouse to overcome this attractive superabundance.

On board, again I've noticed the ages of the pilots going to war. Chiefly absent are the bright-eyed, clean-cut near-youths who roamed the Pacific skies and bars in Korea or WWII. There is only one bright-eyed, bushy-tailed AF lieutenant on board, and he fits the Korea/WWII description of pilots to a "T."

We just hit the coast of Vietnam! The few of us aboard who are pilots are already looking out the windows for check-points and ground references to navigate by, and are also taking note that in this, the "rainy season," there are puffy cumulus clouds all over the place, all of them able to grow and billow into thunderstorms later today. Temperature at Da Nang is 91 degrees.

As we descend, we can see some bomb craters in tight clusters here and there, and many tributaries leading to the big Mekong River and then to the sea. The main U.S. headquarters base at Ton Son Nhut is the grubbiest place I've ever seen; filthy, and old and dingy inside. It was originally built by the French. Now there are burned buildings here and there, and some are very smelly. My first thought was, why would anyone fight over a place like this?

Those of us assigned to Bien Hoa, mostly new fighter pilots, were soon transported by bus the 16 miles north to our new home. The bus had wire screens over the windows to prevent grenades from penetrating, and the bus driver was armed with an automatic rifle. (You'd think this was a war zone!)

April 20 Bien Hoa AFB–This morning I became the newest member of the second oldest TAC Fighter Squadron in the USAF. The 90th Tactical Fighter Squadron, "Pair-O-Dice," was created in 1917, during WWI, and is 50 years old this year.

The C.O. is an impressive guy from what Tip told me at Clark AB, and he said the Operations Officer is very impressive, too.

I am not at all ill or too hot. I'm finally all unpacked and my bags are stored on top of my locker. But I still feel very unsettled, as though everything is all new and ever-changing. I know it all will be much more routine in four or five weeks. Then I'll be able to tell you a lot more about everything going on. Right now I'm not too sure myself.

Bien Hoa is a huge base, several miles square, with six thousand men or more huddled together in the living-quarters section. It was built by the French years ago and all you see any time of day is men in khaki or flight suits by the hundreds, everywhere. With a few exceptions, there is no air conditioning anywhere—only fans. Shower and bathroom are fairly close by, and the Pair-O-Dice Inn is a great squadron bar that's in one of the many squadron "hooches," a combination tent and wooden-slat structured "barracks" where 10 of us are quartered. But the Officers Club is a far more permanent-looking structure. It is nearby, and there is a laundry across the street.

The hooch is a lot like the upstairs of some fraternity houses—a big, open-plan room with each personal sleeping area decorated to make each man's place a bit of a home to suit his taste in decor and reading. Our squadron has three officer's hooches, one of which is sectioned off in front as a wonderful little bar and club, with Mai Ling,

a real honest-to-goodness barmaid, working from 5 p.m. till 10 p.m.

There is a poker table, some bar stools, a few chairs and a whole wall full of books ranging from Reinhold Niebuhr to Ian Fleming. And in the center on the other wall is a gorgeous British girl (looks like a playmate, but isn't) painted on black velvet background in a 4 feet tall by 3 feet wide frame. All around it are pictures, framed in bamboo, of the members of the squadron, organized into each of the four flights. Each guy is standing by his own airplane. All the decor and furniture was scrounged from various places, a living testimony to man's ability to improvise in the sparsest areas of the world for mostly indigenous components (TV included). Together they make up the coolest fighter pilots' lounge I've ever seen. All in a 20x20-foot area!

I'll get away from here about every 75 missions, roughly one week out of every seven, on a permissive "Temporary Duty," (TDY). We all fly about 150 missions every six months. (*In my case, "time away" was far less frequent — I took on an additional duty job some weeks after arriving that had too much paperwork to edit and process, so I skipped all but about three.*)

There is always the looming prospect of getting reassigned to a FAC assignment after six months—depending on "Air Force needs." But if I get to seven months without a FAC job, then I'll stay in the F-100—too little time left to train me on another job.

April 21—I'll be flying in the back seat tomorrow as I begin my check-out program. I'll get one back seat ride, two front seat rides in the same two-seat "F" model, and then one single-seat ride in the F-100 "D-model" before I'm "theatre checked out." After 20 missions, there is another "check ride" before I'm cleared to the Alert Pad, meaning I'm then fully operational.

Today I went in at 8:15 and began by reading some of the many volumes of stuff you have to know to understand the squadron set-up and to do your job in the air. At 11 a.m. I had a briefing on bombs and fuses, and at 12:30 I began a three-hour shift as "Mobile Control Duty Officer," sitting beside the runway to keep an eye on all planes as they approached and landed, to make sure they have gear and flaps down coming in.

Then, at 4 p.m., I went with one of the guys to the "Alert Pad" for two hours and we talked about all the cockpit switch settings, etc. to pre-set for fast starts and takeoffs, and for various weapon deliveries. After dinner at the Club, I helped one of the guys do some administrative writing (for another squadron) and now am going to wend my weary way to bed.

The temperature each day is about as hot as Randolph AFB, Texas, was at its hottest last summer. About that humid, too.

April 22–Well, today was my first mission! The pre-flight briefing before we put on our flying gear was remarkable. I've never witnessed anything like it before. First the weatherman came in and briefed us on the weather for takeoff, in the target area, and back at home base an hour and a half later. Next a guy came in with two covered maps and uncovered them one at a time to give us an intelligence report on all the action by the Vietcong (VC) during the previous night in III and IV Corps (where 3rd Wing flies), and on all current Army operations. He then briefed us on our target for the day and safe bailout areas nearest to it. Both guys were "on and off stage" in seven minutes flat, but they did a very comprehensive job.

Next, the flight leader briefed every detail of how things would go and what we were to do uniformly from start-engine time all the way through the mission and back to when we parked in the protective revetments. He re-emphasized something I'd heard 100 times already, it seems, in my two days here: "If you aren't sure that you have the target in sight, don't drop," and, "If the pass you're making doesn't look right, if you don't have the plane where you want it, go through dry!"

Well, after all this pre-flight briefing, I began the arduous task of getting on all the gear for the mission. It was difficult for a couple of reasons: first, besides the "G-suit," I had to load my new pistol, strap on a gun belt and holster, then put on a survival vest full of flares, survival and first-aid kits and a small, but heavy rescue radio. After that came the "Mae West," which is folded into two little packets that strap on and fit uncomfortably under my arms.

Over all this goes the 35-pound parachute, and in the helmet bag I carry out to the plane goes my helmet, the aircraft check-list, maps of the area and a Wing check-list of local flying procedures. The other reason my "gear-dressing session" took so long is that I found my hands kept shaking, mostly from excitement and anticipation, not fear.

After the cumbersome process of putting on all my gear, we went out to inspect the weapons and then the airplane outside and in. Boy, I felt bulky with all that gear on, and as attentive as a long-tailed cat in a room full of rockers! But as soon as the afterburner lit and we began rolling, I felt much more at home, even if I was riding in the back seat of an "F" model. Until takeoff, though, it was very much like the "rush" I used to get waiting for the opening kickoff at a football game--too much adrenalin!

The first thing I noticed was how long "the lead sled" rolled. Between the heavy bomb load and the hundred-degree temperature, the F-100s used up over 7,200 feet of runway to reach takeoff speed—a lot of that 10,000-foot runway being used, especially for a fighter plane! When we got to the target area, we switched over to the same frequency that the Forward Air Controller (FAC) was on, and when we checked in he gave us a quick briefing on the direction of the winds at bombing altitude, the height of the trees, the target description, and the distance to the nearest "friendlies" (U.S. or Allied ground troops). He then restricted our run-in and our pull-off directions so we wouldn't overfly any friendly areas.

A minute later, way below us, not far above the trees, I spotted the FAC in his small, slow, propeller-driven light plane. He rolled into a dive to fire a marking white phosphorus rocket at the target.

A second later I heard the flight Lead (see next page), 800 feet ahead of us, call, "Roger, I have you in sight, I have your mark. Where do you want the bombs?" He was already part way down the bomb run when the FAC replied, "Roger, put 'em five meters west of my smoke, five meters west."

I was still watching Lead* go down, down, down like he was never going to pull out when we started our own dive. A split second later I heard Lead call "Off left!," and saw his bombs explode dead on target. My instructor pilot immediately called, "I have Lead's bombs, where would you like mine?"

* **Lead vs. lead**—*Throughout, when the word is capitalized, it is pronounced "leed" and refers to the formation flight leader. Pilots flying formation on Lead's wings are referred to as "Two, Three, and Four." While spelled the same, "lead" (in lower case, pronounced "led") means "bullets," outbound from a fighter as he "strafes" in an attack, or anti-aircraft ground fire aimed at any aircraft.*

The FAC replied, "Right between the bombs and my smoke!"

"Roger, I'm in from the southeast."

A few seconds later I could feel the outboard bombs depart the wings, shaking the whole plane slightly. Then on came the G forces as we started the pullout and climb back to the "perch" for the next run. Boy, these guys are real pros, the way they flew the mission, the way they bulls-eyed the target and the way they handled the aircraft. Being one of a group like this, being as good as they are, will be a real accomplishment.

One thing that was kind of funny: I was just a spectator and yet (like "Spence"—Doug Spencer—yesterday), I came back to the squadron absolutely drenched with sweat. I even had salty sweat stains on my "G" suit! It was a bit embarrassing, because we like to play the role of cool, unflappable fighter pilot.

Someone told me that the reason our parachute room is the one air-conditioned room in the building is to provide a dry, cool place for all our gear to dry out. I can imagine how it would smell without the cool room. The place would be unbearable to get near without nose plugs! (Come to think of it, it might smell like our college football locker room after a hot practice.)

Anyhow, the funniest part of the story is that all new guys come back just as sweat-soaked as I was, but the guys I flew with

21

today (all of them with over 50 missions), barely had wet marks under their arms.

April 24—I've been very busy with the checkout phase in the squadron and will be continuing like this for about sixteen more missions. I have four now. Tomorrow I get my last "F" ride and then go solo the next time.

The missions are very interesting, but the weather is quite grim this time of year. It is monsoon season, and there are afternoon and evening rain showers every day for six months; then it's dry as a bone for six.

By the way, our last mission was flying cover for C-123 "Ranch Hand" planes who spray deforestation chemicals (*"Agent Orange"; at the time we thought it was harmless*) over the jungle hideout areas. It was a very interesting, unusual mission circling above the slow-flying propeller planes, then swooping down below them to suppress ground fire when they were fired upon. There were some VC down there. It was my first mission where I knew folks were shooting at me. You seldom see the ground fire in daytime, but the FAC calls it out. We did a good job of protecting the "heavies."

"Spence's" strike yesterday accounted for 22 VC killed by air (KBA) and some other stuff destroyed. The boat (junk) they targeted blew up four times after it was hit. It was obviously loaded with VC ammo. Those "secondary explosions mean you have "struck gold." His was an immensely effective mission.

April 26—I was in our 90th bar talking with our Ops Officer, Major Dale Rook, till 3 a.m. and thus staggered home full of whiskey wisdom and a knowledge that I had to get up again at 8 a.m. for my one orientation briefing from the Wing Staff.

I flew my first solo ride at noon in the "D." It was an utter disaster in every way. I'll try to explain it to you so you'll better understand what is going on, and has gone before, if you suddenly learn that I've been re-assigned as a FAC or as a "Staff Weenie" somewhere.

We arrived at the target area to find it cluttered with pillars of baby thunderheads; which partially covered the entire area and considerably restricted the view. Being "new to the game," I already had my hands very full because I was flying a bird loaded with bombs, which makes it more sluggish, flying out of a base that is still new to me, with gear that I'm not used to wearing yet, and hold a formation position that I've not flown much, called "route formation, spread two aircraft widths further away from the Lead."

To complicate matters, once in the target area, we switch to a different type of formation, 800 feet in trail behind each other. We listen to the FAC's target briefing, confirm seeing him, and his "mark" (that smoke rocket) and then tell him which direction we are coming from as we roll in for our dive bomb or other attack runs.

Like every new guy here, I find that normally my biggest two problems are: knowing exactly which direction I'm coming in from, and, not losing sight of the target marker smoke in the bad weather. As soon as we go into high G maneuvers, the gyros in our navigation equipment tumble and we have to rely on previously identified ground references to serve as our "compass," especially after the first pass. In bad weather, the low clouds sometimes block out both the ground references we've established and the FAC's mark. It seems to be no problem for the veteran pilots here, but we rookies have our hands full.

We were going after a couple of VC bunkers and tunnels.

On my first pass, I saw the mark perfectly well as I rolled in, but I couldn't get the right dive angle as I started "down the chute" through the weather. Unfortunately, I decided to get a steeper angle by pushing the nose of the airplane over to put the gun-sight on the target. (I had been way too shallow.) As a result, I still had negative G force on the airplane when I released the two outboard bombs, and they went almost 200 meters long.

The FAC said "Ooooh Boy! Everybody hold high and dry," and I was horrified, because pilots can face court martial or a Flying Evaluation Board for dropping a "short round" (a bomb out of the target area), or for bringing an aircraft home with a green belly from low pullouts. An "FEB," can mean "bye-bye Air Force wings."

The FAC flew over to the place the bombs hit and said they had fallen harmlessly and had hit "200 meters...Aw...call it 250" off target. My second bomb run was OK (but I was about 30 degrees off the direction I said I was coming in from).

I set up to roll in on the third pass with instructions to put my last bomb between the napalm smokes made by the plane in front of me. I "acquired the target" visually, went by a cloud and thought I saw the same smoke again as I passed the cloud, and rolled in to attack.

What I really saw was the smoke still coming up from my first two bombs, and I then dropped my last bomb very accurately, right between them.

The FAC immediately called out, "Ooopsey Daisy," and I just wanted to die right there in the cockpit. I felt so bad that the crazy thought passed through my head "Why not just take this plane and head it out to sea and crash."

And I felt utterly humiliated.

At the end of the mission, the FAC gave us our Bomb Damage Assessment, (BDA), and then added, "Log three bombs 300 meters from the target."

I'd been flying with the Ops officer, Dale Rook, the Assistant Ops officer, Major Al DeGroote, and my Flight Commander, Lou Daniels—a complete "chain-of-command-above-me" audience. When we landed, we had a long, serious debriefing, with reiteration of the theme "If you're not sure, don't drop! If the pass doesn't look right, take it through dry!"

Then Major Rook tried to cheer me up by saying "You owe us a round of beers for those three out-of-bounds bombs."

However, unbeknownst to any of us, the FAC called Tactical Air Control Center in Saigon (TACC) when he landed, and reported three "short rounds" by me. TACC called our Deputy Wing Commander for Operations (DCO at Bien Hoa and reported one of his pilots had dropped "500 meters off target."

The DCO was in the squadron about 2:30 that afternoon (we had landed about 12:30), and I was called in to Major Rook's office. The DCO, a grey-haired full colonel in charge of all base flying operations, was looking very grim. He sat me down and warned me about the extreme seriousness of "short rounds" and "cautioned" me about how lucky I was because it could as easily have resulted in the killing of innocents. He warned me that it could and would ruin my career if it happened again.

Apparently, Major Rook and the others in the flight had talked to the DCO before he talked to me, and they had de-emphasized the distance the bombs dropped off target, talked of the poor weather, and of my very limited experience etc., so that the blow was softened somewhat.

Nonetheless, that was a very, very grave colonel who talked to me, and I think the only reason that I was given a second chance was that my bombs had gone where I aimed them on two out of three passes.

Major Rook sat in on the "briefing" from the DCO but said nothing to me or the colonel, but afterward, however, he tried to cheer the colonel up with some light and extraneous comments. Later, in the jeep with Major Rook, I was still utterly shattered, and as we drove down the two-mile taxiway toward the hooches for the night, he grinned at me and referred to the jeep's whining sound, said, "I know it's still in first gear. I'm clearing out the carbon." Then he laughed. It helped.

So did Major Al DeGroote, the Assistant Ops Officer, who is in the same hooch with me, as is Tip Clark, my old Montana acquaintance, who is fast becoming a friend. He and I talked about the incident for a short while tonight before he went to bed. Tip's advice was "Don't sweat it."

Well, I will, and I do, very much "sweat it," and I just pray to God that tomorrow will be a better—a LOT better—day than today. I was dimly aware that several other guys had said, "Forget it, shake it off," trying to cheer me up. I'll try to "shake it off," but I know it will be a long, long, time before I forget today

o-0-o

"I know it will be long, long, time before I forget today." How true and prophetic that statement was. Even as I wrote more about it a year and a half later, and for several years after that in what became a very challenging, interesting and often exciting life, I would sometimes still recall how I felt that night. Back then, I thought, but didn't write home:

25

I guess some of the unspoken, unwritten, almost unutterable thought and emotions tied to the very important events in our lives remain with us all. Their poignancy, often bittersweet, is burned forever on our brain pans. That night, for me, was unforgettable. As I lay in my hot, sticky bed, barely hearing the deep throated roar of the outgoing Army heavy artillery that was a nightly occurrence, I retraced the events that had led to my disastrous performance. I went over it all a hundred times in my mind–each time cursing myself for my stupidity and ineptitude.

I could blame no one. It was I who had stayed up too late the night before. It was I who had "pressed" to get the bombs off on that first pass. It was I who then forgot momentarily my lesson in gunnery school about releasing ordnance with negative "G" loading on the airplane. And it was I who had elected to continue the bomb run, thus compounding the mistake.

It was all my fault.

And as I lay there, emotionally exhausted, my mind wandered even further afield, and I began thinking about the training I had received, about the years of experience I already had in jets, practicing, training, then instructing...all of it preparing for just such a job as this. I began thinking about all the elements that go into the making of a competent, productive combat fighter pilot.

How many things contributed to it besides formal training? Family life? College training? My years of "pseudo-combat" on football fields, basketball courts and baseball diamonds–didn't they count for something? What about how quickly I was able to make that Cessna 150 "talk" as I did mock-attacks on freight trains during my 30 hours of AFROTC light-plane training in my senior year at university? How many of these things were important? Were parts of my formal Air Force training somehow a factor?

I didn't know, but that night, in a scrambled, disorganized manner, I reviewed those factors fleetingly....

CHAPTER III

WHEN I WAS A YOUNG MAN,

and COURTIN' THE GIRL...
(1956 - 1964)

"When you're down, get up. If you can't get up, lay there and do push-ups"　　　　　　　　　　　−Loyola High School Coach Bill Murray, Fall, 1958

"The wars of tomorrow are won today on the game fields of Eton."
−Winston Churchill

"HIT THE GLOVE! NO, HIT THE GLOVE...."

Nothing was terribly unusual about my adolescent or teenage years. In sports, I did have two or three advantages: for 15 years, my father was head coach for all three major sports at the Catholic High School in Great Falls, Montana. In the 1930s, he was an All-State basketball and football player from Gladwin, a very small town in Michigan, and then played football at Notre Dame back when that was "something special." When he retired, *The Great Falls* [MT] *Tribune* said he was "the winningest high school coach in all three sports."

Aside from inheriting some of his athletic genes, one advantage was his occasional "suggestions" as he watched me and my brother Frank play catch or take turns throwing passes while the other ran pass patterns.

The second "advantage" had its beginnings on my fourth birthday, my baseball-loving Uncle Nick Mariana said to me after all the presents were opened, "C'mon, Johnny, let's go out and play catch."

I always loved that idea. But this time, and from then on, the game was different. "Today," he said, "we're going to play a new game. It's called 'hit the glove.'"

He then began moving the "target" from spot to spot, insisting each time, "Hit the glove!"

A former college pitcher who was told he was "too short" for the pros, he became a scout, then general manager of a minor league professional team in Great Falls for the Brooklyn Dodgers. For several years, beginning at age nine, my brother and I sold popcorn and programs at home games. Dad was the public address announcer.

The third "advantage" was that younger brother Frank loved the various sports as much as I did, was just as intensely competitive, and hated losing to his big brother at any sport from basketball to badminton to throwing wadded paper at a wastebasket during indoor winter days. We played sports together for hours on end, all summer long and whenever the weather permitted it during the school year. He later had scholarship offers from Notre Dame and the Montana State Bobcats, where he played safety and quarterback until he was badly injured his sophomore year.

Just before I entered high school, my father and uncle decided to become partners in a business in Missoula, so both families moved there and the two men worked together for several years until Uncle Nick decided to return to baseball, this time as general manager for a new minor league team coming to Missoula as a Minnesota Twins farm club. Dad, Frank and I again worked at the ballpark whenever the team was home

Late in my 16th year, just weeks before becoming a senior in high school, my uncle arranged for me to pitch batting practice to his "Missoula Timberjacks" before home games. During my warm-ups, Jim Kaat, the team's star 19-year-old pitcher and a subsequent major league pitching great, would stand beside me offering tips. He showed me how to throw a slider and how to get the most movement out of two-seamed and four-seamed fastballs. Sometimes, Kaat was joined by the playing manager, Jack McKeon, who later managed two major league teams and was for a while the general manger of the San Diego Padres.

One evening as I finished my warm-up pitches, McKeon told me that tonight I was to try to strike out the batters, instead of trying to let them hit. He donned his catching gear, went behind the plate and signaled for each pitch I should throw. Then he called them balls and strikes. Deployed behind me were seven other players in the field. This was clearly to be a five- or six-inning "simulated game."

It went quite well; my fastball that summer was very noticeably faster, and the movement on my three "new pitches" amazed and delighted me. However, I can't say the session went "*very* well" or "perfectly"; the team's huge clean-up hitter smacked one of my fastballs so hard it was still rising as it went out over the left-centerfield lights! I think we beat Sputnik into orbit by two months!

Although I hadn't noticed, a man in the stands wearing a sport coat and straw hat had been taking notes, and he and McKeon met me over by the dugout for a little chat. The gist was an offer to sign with the Twins organization as a pitcher when I got out of high school. I told them I had seen so many outstanding minor league ballplayers in Great Falls and Missoula that I thought would make the Majors, but who were never heard from again. Thus, I thought it important that I get a college degree before going into professional baseball, having the degree as a back-up if baseball didn't pan out. They understood, said it was a "standing offer," and we parted on the best of terms.

Two days later, it was time to change my throwing motion for the football season, which would be coming in mid-August. That fall, our Loyola High School football team won our conference and I was later named to play in the State's East-West Shrine Game as one of the quarterbacks.

A week or so after my high school graduation, a letter from Notre Dame arrived, offering me a football scholarship. Two days later, while my parents and I were still discussing how to raise the "other money" needed for travel and monthly expenses, a second letter came, informing me I had won a full-tuition and books scholarship to the University of Montana Journalism School. It was rated third best in the country at the time. I had nine athletic awards from Loyola varsity sports, and if I was immensely good–and immensely lucky–I might win three more playing football in South Bend, Indiana. But then what?

I knew I wanted to be a foreign correspondent, and the wise choice was to take the journalism scholarship. So I did.

The Dean at Montana's Journalism School was a dynamic, brilliant and very intimidating man. When I met with him a few weeks after his letter arrived, he made it clear that my playing days were over. The J-School had opened in 1927, he said, and no one had ever been able to play a varsity sport and also graduate with a journalism degree; the work was too hard and the courses too demanding. I abided by that agreement until the following spring. But I knew I was blessed with a "freakish" right arm and an ability honed in training with my uncle *("Hit the Glove!!!")* to be very accurate throwing baseballs or footballs.

And I was haunted by the lines from Milton's "On His Blindness," which was among the many poems our Jesuit high school teachers had made us memorize.

Milton had written:

> *When I consider how my light is spent*
> *Ere half my days in this dark world and wide,*
> *And that one talent which is Death to hide*
> *Lodged with me useless....*

To my way of thinking, I had been given a gift—that "freak arm." And it was a talent now "lodged with me useless." The fact that I was 6'2", but only weighed 163 pounds and would be playing on a Division IA football team, never entered the equation. So I went to the Dean, asking him to allow me to "try out for spring football." He checked my two quarters of grades and said, "OK, but keep your grades up."

Three and a half years later I had three varsity letters as a "Grizzly Quarterback." Two of my passing records survived for 27 years. Elsewhere on campus, I had learned to lead and manage by running seven or eight student organizations, had learned to write well under the close scrutiny of the J-School faculty, and while four years with the Jesuits had taught me to think logically, my time at university sharpened my analytical thinking skills as well.

On the college football practice field, without at first realizing it, I had also become "tough" in ways that only college football players will fully understand. The gap between high school and college football is huge. I quickly realized I no longer had any impulses to protect my little pink body from "contact" in scrimmages. Physical fear, which was given some due consideration in my high school football days, disappeared quickly on the Grizzly practice field. What grew in its place was a kind of mental toughness that was to serve me well in combat some years later. To this day I think there was a distinct and strong connection between my practiced determination to plant my back foot and step forward to pass as onrushing linemen 100 pounds heavier than I came at me with bodily harm in mind, and a willingness in combat to press each attack, completely focused on the target in the face of bullets all around.

Thanks to a kind of intellectual toughness that came from being in class with Dean Nathaniel Blumberg, a Rhodes Scholar with a doctorate in History from Oxford, and to a different kind of tough mental attitude learned from Coach Ray Jenkins, himself as tough a man as ever walked, I left college with two bits of internalized "education" that are not on the usual college curriculum.

Before ever going to war, I had already looked *two* tigers in the eye.

o-0-o

Ah, the good old days! It was most likely while in Flight School in 1963 that I wrote this "requiem," looking back on 10 years on the gridiron. "Requiem" was later published as the cover page for the "Sports" section of our Class of '86 National War College Yearbook.

Requiem for a Letterman

We were razor sharp then
Lean and hard as nails–
Ran forever every day
While chewing iron nails
When we were young and strong boys,
When we were young and strong.

Muscles never bulged then
They were hard and flat.
Then we moved with easy grace
Sinewed like a cat,
When we were young and hard boys,
When we were young and hard.

Then we sweat and bled, boys,
Cut, and spun and ran,
Dripped from every pore, boys
And cursed it to a man,
But we were lean and mean, boys,
When we were young and hard.

S'posed to hit the books then,
But hit each other harder.
We were not so fat then,
But we were much, much smarter.
When we were strong and dumb, boys,
When we were strong and young.

Put on pads and flew, boys,
Scrimmaged in the dirt,
Limped for hours afterwards
And every muscle hurt...
When we were young and brave, boys
And wore a letter shirt.

Heroes every Saturday,
From weeks of practice plays,
Where we knocked our teammates
Into a senseless haze—
In Dear Old College Days, Boys,
In Dear Old College Days.
                    — Williams AFB, AZ 1963

o-0-o

A footnote of sorts: *preparing for my Vietnam assignment, I read the memoirs of 27 internationally famous WWII fighter pilots from Japan, Germany. Canada, England and the United States. They were the best hunters, with the highest numbers of "victories"–or "kills"–in the air. From them, I learned much that mentally prepared me for combat, and how to excel in that environment. But I'd already learned far more than I thought about "fear management" and performing under dire threat and pressure at Dornblaser Field, as a 6'2, 165-pound quarterback, foot planted and concentrating on my "targets," with the threat of bodily harm all around. The "translation" of that gunslinger mentality from football to war was quite remarkable.*

Thus, while "Requiem for a Letterman" may leave the impression that there was little or no value gained from bashing brains against brawny bodies on a football field, nothing could be further from the truth. To the contrary, an immense amount of very practical education can be gained from the "playing fields and in the varsity locker room.

For example, my first formal preparation for combat flying began long before I soloed my first airplane, and I did not realize it at the time. In more recent years I've been asked what it is like to fly in combat, how it feels. The answer, for me now, is simple. You are a bit apprehensive--at least I was at first, and the fears or concerns are identical to the ones felt before quarterbacking on a Friday night or Saturday afternoon (in an era when I called all my own plays). First, you worry about how you'll react to the pressure that day; second you are a bit concerned about injury, and third, fear of the possibility that you won't be good enough that day to handle the great responsibilities given you.

In addition, there is a molding process that takes place in the often hot, dusty, hellish cauldron euphemistically called a "practice field." You come to realize that the only way to survive in that world of speed, power and violence is to keep going no matter how thirsty, sore, or exhausted you are. You learn, painfully at times, that no matter how big the guy, or how tough the situation, you can still win if you "stay reckless with your body."That works fine in football. But in combat, it either gets you a medal, or killed, or sometimes both.

AND NOW, IT'S TIME TO FLY!

During my last year at university, of great importance, I had learned how to fly. Not wonderfully, not professionally, but with confidence and an aggressive attitude that far surpassed my limited skills and experience. That opportunity came in my senior year, as a fourth-year member of the AFROTC Cadet Corps. About 180 sophomores had applied for Air Force commissioning and pilot training slots through "advanced AFROTC"; three of us passed the physical and written tests well enough to become "pilot candidates." That meant we would go to the Air Force's 13-month flight training school, provided we showed sufficient aptitude during our 30 hours of training in a Cessna 150 single-engine propeller plane.

When the FAA examiner gave me my 15-hour "progress" check ride, he told me, "Son, you are not flying the plane, the plane is flying you. You want to be a fighter pilot. Ok. But understand this: fighter pilots are called a lot of things, and most of them probably can't be repeated in polite company, but the one thing they are is incredibly aggressive when they fly those planes."

Chagrined, I took it to heart. Over the next 15 hours of flying, every time I was out solo I would quickly run through the maneuvers I would be tested on in the Thirty-Hour Final Check ride.

Then I spent the rest of my flying time doing things with the plane that were utterly illegal and probably dangerous at a level well beyond "stupid." I would fly over to the foothills surrounding the valley around Missoula, and as the daily trains came down through the hills, I would commence what I thought were "diving attacks" and "strafe runs" by cross-controlling the plane's ailerons and rudders so it would "slip," descending very fast and steeply. After "buzzing" very close to the train, I would release rudder, shove in power climb rapidly.

When the check pilot came back for my final exam, some months later, he was astounded at the difference in my flying, and he said so. He also told me he was giving me "the highest score" he'd ever given.

Three years later and 500 hours or more into jet planes, I looked back at the risky, overconfident, dangerous things did in that little Cessna and shake my head in disbelief that I had been that stupid.

o-0-o

Being youngest in my high school class, and at an all-boys school, my "social maturity" was behind most of my peers, particularly where girls were concerned.

That changed rather quickly at college, and I usually arranged a "Coke date" with one co-ed or another every evening for my last two years at university. I found the library rich in fascinating topics, and a great place to meet some smart and lovely girls. Having had some "catching up" to do socially, I obviously overcompensated.

THE THOUGHTS OF WALTER MITTY

Her hair, her lips, her perfect eyes
(To feel your kiss, to hear your sighs!)
Within my arms she glides like air
(Don't stop, band, please keep her there.)

There's such a dazzle in her smile!
(Just stay with me and talk awhile.)
Her laughing eyes -- a friendly glint?
 (A promise there, or just a hint?)

I smile now, "Be seeing you."
(Forgot to say, *"Je t'aime beaucoup."*
"Godspeed, good luck in all you do."
(Oh yes, I'll long remember you.)

You never melted in my arms.
I never tasted of your charms.
In all this world, the things most dead
Are dreams undone, and words unsaid.

Walter Mitty was the fictional hero of a short story, "The Secret Life of Walter Mitty," by James Thurber, published in The New Yorker, *March 18, 1939.*

36

In June, 1962, I was named a "Distinguished Graduate" in AFROTC, giving me a regular commission, and also got what was likely the best job in our journalism class: six months at United Press International in San Francisco before reporting to flight school.

But as with all young men and women at university, I gave a considerable amount of thought to what I wanted to do *with* my life, and what things I wanted to see, do or be as well. Certainly that August evening prior to my sophomore year had established one thing on that list, and that fall and winter I took the series of AFROTC physical and mental exams that would be a first step to reaching my goal to be a fighter pilot.

As time went by, the notion of becoming a foreign correspondent became prominent on my list. That career, or flying jets would satisfy some or all of my desire to see the world, or as much of it as possible, and do so while "somebody else paid for the travel." But during those years in academe, exposed to a wider world of possibilities and places, the list grew longer and longer.

Missoula, Montana, February, 1962—The scene is the campus coffee shop. The girl looks at the boy in wide-eyed wonder and says, "You're the smartest person I've ever known, you're really going to be something some day."

The boy looks at her sadly for a moment, then takes a pencil and notebook and begins to write:

LAMENT

When I have told of many things I know,
Then let me tell of myriads I'll ne'er know.
When I have told of places I have gone,
Then let me tell of hundreds I can ne'er go.

When I've described the wonders I have seen,
Then let me sigh for wonders that I'll ne'er see.
When I have told of those few things I am,
Then let me weep for all those things I'll ne'er be.

And when I am content, or look behind me,
I pray that all these things will soon remind me,
That I am one small candle, unfulfilled,
Faintly flickering in darkness, and soon killed.

o-0-o

In trying to analyze "what to do" with and in my life, I realized it was important to realistically assess what "tools" I brought to each task.

One, I knew, was a rather good sense of humor. Being the class clown in seventh and eighth grade, to the consternation of my teachers, and being one of several in an all-boys high school sometimes full of them had given me good practice. Enough to where I was master of ceremonies at a number of all-university functions.

But there was more to examine:

HOUSE RULE: THE JOKER IS WILD
WITH ACES, STRAIGHTS & FLUSHES

Shuffle the deck of luck and fate
And find your role in life.
Will your life be full of joy—or hate?
And how will you choose your wife?

Or better still, as you riffle the deck,
Decide what you wish to be.
One quick cut, then—what the heck!
Let's see what we shall see:

Now the first face up is the Diamond King,
And this I could never be,
For I was a very poor-born thing.
And the best things in life are free.

So the next dark face to rear its head
Is the Spade King–landsman he.
But it's not for play in the dirt I'm bred,
And toiling is not for me.

Now the handsome face of the King of Hearts
Flips up most charmingly.
But I'm poorly knit -- of awkward parts,
No role for Ichabod me!

But lo! So bold, the Club King stands,
A violent man is he.
But I've fragile bones and skinny hands,
So a soldier I shan't be.

And we can pass each Ace, alas,
· My talents are too small.
They rule the world with grace and class
And that's not me at all.

And now, ill-timed, the Queen of Hearts
In beauty and grace appears.
But since I know my poor, sad parts,
I'll set her aside--in tears.

Then, as I almost reach despair,
One lone, last card appears:
The Joker! See him smiling there?
He laughs away all tears!

And yes, he has more facets: true!
The "wild" Ace is he!
For lo, though you had Aces two,

You now have Aces three!

So I'll be each deck's lone Joker,
I like that role best.
For in life, just as in Poker,
He's more versatile than the rest.
Born in laughter, bred to joke,
To always charm...and win!
Do anything in life I choose...
And always smile within.

o-0-o

THE GIRL - *Ch. III Continued*

ENTER STAGE RIGHT:
THE ONE WHO TOOK MY BREATH AWAY.
(1961 - 1964)

"Sometimes the way to a woman's heart is through the Post Office"
— John J. Schulz, on long-distance courting

o-0-o

This section is written as a tribute to Linda, and to all those spouses who, since the dawn of aviation, married pilots, and then had to watch, wait and worry as they went off to their high-risk jobs each day. The special kind of courage, patience and encouragement of those left behind, while masking their fears, have seldom been fully acknowledged or properly celebrated. You were, and are, utterly amazing people.

THE OTHER CORRESPONDENT: LINDA

We met as student delegates from two of the nearly 100 colleges and universities attending a Model United Nations Conference at the University of Oregon. She was most of the way through her sophomore year at Mills College, an all-women's college in Oakland, California. Her school was representing Israel. I was finishing my junior year at Montana, and had been excused from the first few days of spring football practice to help represent Chad.

It was springtime, and the Oregon campus was stimulating and beautiful, and wow, so was she! She was a standout student; smart, clever, thoughtful, very sophisticated and an absolute stunner.

We arranged to meet for most of those 10 days for a "coke date" during the afternoon break from UN sessions, and then meet again for dinner each night, paid for by the University of Oregon, as I recall. We began to write letters after those 10 days together, where I had made a point to be with her between MUN sessions and every evening. For the next year, we wrote letters to each other from time to time.

Indeed, over the next four years our courtship was carried out almost exclusively by mail, except for one six-month interlude in San Francisco while I worked there for United Press International and she went through the first semester of her senior year at Mills.

We dated every chance we could, and I admit this didn't help her fine grade point average. Now and again, we sometimes talked a bit in "future tenses."

Bidding her a fond farewell at Christmas time, I went home briefly and then reported in to Williams AFB, near Phoenix, Arizona, to start 13 months of Flight School training...and more letter writing.

Often during that flight school year, I fell behind in my letter writing, and would try to make up for it with a special gift, a letter with poems included.

FLIGHT SCHOOL STUDIES

Gee, I wish I had the time
To put, through little words of rhyme,
A lot of thoughts, that in my head
Must soon get out, before they're dead.
The world, though, keeps me in duress;
I don't have time· to "go to press."
But please don't think these silent times
Bespeak indifference, or, worse crimes,
A look of love upon my part—
Just try and stop me, once I start
– Williams AFB, April, 1963

o-0-o

I did find the time on rare occasions during that intense 13 months of training to send a love poem to the girl I had decided was "the only one for me." I know she liked this one a great deal:

THE CHALLENGE

The stars are without symmetry
And birds who sing from every tree
Will miss a note sometimes, I fear,
But no light anywhere, my dear,
In all the midnight summer skies
Has half the twinkle of your eyes—
Nor any of the complex flashes
That come from 'neath those lovely lashes.

43

And as for tones, you see, my love,
I've studied Robin, Thrush, and Dove,
And not one sound is sweet or true
As your "My Darling, I love you".
The stars are just old rock formations
Where grandsons will run service stations,
All mysteries of birds are gone
Thanks to Mister Audubon.
So now the biggest mystery
Existing in this world for me,
Is you, and unless calculations fail,
Or problems unforeseen assail,
I'll understand your spell on me
By late in 2093.

– Williams AFB, September, 1963

o-0-o

In February, 1964, the day of our Graduation Ball to celebrate winning our Air Force Pilot's wings, Linda flew to Phoenix, stayed with a couple in my class and was my date to the Ball. That night, we became engaged. The next day, Linda flew home to continue her graduate studies in counseling at San Francisco State, and I drove to Waco, Texas, to attend three months of Instructor Pilot School before reporting to my new job at Vance AFB in Enid, Oklahoma. So, yet again, it was time to "live on letters."

I had wanted to graduate high enough in my flight school class of 50 (reduced to 38 during the year) to select one of the six fighter assignments. That decision was rendered moot: all six fighters were taken when it was my turn to select. But the good news was that I would still be able to stay in "high performance aircraft"; I chose one of the three Instructor Pilot slots, which would keep me in Air Training Command.

My academic scores had been fine, and I was once told by my last instructor pilot that I could fly better acrobatics and formation than he could, but thanks in part to an oversensitive balance system that prompted vertigo, and peripheral vision that was "too good" when I flew instruments under a visor or in the shrouded T-38 cockpit, I struggled mightily with instrument flying, fighting vertigo every second.

My decision to take an instructor assignment turned out to be as wise as it was fortuitous. Linda and I were to be married in July of 1964, but we had lived on letters during most of our courtship. Even before Vietnam heated up, the average fighter pilot was away from home on temporary duty (TDY) sometimes for up to half of each year. No doubt that was less of a problem than the high mortality rates involved in fighter flying, and most especially in the "Widow Maker," as the F-100 Super Sabre was often called.

Instead, I was going to be a "Tweetie Bird" pilot—as the subsonic T-37 Primary Trainer jet was nicknamed, due to the high-pitched whine of its engines. I would be sitting beside the student, flying the bubble-topped, twin-engine, highly maneuverable T-37 trainer jet.

And although the laughing epithets from some fighter pilots, who called us "Air Training Commandos" and "Training Weenies," were a bit tough on the ego, it was the best possible place to polish my flying skills in a safe and stable aircraft. More importantly, it allowed Linda and me to be together for two full years, interrupted on only rare occasion by brief cross-country TDY training flights with students. After all, most of our courtship had been conducted by mail.

During the five months before our wedding, with both of us again in school and with Linda also preparing for our wedding, I knew she retained certain qualms about her husband-to-be being in the same sort of fast-moving business as Grand Prix race drivers. Knowing that, I sent her the following ditty in one of my letters from Instructor Pilot School in Waco, Texas, designed to provide some reassurances.

AIR TRAINING COMMANDO
Some men work at selling shoes
And others pack the mail,

And some men earn their monthly dues
By helping guard the jail.
But do not fret, or get upset,
  Your man has learned to fly!

The world has seen its fill, I'm sure,
Of scavengers and kings,
But never were there men so sure
As hotshots wearing wings.
Now do not fear, my little dear,
  I'm much too young to die.

There's handsome men the world 'round
And clever men a'plenty...
But no Marine has yet been found
Can lick us, if there's twenty.*
Now do not fret, my little pet,
  I'll get this darn thing landed yet!
Next time you see a throttle jock
A'lookin' drunk and lonely,
He's scared to death, can hardly talk,
He drives one engine only.
Collections please, for my young wife.
  She's stuck with pilots all her life.

The fighter pilot spun in flat,
And all we heard him say,
"Just one more bad mistake like that
Could ruin my whole damn day".
But I'll be home and don't you fret,
  We haven't lost a "weenie" yet.

For no big deal is pilot me,
I fly a glass balloon.
My soul belongs to ATC**
I'm just a gunless goon.
It's just a Classroom in the sky;
*home nights... and never TDY****
− James Connally AFB, Waco, TX April, 1964*

----
* 20 of us vs. 1 Marine
**Air Training Command
*** Temporary Duty, some of which could last up to six months.

o-0-o

As I contemplated our relationship and our forthcoming wedding, I realized that during those intense 13 months of flight school, I had not always been very good at letter writing. As a result, during that year, our "pen pal relationship" had withered a bit, but we made a nice recovery as my early February graduation neared.

I tried to sum up the ups and downs from the time we met until "now" in one letter from Waco, TX, after we were engaged. It was sent as an apology of sorts for my part in what was, for the previous year, an "up-and-down" relationship to some degree.

OUR PHOENIX LOVE
Abysmal depths and towering heights,
Black, black days, and glittering nights,
Momentary towering spires
Of ecstasies, of deep desires.
Times without you, colored blue,
And memories of other hue,
All intermingled, blurring fast,
As dear dead days go streaming past:
A flash, blood red, of number Ten*
(My bruised friends had an odor then

47

Of tension, mixed with wintergreen,
And other things they might have been.)
The knotted twist of growing fear
That breaks when thousands stare and cheer.

Blend now with these,
The burning 1eaves
Of autumn and another time
When all the world appeared to rhyme**
As hand-in-hand in fall's delight
Day's plans were laid to last the night.
Then dash it all with bolts of pain,
As thundering, an airplane
Arcs across the growing dusk
And men go forth, as young men must,
Combining blazing, screaming motion
With young men's dreams of deep devotion.

Warmed by spring, grown summer tall,
A weary Love by chilly fall
'Till dear dead winter's frozen night
Extinguishes each tiny light...
Ah, strange it is—but nonetheless
A key to New Year's happiness:
That easiest do new flames soar
Where once a fire blazed before
And blurred and faded memories
Need never be vain reveries.
For memories can spring anew—
And every dream is someday true
If lovers only dream awhile,
Remembering that distant smile,

Enduring all ensuing pain
'Till soft, warm lips are close again.
—Waco, Texas, March, 1964

----

*   My uniform number in college
**   Our fall together, before flight school.

o-0-o

Without question, those five months of yet more separation before our wedding were frustrating. Phone calls in those days cost far more than they do now, in relative cost terms, so those were infrequent. In one letter, I expressed the wish that somehow I could magically be at her side, just by wishing it so. But as I realized, and mention in the poem, there was one "catch"—how to wish myself back.

THE COWARDLY MAGICIAN

Bound on all sides by the circumstantial fate
Of having three dimensions, I now hesitate
To brook the limitations so imposed
On human beings not so far deposed
To dusty death, that freer state
Allowed to beings who have passed the gate
Of growling Cerberus. (For they,
Unimposed-upon by night or day,
Or any two dimensions, three, or four
Are free to knock at whim on any door,
And talk with Socrates, or any other name
Whose wisdom, grace, or strong arm gave them fame.)
But, being as I am, still quite alive,
There are two things from which I can derive
Sweet, secret pleasure—all unshared:
In knowing, first, that if I dared
Beyond the heights of human comprehension,
I'd think myself into the fourth dimension

49

And quickly fly to you; but then, alack!
I'm not so sure that I could think me BACK.

Thus, Loved One, my last consolation lies
In knowing only this: that old time flies,
And with each new red dawn an old pain dies,
And fresh hope climbs the distant azure skies;
And with each sunset our planned meeting day
Is one less long and painful day away.
— Waco, Texas, March, 1964

o-0-o

On the night of my parents' 25th anniversary, a full four-and-a-half years, reams of letters, and several visits after meeting, Linda Lao ("Beautiful Flower" in Spanish and Hawaiian) changed her last name to mine in ceremonies at the Treasure Island Naval Station, near San Francisco. Our time together in Air Training Command from 1964 to 1966 allowed us to build a solid foundation to our marriage without the strains of long separations—quite the opposite of what we had already undergone.

We were married just over two and a half years when the letter writing began yet again, this time with a post mark stamped "Bien Hoa Air Base, RVN."

Three weeks after my arrival in Vietnam, Linda sent me news of a "special gift" in the form of our new baby daughter, Melinda Marie--whom we nicknamed "Molly." Ten months later, "The New Addition" and I were introduced, in Hawaii, on my R&R.

That year-long combat tour was followed by three years at RAF Lakenheath, in England, where our squadron was elsewhere in Europe for a month at a time every third month—and, at home, we took turns on "alert" duty away from home as well. This meant that our total time separated during those three years in England was close to 40 percent.

CHAPTER IV

THE LONGEST YEAR OF YOUR LIFE
(January 1963 - February 1964)

"Schulz, see that little farm down there below us? You are going to spin in and 'buy that farm' someday real soon if you don't keep your nose down and your airspeed up in these base-to-final turns."

−Lt. Molinelli, my first T-37 Instructor Pilot, February, 1963

While I was an instructor pilot at Vance AFB, Oklahoma, from 1963 to 1966, Linda and I made a point of observing each new flight school class that checked in every six weeks. Invariably there would be a handful of particularly baby-faced looking new lieutenants in the group. We made a special effort to note how they looked–all bright-eyed and bushy-tailed –most resembling brand new college sophomores.

But oh, what a change a year and a month at flight school made!

Because of the long, long hours, the day-in and day-out grind of academics and the strain and rigor of the flying training program, the change in these young men's physical appearance was startlingly evident. Invariably they developed deep lines around the eyes, trimmer waistlines, deep tans (usually just on the faces and arms, due to the baggy flight suits they wore) and an aura of self-confidence and maturity that was striking, and that none possessed 13 months before.

There are definite reasons for each aspect of this evolution: The deep lines around the eyes come as much from many late hours on the books and a year of relentless pressure, as from "scanning the distant, sun-swept horizons."

There are literally thousands of pages of textbooks, manuals, and regulations to be read and digested during the year. The "relentless pressure" comes from having to take many tricky examinations on often very technical material before moving on to the next subject. The harried college undergraduate who finds "Finals Week" at the end of each semester to be a trying experience would go berserk when faced with a mid-term or final examination every 10 to 30 days for a year. The subjects include "aircraft engineering" (taken twice, once for each trainer jet), flight physiology, navigation, meteorology, aerodynamics and supersonic aerodynamics, and more. One test even requires students to tread water and float for five minutes. (I was so skinny and low on body fat, I nearly flunked that test. At exactly five minutes I was "going down" a third time.)

And Oh, those written exams! The test administrators assume a high degree of knowledge and understanding among the fledglings they are testing, so they purposely make the multiple choice exams tricky, with the three "wrong" answers becoming real "teasers," because they are almost right, or even absolutely correct—as far as they go. As a result of the keen competition, a young man could sometimes miss only two of the 50 questions and find himself with a grade of 86, *just from missing two or three questions*, because of the grade curve. Students always worried about making a score on tests of at least 78, because a 77 or below is a failing grade, and three failed exams meant elimination.

While the academic section is hammering away at the students, the Instructor Pilots (IPs) down at the flight line are demanding more than equal pounds of flesh from "the studs," as they are called. The IPs expect verbatim memorization of the 15 or more four-to-six-step Emergency Procedures, complete knowledge of the aircraft and its systems, and complete procedural knowledge of every flight maneuver and power setting from simply landing the airplane to acrobatics like the complex cloverleaf maneuver. As one example, I once calculated that there were 61 power settings from three to 100 percent that were required knowledge on the RPM gauge alone. And for the poor student who doesn't know the answers, there are penalties ranging from a "boner" to a "pink slip" and an automatic grounding.

"Boners" were always handed out at least five at a time, for which a nickel a "boner" was contributed to the "bonehead fund" and used at the graduation party. A "pink slip" was given for an unsatisfactory flight, lack of sufficient knowledge during a ground briefing, improper recitation at the daily emergency procedures quizzing or for failing to pass one of 13 flying "phase check-rides" during the year.

The "boners" were treated lightly by the students and the instructors. The "pink slips: were another matter entirely. Three "pink slips" in a row on any daily flights, or one on a "phase check-ride (such as "instruments," etc.), meant that the student would meet the elimination board. The "studs" face the threat of a "pink" on every flight they take for 13 solid months, and can get one for just one minute of goofed-up, unsafe flying in their 260 hours of training. It's a pretty rare student who graduates without at least one "pink" on his record. Two to four "pink rides are average during their many "dual flights" in their two phases of training (in two aircraft types).

Our class (designated 64-E) entered Williams AFB, in Arizona to begin training on January 12, 1963. There were 54 students in our class, and we were immediately separated into two "sections" so that while one half of the class was on the flight line, the other half was in the classroom for half a day. Thirteen months later, 34 of us graduated, including our six German Luftwaffe pilots. All the rest of the original 54 had been eliminated because of fear of flight, air sickness (called "Manifestations of Apprehension" in Training Command parlance), or, very rarely, they were washed out because of academic problems. Most of those eliminated were victims of the first flight exam, the 30-hour check ride, which was treated as a watershed event. Most who got through it would "make it through," and were at least deemed worthy of the further time, training and the costs involved in keeping them around for further training.

Our first six months of flying, called "Primary," was done in the Cessna T-37. With its bubble cockpit, side-by-side seating, subsonic wing and fine acrobatic capability, it was the ideal trainer to introduce students to the rigors of jet flying. After the first six months, those who had not been eliminated moved on to six months of "Advanced" training in the supersonic T-38 Talon.

The typical schedule for a week was as follows: Academic classes from 7 to 10 a.m., physical training for an hour (ranging from calisthenics to basketball, soccer, flag football or half a dozen other sports), lunch, and then off to the flight line for six to seven hours. There, when not flying, students had to study, run the squadron snack bar, or handle the job of "Dispatcher," logging and totaling the daily flying time. The following week the students in one section switched with their other 64-E classmates in the other section, moving to "morning flying." We then reported first to the flight line–as early as 4:45 a.m.–and stayed until noon or 1 p.m. Then, began our classroom academics from 2 to 5 p.m., and then headed off to "hit the books" at home for two to four hours or more.

The eight Undergraduate Pilot Training bases were then located in the South and Southwestern states, where the flying weather tends to be better. Williams AFB, near Phoenix, where my class trained, was ideal in that regard. The downside is, an hour of soccer can get pretty grueling in those 115-degree temperatures, but it is geared to help the fledglings pass the biannual physical training exam, which includes sprints, sit-ups, and pull-ups. The maximum score on sit-ups was 114–one point per sit-up. I've never heard of a student *NOT* scoring 114 at testing time.

The flying is exacting, demanding, precise, and nerve-wracking. The Instructor Pilot sees that each of these clichés becomes reality. If the final approach speed for the T-37 is 100 knots, that does not mean 101 or 99–it means "peg" the airspeed indicator at exactly 100. And oh, by the way, at 99 knots on the gauge, the student flunks the ride for the day–the dreaded Pink Slip for unsafe flight.

The academic examinations are very comprehensive and extremely competitive. While I was at Williams AFB, a team of three professors from civilian universities came and surveyed our academic program and pronounced the one year of academic education to be the equivalent of three years of coursework material at a good university. Note that all of this process of "drowning in information" comes while spending only three to four hours a day in class, five days a week, and then six to seven at the flight line, where MORE learning, written and in the cockpit, was going on.

As I indicated, the environment is not just demanding, but intensely competitive because class standing is derived from the results of academic achievements and the flying check-ride scores. The post-graduate aircraft assignments are chosen by each student. Each class chooses from a block of aircraft assignments announced shortly before graduation. Selecting aircraft assignments was based solely on class standing: The number one man in class gets first choice of all available aircraft, and so on down the line, to the last B-52. Fighter and Instructor assignments usually went first, because after a year in fighter-type (high performance) trainers, most students desperately wanted a fighter assignment. There were never enough to go around.

The aura of confidence each student develops stems from having met and handled each challenge. Meantime, back when we were in training, almost one quarter of each class washed out–despite having gone through such demanding written, physical and psychological screening that each new pilot candidate was already one of "the handpicked few." Those of us who won Air Force silver wings were not only justifiably proud of ourselves. Each new graduate was, and these days likely still is, the product of a three-year process of "creaming" that eliminated the 199 other applicants who originally applied and tested for commissioning and flight school appointments. The last elimination process is flight school itself.

As an instructor, I used to tell my students on their first day at the flight line that their first assignment was not a reading task, but a writing task. "Go home tonight and write a letter of goodbye to everyone you know," I'd tell them, "because the guy who comes home a year from now just won't be the same person." They used to think I was kidding. Six months later, when they left me and the T-37 to begin six more months in the supersonic T-38, I'd always remind them of what I had said that first day. Each time they always agreed, I hadn't been kidding at all....

FLIGHT SCHOOL BLUES

It's four a.m. and you're fast asleep,
When, drawing you from your dreams so deep,
Comes the horrible jangle of your alarm.
Then somehow, all the glamour and charm
That surrounds a jet jock doesn't seem
To have that recruiter-poster gleam.
And you wonder why–oh why, oh WHY
You ever began to learn to fly.

"LOOK AT YOUR AIRSPEED -- YOU WANNA DIE?
DAMMMIT, YOU'LL NEVER LEARN TO FLY."

You stumble into your flying suit
And put on the same ol' dirty boots
Then you drive beneath the starry sky
To the shack where fledglings learn to fly,
And where they study, dispatch, and take
Ten Boners now and then, and make

56

The squadron's coffee and 'burgers and such
That help your flying touch so much.

"USE YOUR HEAD, WILL YA? STOP 'N THINK!
YOU'RE RIDING TOWARD ANOTHER 'PINK'."

Soon, with helmet and 'chute you're ready,
With gauges checked and needles steady.
And coming along for your jaunt to the sky
Is a quiet, smiling, unruffled guy
Who never swears or shouts or screams--
Until your err--But it sometimes seems
That your every move is a bad mistake,
And his shouting makes your poor ears ache.

"WHAT ARE YOU DOING, YOU KNUCKLEHEAD?
KEEP THAT UP AND WE'LL BOTH BE DEAD!"

Soon you land, and debrief, and sigh,
And wonder if ever you'll learn to fly.
Then soda in hand, you join the guys
And tell a pack of flying school lies
For an hour or two, 'til it's time to scram
And read ten chapters before your exam.
But you shrug instead and go off to chow...
Each choice on the test is wrong anyhow.

"A NEW A.T.C. QUIZ!" HE SMILES SO BRIGHT,
"THE TEST'S ALL THE SAME–A NEW ANSWER IS RIGHT."

Somehow you manage to come through it fine
With a safe and acceptable seventy-nine.
So undaunted you hurry to change for the fun

Of one-fourteen sit-ups in one-fourteen sun.
As wearily homeward by sunset's light
You trudge to study--for half the night
Some screwball calls out "No girls do I need,
I live in a world of dazzling speed."

YOU LAUGH, "BIG DEAL--JET PILOT! GEE WHIZ!"
THEN A VOICE INSIDE ADDS, "YOU KNOW--IT IS!"

o-0-o

ACROSS THE TABLE...
from me sat one of the first real jet pilots I'd ever seen: my Instructor
Pilot. As I look back over the years to that important day in late
January, 1963, I can still visualize Lt. Marianaro with his feet propped
up on his briefing table, flying suit unzipped halfway down to his
navel and hat balanced precariously on the back of his head. He
appeared to my wondering eyes to be the ultimate in "cool."

For six long months, this would be the man to whom I would
entrust my very life and my future as a jet pilot. As he sized up my
three table-mates and me from beneath his shaggy dark eyebrows, I'm
sure he was wondering what new ways we would come up with to try
to kill us both in our little "flying classroom."

Each of us, in turn (who weren't eliminated), would sit with him or
another of the "IPs" through a long list of "dems" (demonstrations) and
practice. We started by learning to handle all the "basic maneuvers,"
and quite quickly moved on to various acrobatic maneuvers such as
barrel rolls, cloverleafs, Immelmanns, and the "Split S." In that last
maneuver you smoothly rolled the plane inverted and then pulled up to
six Gs so that the nose of the aircraft went down through the vertical
dive, and then back up to level flight, well below the starting altitude,
going the opposite way.

To accomplish the transformation from fledglings to polished
military pilots, the IPs would resort to every teaching technique and
motivational device known to man, despite our contention that it was

limited to an hour and a half of sarcasm and ridicule every moment we were airborne.

Graduation night, in gratitude to my two instructors, (one in T-37's, one in T-38's) for the hard hours of sweat and tears they had undergone on my behalf, I presented them with a framed print of the poem, "My IP." I couldn't help "getting even" at the same time by reminding one of them he'd often said, "I'm a nice guy on the ground but the minute the canopy closes I turn into Simon Legree."

MY IP

You may talk of flying cheer when it's VFR and clear,
And you've earned your wings and flying is such fun.
 But while you're trying to earn 'em,
You sometimes wish they'd burn 'em,
And you dread the day that you had e'er begun.

Now In Willie's sunny clime, where I used to spend me time,
A'trying to make the Tweetie Bird like me,
Of all that tough old crew,
The meanest man I knew,
Was me dear Instructor Pilot, Sam Legree.

Oh it was din, din, din in the cockpit where me earphones shoulda been.
"Now watch your blasted air speed and get off that topside rudder,
Or you'll kill us both in just one little spin."

Now I shan't forget the day
When we went upstairs to play,
When a bogie right at twelve swung on around,
Sam was going through a "dem"
When I grabbed the stick and then
I yanked five G's and pulled 'er toward the ground.

It happened in a blur,
And without "I've got it, sir,"

59

But we got away from that old Tweetie clean.
He knew we'd near been hit,
But he didn't smile a bit,
"That's about the worst "Split S" I've ever seen."

So I'll meet him down below,
In the place all pilots go,
Where we all fly IFR from eight to three.
He'll be teaching Satan's crew
How to fly in squads of two,
And I'll get more chewing out from Sam Legree.

Oh It was din, din, din in the cockpit where me earphones shoulda been.
Though you've yelled at me and grayed me,
By the livin' God that made me,
I can fly as well as you can, Sam Legree.
                                    – Williams AFB, Chandler, AZ 1964

"THE GREAT WHITE TRAINING AID"

The T-38 "Talon" was built by Northrop Corporation as the first supersonic trainer to introduce student pilots to the characteristic of supersonic flight they would encounter in our post-Korean War Air Force inventory. The "Talon" lived up to all the expectations...and then some! As we would describe it to guys coming in to the new classes behind us, "It taxis like a Cadillac, drives like a Ferrari and lands like a white crowbar." These landing characteristics were specifically designed into the bird. They are an inherent drawback, especially during landings, that are part and parcel of every supersonic aircraft. A supersonic wing must be as small as possible, be swept back from the fuselage on about a 30-degree angle or more, and must be thin, and symmetrical, top and bottom. The result is a plane that flies high and very fast, but which staggers through the air, with power nearly at full throttle when it is slowed to landing speeds. In sum, flying 188 miles per hour may seem like a lot to other aviators and those who don't fly

60

at all, but to pilots riding a supersonic wing, it's time to land—whether they want to or not!

As if getting through this toughest course in the Air Force were not enough reason, the students were also quite proud of conquering the T-38 "Talon," and well they should be. They have sometimes flown it over 1000 miles an hour, above 40,000 feet, and often have flown the sensitive machine in tight formation with skills that, in some cases, would make an aerobatic team proud. They can guide it through acrobatic maneuvers that call for exact speeds and smooth precision at all times.

They have also learned to land a supersonic wing, where descent is controlled with the throttle, where the landing speed is "pegged" exactly—no faster and no slower—and where the touchdown area is circumscribed. Landing too long can result in a roll-out that goes off the end of a very long runway. Most of all, they have learned to "stay ahead" of the milk-white aircraft with its blue and orange trim as it raced skyward at a dizzying rate. During its testing phase, the "Talon" set a world's climb record (since broken), going from brake release to 30,000 feet in 59 seconds.

THE TALON

The Talon sits in the pre-dawn chill,
Streamlined, sleek, grey and still.
Then somewhere down along the line
The starters begin their high-pitched whine,
And soon with a deeper, richer sound,
The Talon prepares to leave the ground.

Slowly it taxis, and in the light
Its flashing colors, orange, blue, and white,
Begin to gleam, and its silhouette
Seems to suggest the pirouette
That the Talon can do in the distant blue
Where the sky takes on a darker hue.

Encumbered by gear it waits to soar,
Trembling, it stands through the run-up roar,
Then gauges and lanyards check—and Go!
With burners lit in a pale blue glow.
In an ever-accelerating race to the sky
The Talon leaps—gear, flaps, and fly!

Streamlined now, and home at last,
The fetters now of the earth are past.
The Talon wheels with easy grace,
Sketching the edge of outer space
Eight miles up in the azure sky
Where never an eagle could hope to fly.

Diving, climbing, rolling, soaring,
Now in tight formation roaring,
Dancing a carpet of Stratus white,
Skimming the deck in the morning light,
Chasing a contrail's puffy trace,
Challenging angels to a race.

Plummeting now, the Talon glides,
Skimming the craggy mountain sides,
Then gear and flaps and once around,
Too soon returning to the ground,
Restrained by chocks and pins and ties,
Kept from its home in the distant skies.
                    — *Williams AFB, Feb. 1964*

o-0-o

THE TABLES TURNED: "BRACE YOURSELVES–HERE COMES THE NEW CLASS OF IDIOTS"
(1964 - 1966)

Situated three miles south of Enid, Oklahoma is a small, pretty Air Base where I began my career as an operational pilot in the Air Force. It was here that I brought my bride, here that I really learned how to fly instruments in weather, here that I flew most of my 1,500 jet hours, and here that I almost "bought the farm" on about two dozen occasions, thanks to student mistakes.

It was an interesting, enjoyable, maturing experience having to "play God" for a bunch of young men just out of college (and only about two years younger than I was), as they began the progression I had just been through from "learning to crawl" to jet flying at its most proficient. Each instructor had four students–referred to as "the studs" at his table, but also flew with others, so that students got tips and critiques from other IPs in the Flight.

Although most aspects of the tour were extremely enjoyable or beneficial, the tornadoes in the spring and fall were a bit scary when they hit only 200 yards away, and the thunderstorms were very frequent in the summer months and in the middle of winter. Because of these weather phenomena, we sometimes could not fly for days on end and thus sat around the "IP Desks" and went through hours of "hangar flying" and ground instruction referred to as "table briefings." Moreover, when we got behind in the flying schedule, we had to make up for it on good days, and this meant flying three times a day for the IPs, with the last takeoff at 6 p.m., just as sunset was turning into darkness. It made for a long, tiring day from 10 in the morning until nine at night.

Often, at this very friendly base, the squadron instructor pilots and their wives would get together at Officers Club parties. I recall our having a "Gay 90s" party, preceded by a mustache-growing contest, a Dogpatch party with Kickapoo Joy Juice, and a Beatnik party with appropriate decor and dress. Part of the program that night included poetry readings and some pretty "way out' stuff composed by yours truly, as the next three poems illustrate.

64

WELCOME TO VANCE, FELLA!

Cacophonous radio blaring,
Mindless eyes at gauges staring,
Labyrinthine mazes of mass illogic
And tedious briefings, dull and stodgic.

Quavering horses on run-up's roar,
Aerodynamically built to soar;
A Pegasus in candy coating
Up at forty thousand, floating.

Dive and soar and wheel, you clown,
When gas runs out, you're coming down.
So, 400 up and a mile out,*
No let it fall, and don't round out.

Brief, brief, brief, and now for practice,
Brief some more till SAC extracts us.
Or maybe you'd like ocean shore,
Then, Vietnam, and brief some more.

Of thunderstorms, we've just a few,
Tornadoes today? Just one or two.
Gentle breezes wafting by**
Lovely weather! Solos, fly!

----

* *To fly proper final approach to landing in a supersonic aircraft, it's best to arrive at 400 feet above ground a mile from the runway, then hold constant airspeed while using the throttle to control the rate of descent. This was true for the T-38 and for the F-100.*
** *Less than 40 knots. Unfortunately, most of the time the near-constant wind was blowing about 90 degrees to the runway, and it was said that pilots from Vance AFB always landed one wheel at a time, crabbed into the wind, even if at other bases there was no wind!*

ODE TO THE STUD

Programmed idiots, wearing green,
Stammering procedures they've never seen.
Jaws cheek full of bubble gum,
Trying to land with gear un-hung.

Turning final, nose straight down,
Campus hero, village clown.
But, compensation at my table,
One young boob who's truly able.

Behold yon Cassius: beetle browed
And sullen, never joins the crowd;
Magic hands* but half-baked mind,
Shoddy dress and shoes un-shined.

Dully, at the world staring,
Bad hangover--never caring;
No doubt what this young lad will be:
Another A.T.C. IP. **

Magic hands--exceptional feel for the aircraft, a precise pilot.
*** Air Training Command Instructor Pilot.*

o-0-o

THE COLUMNIST

During my first two years at Vance AFB, I was able to use my journalism schooling a bit by writing a column for the weekly Base newspaper. One of those was a "guide" for the 400 new second lieutenants going through flight school. It provided them with the "real" meaning of the terminology used in flying training reports:

TERM	DEFINITION
Exceptionally well qualified ••••••••••	Committed no major blunders to date.
Exceptional flying ability ••••••••••••	Equal number of takeoffs and landings.
Indifferent to instruction••••••••••••••	Knows more than his IP,
Expresses himself well••••••••••••••	Speaks English fluently.
Slightly below average••••••••••••••	He's really hurtin'.
Meticulous attention to detail••••••••••	A nit-picker.
Demonstrates qualities of leadership•••	Has a loud voice.
Character, integrity above reproach •••	Still one step ahead of the law.
Quick thinking••••••••••••••••••••••	Offers plausible excuses for errors.
Often spends extra hours on the job••••	Miserable home life.
Socially active••••••••••••••••••••••	He really hits the sauce.
Approaches difficult problems with enthusiasm••••••••••••••••••••••	Finds someone else to solve the problem; he just approaches it.
Outstanding••••••••••••••••••••••••••	Usually in the rain

o-0-o

A POINT OF GROWING CONCERN

Perhaps more than in any other profession, military pilots are alienated from the mainstream of American society. It is an unfortunate situation, because this communication gap breeds misunderstanding and even resentment on both sides.

The gap is understandable for several reasons. First, the pilots and their families are often living on an air base, in what is a relatively close and closed society—an enclave within guarded gates. They will move at least once every three years on average to another community elsewhere in the world, seldom, if ever, to return. For this reason, "community relations" are difficult to develop or maintain. Further, the pilots themselves are gone from home a great deal, often on temporary duty for weeks or months at some other enclave in the United States or abroad.

This, combined with the natural subculture that develops in any demanding and difficult profession, causes them to feel quite detached from ordinary or civilian life. Doctors or lawyers, to take one example, after years of intensive study and extremely rigorous training develop vocabularies—jargon—and an outlook that is modified over time when they begin dealing with patients or clients. Military pilots, in contrast, after leaving their intensive training and class work, deal almost exclusively with other pilots on the ground, in the air, and after work at social gatherings. The standard description of a squadron party is a large group of men in one corner of the room "talking airplanes" and a large group of wives in another cluster "talking babies."

As with any technical and demanding profession, much of a pilot's time is taken up with flying briefings before and after each flight, study to prepare for the next check-ride, and focus on technical literature.

Naturally, in their leisure reading in daily newspapers and magazines, items about flying will catch their eyes. Because they mistakenly assume that the general population has read much of the same information, the pilots are often quite amazed at the many naive, elementary questions they encounter in their occasional encounters with civilians, and even with ground support officers and enlisted men.

Small wonder that after two or three years in this environment, civilian life, or as a non-aviator in the military, seems dull, alien and very remote.

Nowadays, some 50 years on, that gap and do doubt worse sense of alienation, for many complex, other reasons, now may best describe almost all our military forces. While it may have been somewhat exacerbated in 1972, with the discontinuation of the Draft, in too many cases it is a bigger divide now, because our "all volunteer forces" are, in the case of combat units, doing multiple "tours" in war zones, threatened by loss of life and limb, and the loss of friends

CHAPTER V

THE MACHINE
(April 12 - 26, 1967)

A TRIBUTE TO THE F-100 SUPER SABRE

This is about my first fighter, the F-100 Super Saber.
I checked out in it at the age of 21 and flew it for 10 years, compiling
2,000 hours in it, a combat tour and 11 of my 13 ocean crossings in it.
I sat many hours of alert with nuclear and non-nuclear weapons
in it, far from home, civilization and my family for months that
cumulatively amounted to years at a time.
I have been joyous in it,
triumphant in it,
lost in it,
and terrified in it.
I crashed the first one I soloed...
but accomplished many victories in it as well.
It took me to nine different countries
and brought me home in impossible weather.
It was the most difficult to fly
and least forgiving of all jet fighters,
and, from time to time
it scared all of us who flew it.
It was the backbone of the Air Force fighter corps for many years,
and even after it was technically obsolete,
it was the favorite jet of those troops in Vietnam who
needed help when things got tough.
There are a lot of aging vets—former soldiers and
Marines—walking around alive and well today
because I and a lot of guys like me were very good in it
and could visit deadly destruction on the enemy with it
when called upon.
It is gone now,
but still alive in my heart
and in the memory of those who flew it.

– Norm Turner, IP at Cannon AFB, NM; later, a California Federal District Judge

PLEASE DON'T THROW ME IN THAT BRIAR PATCH....

I was sitting in a dental chair at Vance AFB in September, 1966, when my squadron commander called, telling me I was being reassigned to the F-100 and to Bien Hoa Air Base, Vietnam. He could tell from my response that this was very exciting news to me: the F-100 was at the top of my very short list of desired assignments. In fact it was the *only* plane on my list.

He also told me I would be going to Survival School at Fairchild AFB in Spokane, WA before starting my checkout in the F-100 at Cannon AFB, near Clovis, NM.

Ah, what a charming place, Survival School! In two weeks of classroom work we learned the principles of survival anywhere in the world. And the last week, we got to practice what we had learned. Armed with a knife or hatchet, a 40-pound pack, a pair of fish hooks and some leader, we headed off to the Sullivan Lake game preserve in the Bob Marshall Wilderness Area, high in the northern Rocky Mountains.

Oh, did I say we had food for the week? No, we didn't.

Despite the bitter cold and snow of November near the Canadian border, I faced the coming week with some confidence. After all, hadn't I been raised in this neck of the woods, just 120 miles away, in Missoula, Montana? And hadn't I been on Boy Scout camping trips in mid-winter in nearby Glacier Park?

Well, the Boy Scout experience, my two summers of working for the Forest Service as a firefighter traveling to several western states, and my many excursions into the Montana mountains in various seasons did little to prepare me for what lay ahead. The Bob Marshall Wilderness Area, which included Sullivan Lake, is one of a handful of virgin wilderness areas in the country, and remains untouched by human efforts at any changes whatsoever.

What a gross travesty in terms of accurate reporting the preceding understated sentence is! How can you describe a tangled horror of underbrush, branches, trees, snow, ice, rocks, fallen logs and wild, icy creeks? Hannibal may have crossed the Alps–but *WE* crossed Sullivan's Lake game preserve!

Elsewhere, when I traversed heavily forested areas, I frequently had to part tree branches to make my way. Often, over that six days and nights, I bent small trees apart in order to continue. And all this in 14 degree Fahrenheit temperatures with snow and sleet.

Beauty spas and slenderizing clinics take far too long to achieve their goal. Six days and nights "on the trek" and two days and nights in the "Little Camp for downed and wayward flyers" and I'll guarantee most of you will lose 15 to 20 pounds. *(As for that "little camp," suffice to say it is a subject about which I can say no more, even now.)*

When it was all over, they asked us for a written course critique. Here was mine:

SURVIVAL SCHOOL CRITIQUE

Please, Sir, I'd like a word with you,
Now that I'm through your course.
There are some things I could suggest:
The first one is a horse.

Way out here in this wilderness
I didn't want a car,
But running everywhere is bunk–
And just where is our bar?

Then, too, I must confess that your
Cuisine was rather needing
More flavor and variety
And more bread with each feeding.

Furthermore, you advertised
Rooms spacious, long and wide.
And fresh air and a gorgeous view,
But Man, it's cold outside.

71

And, Sir, there are two other things
I think that I should mention.
They're things that we've all noticed
And they will need your attention:

Out here you have the loveliest
Of views in all creation
Undoubtedly the prettiest
Golf course in this whole nation.

But, nonetheless, the planners here
Made all the fairways longer
By miles than I have ever seen
And nothing could be wronger.

And you'd best fire your gardener,
For, nowhere, I would guess,
Are fairways more in need of care,
And your Greens are a mess!

I've always been a golfer fair,
On courses that are tough,
But this time I guess I just played
My whole game in the rough.

So, Sir, between your lodgings
And poor food and transportation,
I don't think I'll come here again.
Oh—have my last "C" ration.

                         – November, 1966

o-0-o

NOW IT BEGINS! I GET TO FLY THE F-1OO SUPER SABRE

"Welcome to the F-100.
It takes off funny, it flies funny, and it lands funny."
— 481st Squadron Commander's Initial briefing,
Cannon AFB, NM, 1966

o-0-o

Immediately after Survival School, Linda and I packed up for the move from Enid, OK to Cannon AFB, near Clovis, NM. It was time for my "combat crew training," which is fancy way of saying that I went to an advanced flight school to learn to fly and fight in the F-100. This involved first learning how to fly "the most dangerous plane ever built." "The Hun," nicknamed with reference to the "hundred" in its numerical designation, killed more pilots per thousand hours of flying than any plane ever built. Second on that grim list was the Sopwith Camel, followed by the F-104 Starfighter, with its very stubby wings and extremely high landing speeds.

My 16 classmates and I were all experienced pilots with at least 1,000 jet flying hours before we came to Cannon for this checkout. Thus, we were expected quickly to master the "routine" tasks of landing, takeoff, close formation flying, instruments and basic acrobatics so we could move on to learning the "real stuff." That included air combat tactics, air-to-air and air-to-ground gunnery, dive and skip bombing, low- and high-level navigation, air-to-air re-fuelling and high altitude spread formation and dog fighting tactics. This was combined with a daily classroom program to teach us the basic engineering of our new "vehicle," including its many unique features and sometimes deadly proclivities. The objective was for us to learn the Super Sabre "inside and out." Given our knowledge beforehand of the challenging and dangerous plane we were now attempting to master, we were all highly motivated to achieve those academic objectives and learn our classroom lessons very thoroughly.

There was one rather steep mountain to climb as we transitioned. The F-100 was at least three times the size and weight of the T-37, which many of us had spent most of our time flying until then. And for the few instructors from the "advanced phase" of flight school, their T-38 Talon was quicker, about as fast at top speed, more agile, and only about half the size and the weight of the "new bird" we were learning about. Simply, the T-38 had a far safer thrust-to-weight ratio, and added power would get students out of most of their dangerous situations in the landing pattern. Most of all, for all of us, there were easily three times the number of buttons, switches and circuit breakers in the cockpit of the F-100, and before we even got to ride on our first flight with an instructor, we were expected to pass a "blindfold cockpit check," were we could move deftly and accurately to every switch, button and gauge as soon as our instructor pilots named them. The blindfold cockpit test, by the way, is a standard part of the checkout in any AF airplane, beginning before a student's first flight in the T-37 in the Primary phase of flight school. Any "negative motivation aside," for me and for most of my classmates, this chance to fly the Super Sabre was a dream come true; we had all long been fascinated by this challenging and impressive bird.

In Tokyo, some years after my last flight, I found myself combining things we learned in our initial classroom lectures about what to expect from "The Hun," and contrasting that with the more recent memories of things that had happed over the years...some of those "close calls" we all had flying that bird.

Nota Bene: *Before reading the next poem, go to **pp. 77-8:** "Tricky Handling Characteristics." There's prior context to all other poems.*

SUPERSABRE: OUR FIRST CLASS LECTURE

Supersabre sits in the velvet night
Awaiting day, armed for any fight.
"The men who designed it planned from the start
To put fire in its mouth and steel in its heart."

Supersabre cart-starts and roars to life;
Shark-like, functional, ready for strife.
"Its long, husky body, hollowed from lead...
It'll bite you the instant you give it its head."

Supersabre ripping through silver dawn,
Paired with his Brother...soon both are gone.
"Each switch and each line was built with a mind
That this is a War Bird...and no other kind."

Supersabre staggers for speed and height...
Soon we'll soar, soon we'll know Flight.
"Lead Sled, Widowmaker, call it what you may...
Just get decent airspeed..then watch it at play!"

Supersabre swift now--smooth, agile, light...
Gliding o'er the meadows of wooly white.
"Lieutenant Killer?"...yeah...but what a beauty!
Such a lovely brute for fun...or Duty.

Supersabre knows now: War up ahead...
In it now, Thunder Bird, roar with your lead.
"Shrapnel and ack-ack it takes by the score,
Wheels, soars, dives again...too tough for any war.

Supersaber's sideways, nipping at the stall,
Snapping nose downward, hearing War's call.

"It has adverse yaw at high speed and low...
And if you don't fix it...Boom Boom..out you go."

Now I'm hit...WE are hit...are we dead?
Sabre, will your fire light scream in red?
"Now when the fire light decides to come on,
You've got about ten seconds before you're ...gone!"

War Bird, you're wounded, smashed beyond repair...
Ninety miles to the Base. Can we get there?
"Remember, bailout may just be the way
To make sure you're around to fly another day.

Supersabre: Need this...must still attack..
(When the battle's over, we'll go back.)
"Forget all your science, throw away your charts...
The Hun is the sum of more than all its parts."

Supersaber's shot up, taking some more,
Giving violence tenfold, up...up...soar!
"Just remember, students, now starting to yawn:
It'll make it home with half its engine gone."

Supersabre, Base is near, gear down, Now!
Quit your buck and stall act! Fly! (Somehow).
"Gentlemen, this bird is old...tough...and smart.
So be the same and this old Hun will steal your heart."

Supersabre, you and I...up at play!
I was careful...but you got me anyway.
"Now Gentlemen, I warn you..do not shrug:
Old Supersabre...is a habit-forming drug."
                    -- "remembering when," Tokyo, 1976

EARNING THE "WIDOWMAKER" NICKNAME:
THOSE TRICKY HANDLING CHARACTERISTICS

Because it could perform many missions and fulfill many roles while flying in any weather, and with various types of ordnance, the Super Sabre was truly an engineering marvel for its day, and a military strategist dream.

But inherent in its supersonic, swept-wing design were a number of handling characteristics foreign to even the most grizzled veteran pilots. A swept-wing, supersonic aircraft simply flies differently from other aircraft, and any attempt to land it from the far tighter overhead, circular "pitch- out" pattern of prop-driven or subsonic fighters is usually fatal, particularly in the F-100. The supersonic jets also flew an overhead "pitch out" pattern over the top of the runway, but instead of continuing in a descending, circular turn, pilots extended the downwind leg before beginning a descending turn that put them 400 feet above ground a mile out from the runway. From there, with the nose above the horizon, and the speed now pushing down close to the stall, pilots advance the power to control the rate of descent while holding a constant final approach speed. In simple terms, you "control the crash to the runway," and just above it, the air off the wings hits the ground and bounces back up to the fuselage, causing added life, called "ground effect" to cushion the landing quite effectively. To try to land from too tight a circular pattern descending in too close and with too tight a turn, is deadly. Or, to put it more euphemistically, but in the phrase familiar to all military pilots, "*You do that and I'll guarantee, you'll buy the farm!*"

"The Widowmaker," as it was sometimes called, had some unique idiosyncrasies. First, and put simply, at slow speeds, such as in the landing pattern, or in high G maneuvers, the plane rolls opposite the direction from the way the pilot moves the stick, and all the while the plane is nibbling at the stalling speed, due to its "high angle of attack" in relation to the direction it is actually flying. This little trick–known as adverse yaw–gave many F-100 pilots a "rough go of it," or worse...until they learned, and learned quickly, how to fly with their feet by pressing the appropriate rudder, while blending in their stick movement to roll the plane to fly the landing pattern or complete high G maneuvering turns at greater speeds. Sadly, a few neophytes flying at slow speeds, low to the ground on takeoff or landing, discovered too late that adverse yaw can result in a sudden snap roll to the inverted, spinning the plane and pilot into the ground almost instantly, with no time for bail out or recovery.

There is another danger, and every F-100 pilot, and most AF pilots in general, have seen the infamous "Sabre Dance Landing" film. This "dance" can occur any time a pilot on final approach to landing, with the nose of the aircraft above the horizon and a steady sink rate toward the runway at a speed very close to stall, decides to raise the nose a bit more to slow descent or to round out for a softer landing.

In either case, the F-100 starts to roll off on one wing, then the other, and the pilot trying to fix this and to avoid the increased sink rate, advances the throttle and fights to stop the rolling. But he is by now "caught in a corner" where to recover flight, he must lower the nose, but that will mean certain death that close to the ground.

Pulling on the stick to try to climb away is not an option either, because lift is near impossible and raising the nose just makes the sink rate rapidly increase, resulting in a deadly fireball at the approach end of the runway. That is precisely what happened one day, early in the life of the Super Sabre, when a camera crew just happened to be filming at the end of the runway when a pilot came in to land his "Hun," and was then killed. The Sabre Dance, as we saw in that "horror movie," rapidly becomes the "dance of death."

Yet I know of no other aircraft built that I could ever love so much ...or pay so much attention to every moment I was in it. And when it became obsolete and I had to think of moving to another airplane, my strong desire was to get to the A-7, the only other single-seat, single- engine fighter in the inventory at that time.

The F-100, to me, was a powerful, tough looking plane whose every line bespoke muscle and power and aggressiveness. While the Navy inherited a tradition of calling all its ships "she," a practice that has transliterated to airplanes, I could never find anything the least bit feminine or petite about the F-100, parked or in action. And I could only think of it in the masculine gender, or a very formidable "it."

78

THE WIDOWMAKER

The silent Super Sabre sits,
Its mouth a gaping sneer,
With speed and grace in every line
It dares you to draw near.

With swept and supersonic wings
Its beauty takes your breath,
But if you let him "have his head"
He'll spin you to your death.

That moment that you first forget
Exactly what he's made for
He'll plant you in a piece of farm
That is all bought and paid for.

So listen now, young fighter jocks,
And fighter-jocks-to-be,
You won't get into trouble'
If you heed these words from me.

"That bird you see a'sittin' there
With guns and gaping jaw,
Can do a trick that ruins your day,
So watch its adverse yaw.

"Those four guns you see beneath
Can sing a deadly song
But when it starts its "Sabre Dance,"
You won't be livin' long.

"In any venture, one sour note
Can ruin the melody,
And this great beast can ruin the song
By running through a tree.

"There's many a Sabre lesson taught,
And each day do you learn,
For many a man has failed his class
in 'Base-to-final-turn.'"

No, I don't trust you, Mighty Beast,
You won't get me today.
I love you, but respect you more,
When we go up to play.

MID-AIR!

One of my most unforgettable experiences during the F-100 checkout program was my first air-to-air refueling mission. I'm sure it leaves an indelible impression on every pilot who has tried it because, for most of us, it is our first mid-air collision. And, of course, every pilot internalizes the notion that a principle of survival is to *avoid* mid-air collisions. But now, a collision is precisely what we must arrange, and it goes against every instinct and bit of common sense we have.

In principle, the concept of air-to-air refueling seems simple, but on the first try, or the first time in turbulent conditions, it begins to seem like it will take years of practice before it becomes so.

On that first flight, the neophyte finds himself up around 20 thousand feet trying to fly formation with a gigantic KC-135 refueling aircraft (tanker). Before he can think of a good reason to abort the mission, he finds it's now his turn to refuel. So he drops down to the left from his perch beside the tanker and begins the painstaking process of driving his steel refueling probe, located on his right wing, into the "Drogue" on the KC-135, which is operated by a "boomer," who sits in a small place at tail end of the big plane. The result of the pilot's efforts is a mid-air collision that rattles to the marrow of his bones, and an ensuing five-minute formation ride with the big and bouncing basket while fuel is pressure-pumped into the fighter.

Because with any decent pressure on the control stick of the F-100, you can gain or lose a hundred feet—a 10-story building—in about a second, you begin to imagine how delicately and precisely one has to control the aircraft to keep it inside error ranges of inches. And now the amazing part: most students selected to fly fighter planes are already excellent formation pilots, ranked very high in undergraduate training in the first place. So, while it may run contrary to everything said in the previous paragraphs, the reality is that by the second or third flight involving air-to-air refueling, it ceases to be much of a challenge at all; rather, it becomes a quiet source of pride. Or as a fighter jock might put it to the neophyte: "It's a piece of cake."

A note of explanation must be interjected here regarding the term "Flying Evaluation Board. An F.E.B. is convened whenever an aircraft accident or incident occurs where a "pilot error" may be a factor, or whenever a pilot fails to pass his semi-annual Flight check ride. The pilot then can be congratulated, grounded, moved to another aircraft, fined, or given a medal as a result of the Board's findings. Needless to say, an F.E.B. is the bane of all Air Force pilots' existence.

Mindful of one of my favorite hit songs, *Ghost Riders in the Sky,* written by Stan Jones in June, 1948, I was inspired at some point to scribble this parody to amuse my classmates and instructors at Cannon.

GAS STATION IN THE SKY

A Fighter Jock went ridin' out
One dark and cloudy day.
Within his jet he rested
As he sped along his way,
When all at once a Mighty Bird
With monstrous wings he spied,
With 14 engines mounted aft
And 12 crewmen inside.
Yippie-aye-aaaa, Yippie-aye-oooo
Gas Station in the Sky.

Their faces blurred, their eyes bloodshot,
Their flight suits soaked with sweat,
They'd like to land this big Gas Pump,
But they can't land it yet.
'Cause they've got to ride 12 hours
In that monstrous hunk of tin
A-givin' gas to fighters
As they ride on, hear the din...
Yippie-aye-aaaa, Yippie-aye-oooo
Texaco in the Sky.

The "Basket" dropped, the jock hooked up
With only 15 tries,
And rode that blasted probe and drogue
Through herky-jerky skies.
It seemed he rode forever
On that rack up in the blue,
Just how he got his load of gas,
No one ever knew...

82

Yippie-aye-aaaa, Yippie-aye-oooo
Next spastic in the Sky.

As the jock stowed all his Green Stamps,
He heard the "Boomer" say,
"If you wanna save your soul from SAC,
A-givin' gas all day,
Then fella, don't get F.E.B.'d
Or with us you will ride
With a gas hose trailing after us
Across these endless skies."
Yippie-aye-aaaa, Yippie-aye-oooo
Gas Station in the Sky.

o-0-o

THE WORKHORSE OF VIETNAM

The F-100 was originally designed as a supersonic air superiority fighter to follow the North American Company's famed F-86 Sabre Jet. This "A" model was purely a "day fighter," but it was soon replaced with the "C" model. While retaining its excellent air-to-air fighting capabilities, the far more versatile C model was also capable of air-to-ground, close-air-support, and of great importance in that era, tactical nuclear weapon delivery. Over time, the D model was added to the inventory, and soon became the most widespread F-100s in use in our Air Force. The D model had flaps, allowing it to land at slower speeds, and much more advanced conventional and nuclear weapons delivery capabilities. Critical to the initial training of new pilots, North American also built the two-seat "F" model, which could handle all the missions of the single-seat D-model.

The F-100s were in active duty Air Force units from 1954 to 1972, and in a number of Air National Guard units until 1979. Over time, 2,296 F-100s were built, including two prototypes built initially

and seven RF-100As that were modified to go on reconnaissance missions during the late '50s.

F-100s also gave a multi-mission combat capability to allies in Turkey and Denmark Nationalist China and France.

That added nuclear delivery ability not only meant that F-100 squadrons were deployed to strategically important bases in Europe and North Asia, it also drove the life style of the pilots and their families stationed at those bases and at F-100 bases in the United States. Pilots in those squadrons could expect to be "forward deployed" to places where the primary mission was "nuclear alert" to deter the outbreak of WWIII. And it also meant a great deal of family separation, up to half of each year, for the pilots.

In June of 1964, eight F-100s conducted the first official combat strike in Southeast Asia, striking anti-aircraft artillery (AAA) sites in Laos from their temporary base at Da Nang, in South Vietnam. By December 14th of that year, temporary duty units deployed from other bases began regular combat operations, providing air patrol support to protect the F-105 Thunderchiefs, which began covert attacks over North Vietnam from Korat Air Base in Thailand.

As the war in Vietnam escalated rapidly, so did the role and numbers of F-100 squadrons deployed to Vietnam, first on temporary duty for up to six months, and then to full tours of duty for a year. Close air support became the Hun's primary mission, and from "in-country" air bases at Bien Hoa, Da Nang, Phan Rang and Phu Cat, full wings of F-100s—usually about 68-70 aircraft for three squadrons—the numbers of day and night combat sorties increased steadily, as did the size and number of U.S. ground units based throughout the country. During the nearly six year involvement of F-100s in Vietnam, the Super Sabers also played the key role in two special, very dangerous programs over North Vietnam. The "Wild Weasel I" program used highly modified "F" models focused on electronic warfare to fly North to seek and destroy AAA and Surface-to-Air Missile (SAM) sites. Later, F-100Fs were chosen for the Fast Forward Air Controller (Fast FAC) program, soon labeled the "Misty" mission, after their famous radio call sign. The Misty pilots flew up to four hours or longer at low altitude over North Vietnam, locating targets for the Air Force, Navy and Marine fighter bombers coming into North Vietnam from Thailand or off aircraft carriers in the Tonkin Gulf. (*For amplification on the Misty mission—widely considered the most dangerous air mission during our Vietnam involvement, see Ch. VII, "The Men," and the profiles on Gary Tompkins and Jack Doub.*)

By the time the last F-100 unit, the 35th Tactical Fighter Wing, departed Southeast Asia in July, 1971, the F-100 Super Sabre had well earned its reputation as "the workhorse of Vietnam." F-100s flew 360,283 combat sorties in SEA (more than all other USAF fighters combined), and suffered 242 losses.

(For more information, see "USAF Fixed-Wing Losses in Vietnam," on the final few pages of this book.

o-0-o

TIME TO GO TO WAR

In March, 1967 our class graduated from the Replacement Training Unit (RTU) course at Cannon AFB, New Mexico. Our instructors were all veterans of a long TDY assignment to Vietnam prior to becoming Instructor Pilots at the new RTU site at Cannon. Until shortly before we arrived at Cannon, all F-100 training for new flight school graduates and the "checkout" for experienced pilots transferring from another airplane had been done at Luke AFB, near Phoenix, Arizona.

Before heading out across the Pacific to our new assignments, our class had a month of leave, so we visited my parents in Montana and hers in San Anselmo, California, where Linda then stayed for the year I was gone. When I left, she was over eight months pregnant with our first child.

Once again, we would have to "live on letters."

o-0-o

CHAPTER VI

LETTERS TO LINDA (CONT.)

Within a Fighter Pilot's Letters (From Vietnam)

Part Two

(April 27, 1967 - March 13, 1968)

Between the lines you'll have to see
Some things I dare not write to thee.
I will not write how many died
Nor can a man admit he's cried.

Dear Linda,

April 27, 1967—I had my seventh combat mission today and did much better with my bombs, but it will take some work before I am confident that I can "put 'em where I want 'em" every time.

I have a very impressive guy for my Flight Leader, Major Lou Daniels. He is very quiet, extremely thorough, and an outstanding officer, widely respected. He is one of the few people in the Air Force who made Captain two years below the normal 4.5-year zone a number of years back, when promotion to Captain was on a competitive basis instead of just automatic at four-and-a-half years if you were deemed "fully qualified." Nowadays, competitive promotions start at Major, where only the "best qualified' are promoted—sometimes only 48 percent of those eligible.

I am now the flight publications officer; the squadron information officer and assistant awards and decorations officer. I'll be happy to take all the work I can get because the time passes so much more quickly that way.

Bien Hoa is really not much of a hardship assignment compared to an awful lot of the places a man could be in a war. There are TVs in many of the hooches, a locker bigger than the number of things I've stored, good hi-fi sets being played in almost every hooch, an excellent BX with plenty of opportunity to buy the things you need, except for a fan, a lamp, a small tape recorder and a set of shower clogs—which is what I need.

The biggest thing you have to fight on many missions is complacency. Right now, rare are the times you see anyone shooting at you on daytime missions. That's because of our speed and the color of the ammo in daylight. Also you get the feeling you are on the gunnery range with no one down below. I've heard it's different on the Alert Pad, where flights of two are always sent to tense situations and hot gun battles; and seeing anti-aircraft fire is more likely at night.

On routine flights, though, our mission seems to be to search—(via the FAC, who is in FM radio contact with Army commanders on the ground)—and destroy (that's us). We go after all supply storage deposits and hideouts that would be of aid and comfort to the enemy.

A couple of days ago I got seven lean-to's with my napalm down in the mangrove swamp we call "Tiger Swamp." Often our bomb damage assessment (BDA) amounts to a certain footage of trenches and tunnels, which may have VC in them, or which provide ambush sites for the enemy when our Army guys move into a given area. Note, however, that I speak with all the wisdom of an "expert" with a week in the war and seven missions behind me.

But as I see it so far, it seems the prices we pay for being warriors are: frustrating BDAs, no women—especially our own, heat and humidity, weight in the cockpit with all our survival gear on and the tensions of fearing a bad bomb-drop or some other goof-up. Worse than any price, I think, is the knowledge that we are the source for so much pain and agony for those at home in the United States, who worry about us and miss us.

April 28—Well, my checkout in the F-100 here is still challenging: I'm still not putting my bombs perfectly on target consistently yet, and target acquisition (re-finding the target after going through rain storms) is a big problem as we zig and zag around in the heavy clouds and monsoon rain. I *am* seeing good progress, and I hope to eliminate any small problems in the next few days and hit bull's-eye every time. At least I'm doing a thousand percent better than I did on that nightmare sixth mission.

April 30—I have nine missions now and delivered napalm yesterday in support of Operation Manhattan. We got a BDA of 20,000 pounds of rice, 100 meters of trenches and three hooches destroyed, credited to our three planes.

Later on April 30—Spent the late afternoon scrounging and came up with some lumber, boards, a broom, some nails, two *Playboy* magazines and some 2x4 blocks. The result is a writing desk in the corner of my cubby-hole, which, when completed, will house a small library, pictures of you, my writing equipment, a lamp, and some pinups so I don't forget what a girl looks like and can appreciate you all the more when I see you again.

May 2—I had my Stanboard (Standardization and Evaluation Board) ride yesterday in a single-seat D-model (with my roommate, Pete Robinson, leading), and it went beautifully! Later the same day, I flew an F-model two-seater to get further technique instructions in dive bombing from Major Daniels, one of our best combat pilots. I did really well at that, too, so yesterday was a very good day. One of the three Wing "Check Pilots" flew "chase" in the number three position, behind me, on each pass during Stanboard check ride. But they dispense with all of our usual annual instrument and proficiency check rides over here and the written tests as well.

Later on May 2—All the checkout flights/exams are just like any other combat missions we fly. Alert duty is a 12-hour shift at the alert shack, sitting in readiness for a call on the red "scramble" phone. Two birds from each squadron are "cocked," i.e. pre inspected and with the weapons already armed and ready so we can be airborne in under five minutes—closer to two or three—headed off to help anyone in the southern half of South Vietnam who needs help. They roll about two times per day per squadron, or about 12 sorties per 12 hours from the alert pad. That's a bunch, especially when most of the missions are pretty hot and sometimes damn scary. The outgoing "boom boom's" from the SVN artillery unit begin their evening lullaby, so it's bedtime.

(NOTE: as the year progressed, the numbers of times all three squadron alert teams were called out three times per shift sporadically increased. By the end of my year-long tour, all but three of the 27 F-100s lost at Bien Hoa were from the alert pad.)

May 3−It is pouring rain at the moment and the guys coming into our squadron bar and lounge are still flushed with excitement because the fighting activity picked up considerably in the rain and clouds we had today. One flight was credited with 200 to 500 "killed by air" this afternoon. This is very different from our "tree busting" targets of the last few days and from our intelligence reports we are hearing we will have a lot more enemy troops massed and many more Army troops "in contact" as we fly our missions in the monsoon weather of the next four or five months.

All things considered, I'm holding up very well so far, and if it weren't for being apart from you, this wouldn't be too bad at all.

May 5−I have been trying to reach you by phone almost steadily for the past 20 hours, ever since I received your letter. I got it in my mailbox about 6:30 last night on the way home from Mass. Our radio-telephone station was struck by lightning the day our Melinda Marie was born, so no word could get here, except through via a Red Cross message. Put mildly, I was thunderstruck to hear we have a daughter and stunned to realize that "Molly" was already five days old before I knew about her.

The other letter in the mailbox was from my folks in Missoula telling me how proud they were and happy to be grandparents. I opened it first and thought, "There has to be some mistake−but they know her name!" So I tore open your letter and got the word that I am a daddy.

How are you? How is she? I've tried and tried to call−all night− but I can't get a call overseas! I've tried Ton Son Nhut HQ in Saigon, the Red Cross, USO, and a hundred other things, but the phones go dead, the connections disconnect, people tell me I need a chaplain's letter or a Red Cross bona fide emergency letter, etc. etc. I can't even get a commercial phone line anywhere to get through of you.

Frustrated though I am, I can't tell you what wonderful news it is and how excited, proud, and worried about you I am.

May 6−I haven't yet figured out our Squadron Commander−he is non-communicative with me, so I'll just let him make the next move. I've tried several times. I think it is just that I'm still "on trial" because of the bad bomb I threw when I first started. He was away when it happened, but I know he knows about it. Be that as it may, I 'm getting along beautifully with everyone else as far as I know.

May 7–We were attacked last night, I guess, and almost everyone on this huge base went out and sat on the bunkers taking pictures of the tracer bullets and turned on tape recorders to capture the gun battle. But not your dear husband. No, he slept through the whole thing and knew nothing about it until this evening when the topic came up in conversation.

May 11–Yesterday I had had a pretty good mission. Ray S. was the FAC we worked with. Such a shock! At the end of our air strike, he called and said, "Hey, number Two," your first name wouldn't be John, would it?

"Roger, that," I replied.

"This is Warlock Two." (That was the call sign of my former Assistant Flight Commander.)

"Hello, Two," I replied, "This is Warlock Nine!" (These "Warlock" call signs were assigned to us as Instructor Pilots for "Warlock Flight" at Vance AFB, back in Air Training Command.)

He replied, "I can always tell your voice, John, no mistaking it anywhere!" That was all, but it was a bit fun, and certainly an unexpected "reconnection" here in the war zone.

o-0-o

I got an Information Office poster put up today in our Squadron Parachute Room. Over on the top right was a bikinied Las Vegas Show girl waving to them as the guys go in to hang up their parachutes. It reads something like this:

> "Hi, you Big Hunk of Handsome Fighter Pilot!
>   Did you have a mission that was pretty good?
>   Then, after Intel debriefing, please, if you would,
>   Taxi over next door to the IO's place
>   And tell your tale—they will make you an ACE!
>
> If you had:
>
> 1) Troops in contact   4) Confirmed KBA*
> 2) Secondary explosions   5) A very good BDA*
> 3) Something else   6) Your 100th, 200th or 300th
>   mission
>
> ...They'll love to hear from you! It only takes a minute—and
> damn!—it sure helps my OER!**
>
> *(Paid for by the Society for the Prevention of Unemployed
> Information Officers)*
>   —J. Schulz, President
>   —Alfred E. Newman, psychiatrist in attendance.

KBA--Killed by Air; BDA--Bomb Damage Assessment
**OER--Officer Effectiveness Report*

    I think our squadron commander liked it. When I walked into the Dice Bar tonight he yelled, "Here comes our crazy Information Officer," and then he roared with laughter. As I indicated before, he is a real "hale fellow well-met." He's so dynamic that he "fills the room" with his boisterous voice and manner. He's full of life, a larger-than-life personality and I could certainly see him leading his Musketeers and loudly ordering, "Innkeeper, hay for my horses and wine for my men, for tomorrow we ride!"

May 12–Well as you know by now from the papers and TV, we were badly shelled here last night from 1:07 to 1:21 a.m. Such a short time! The base took a horrible shellacking with six killed, 32 wounded and 100 more with stubbed toes and cut feet from running barefooted to their bunkers in terror and darkness. Terror is the right word. This is a huge base, the runway alone is two miles long, but at least one shell landed close enough to wake and terrify, damage buildings and maim or kill people in every corner of it.

Again I slept through half of it. But it woke me, briefly, because this was an attack that included the indescribably noisy 122mm rockets, plus 81mm mortars and .50-calibre recoilless rifles all hitting at once. At 2:30 this afternoon the known count was 325 mortars and rockets in that 14-minute period...and still counting!

One F-100 was literally turned into ashes. The revetment housing it looked like a giant cigarette ashtray that was also holding about four smaller pieces of recognizable metal. And two A-1E propeller-driven Vietnamese AF fighter-bombers were also wiped out. A fuel truck blew up. Enough ammo for a battalion of army troops was also blown sky high. Our 90th Tactical Fighter Squadron building

had broken glass, smashed wood and lots of shrapnel everywhere and all our trophies fell and smashed, separating them from their metal plaques. This was especially sad because some of our trophies date back 50 years or more to WW I and had survived four wars.

I woke when, up in our hooch area, a 122mm rocket blew up the Air Police Shack up the street, killing two guys. But I didn't know how close it really was, just a lot louder than our nightly serenade of outbound 105mm howitzers fired each night. When I didn't hear anyone in here moving, I thought, "Well, they must know there is no danger or they'd all be running for the bunker." Each bunker, just outside each building, is a fortified and sandbag-protected little fort; there are dozens all over the base, just for this purpose. I found out later everyone was out huddled in our bunker and they thought I was right there with them.

At the time, I decided:

1) If I'm going to die, then I may as well do it in bed, asleep if possible;

2) Running out there now would be more dangerous, and,

3) I have to get up at 7 a. m. and I need the sleep.

So I plugged my ears and quite literally, sweated it out, but soon forced myself back to at least semi-sleep. A few minutes later, the Seven Dwarfs appeared at the foot of the bed of Snow White–or Sleeping Beauty (to mix fairy tales). They couldn't believe I'd done it again–sleeping through the second bit of nocturnal excitement here in two years.

Needless to say, the next time I hear a sound I don't like, I'll take those 15 steps from my bed to the bunker in record time! The only ribbon I want over here is a cluster on my longevity ribbon---for four more years of service.

Incidentally, the only sign or poster in our squadron building that wasn't peppered with shrapnel holes was mine. Ours was the only fighter squadron building even touched.

o-0-o

Al DeGroote's Story (and he's sticking with it)

(In mid-2013, in the midst of revising this book, I received a book in the mail from an old friend and squadron mate. In his memoir, *A Flight Through Life*, published in 2013, Col. Al DeGroote, our Assistant Ops officer at the time, had this to say about the attack that night):

On May 11th, I went to bed early, having scheduled myself for an early morning takeoff. Unfortunately, the VC decided to interrupt my deep slumber at around 0100.

Almost all of us were accustomed to sporadic mortar attacks hitting the base and everyone pretty much ignored them after their first few weeks in country. But this was different. The rockets were very potent and would dig craters about eight feet deep. I had long ago learned to sleep through the outgoing artillery that the army fired all night, every night and was annoyed to be awakened.

It took me some time to realize that this was incoming, and for some reason I decided that it was more important to don my boots and carefully lace them up before proceeding to the sand bag bunker. I finally went to the bunker looking quite debonair in my underwear and neatly laced boots, whereupon I transferred my anger from the Army to the VC. After about 15 minutes the barrage ended and we went back into the hooch.

I was taken aback by the sight of John Schulz, a newly arrived pilot, stretched out on his cot. I immediately thought he had been hit by shrapnel and I began looking for a wound. This caused the "corpse" to arise, sleepy eyed, asking what was going on. It seems that despite being in country for only a few days, John had acclimated so well to the noise of the artillery that he slept through the entire barrage, with its earthquake-like impacts all around. I decided that in the future I would knock John out of bed on my way out the door. I also resolved to skip the footwear next time.

(Extract from *A Flight Through Life*, by Col. Al DeGroote, 2013)

May 15−One of the guys in another squadron took a hit on a mission down in IV Corps and couldn't quite make it back; he had to jump out 12 miles from Bien Hoa. He was only on the ground about four minutes, maximum, then back at Bien Hoa 15 minutes from the time he had bailed out. It was Sammy Winborn, who is a real character. He came over to our bar about 10:30 that night, gassed out of his skull from all the champagne people had bought him, and he wanted to thank the Dice troops who had flown "top cover" over him during the helicopter rescue operation. So, we played tapes and sang to guitar accompaniment till midnight.

This morning I went on Alert for the first time. That means that except for night alert, I've arrived! Well, I got to the Alert Pad about 11:30; at 12:15 we were scrambled on a very hot target. The mission was effective enough to be sent over to the Public Information Office (PIO) and they interviewed me on tape. Our troops on the ground were under heavy fire from fortified gun positions. I put my two napalms (one pass) just past the water and hit a whole fleet of VC or North Vietnamese Army (NVA) boats on the beach. Then I dropped a bomb that blew up a protected gun site, from which our troops–and the Forward Air Controller (FAC)–had received heavy fire. On the next pass, I dropped my last bomb right in the doorway of the other building, blowing it to kingdom come, damaging the building next to it as well. "Bad guys" had been firing from all three buildings. When I landed, the drag parachute in the tail section didn't deploy, so I got my first Alert Pad scramble, Pad, first "troops in contact," and first "barrier engagement," *(below)* all in the same day...on my 20th mission.

The Hun has a tail hook, by the way, and there are cables clear across the departure end of the runway attached to heavy ship's anchor chains. Anyone in danger of running off the far end of the runway because of brake failure or drag chute malfunction, drops the tail hook and the plane is stopped by the cable "barrier." Navy aircraft carriers have far more complex systems, far more abrupt stops, but have the same objective.

May 17–The guy from our squadron who now runs the "Wing Awards and Decorations Office" is Bob Baxter, who was a Rhodes Scholar at Oxford. He is a 1962 Air Academy grad, was an All-American football player–at tackle–and is an outstanding bomber and fighter jock as well. He has the bunk right across from mine and we've had some very interesting talks, some of them comparing notes on our college football experiences.

I find it "interesting" that I still feel the urge and inspiration to write poetry at times, but none of it much like my previous efforts to write with humorous, wry, or rather moonstruck themes and word choices. Instead, it's all focused on missions and combat and war, and occasional brief encounters with terror. Sometimes I do an ode to a fighter jock or to the F-100. While this by no means obviates the love I have for you or the immense curiosity I have about our little Melinda Marie, it still says something, I think, about how war changes a poet. Siegfried Sassoon and his brilliant WW I poetry comes to mind.

May 19−Well, at 7:30 this morning, Gary Tompkins and I reported to the Alert Pad, and at 7:45 we scrambled. We got three probable killed by air and a secondary explosion with my napalm. When I hit it with my napalm, the target just went "kablooie." At 11 a.m. a group of high-ranking British and Australian generals arrived at the Alert Pad and they were standing around drinking coffee with us and asking many questions when the red "Scramble" phone rang. The guy who answered yelled, "Scramble Dice," so Gary and I put on a show for the visiting dignitaries as we raced out to our "cocked" planes and rolled out to the runway in about 40 seconds flat. We flew down to the U Minh Forest (in IV Corps) and hit a place where 300 VC−more likely, NVA−had been spotted. We were credited by the FAC with destroying six enemy bunkers and 14 fortified positions in about 20 minutes of "work."

So we came back, ate lunch at the club for 20 minutes while they serviced our birds, and at 2 p.m. we "cocked" them (inspected outside the planes and inside the cockpits and set all the switches to the "on" position so the planes could be taxied in about 30 seconds from the time we hit the ladder).

At 2:40 p.m. we were scrambled for the third time. This mission was to suppress ground fire during rescue of a downed helicopter crew. The FAC, with reports from the Army on the scene as well, said we got six VC, caused another secondary explosion, and also destroyed two military structures. The regulations say only three flights are allowed per day or night, so by 4 p.m. we had a full day and I had my 26th mission.

May 23–We lost a pilot late today from another squadron, and one of our Dice squadron aircraft came back with major battle damage (our fifth in two weeks for the Dice). I'm told we only had five hits total in the squadron from 1 January until 10 May this year. It is now Monsoon rain time and the bad guys are coming out to play! So that's three F-100's down in three weeks now, and one pilot fewer in the 3rd TFW. Still, though, the odds are very good here. We have around 70 day-to-day pilots in the Wing and may lose four or five in the year I'm here.* Those are darn good odds–better than at the F-100 training wings at Luke AFB in Phoenix and Cannon AFB, NM, where two pilots were killed the week my class graduated. *(*Note: my estimate was way off mark as the year progressed).*

May 24–Earlier tonight on the Alert Pad, two of the "Silver Knights Squadron" pilots were sent to sink a couple of U.S. boats that the VC had captured a few minutes before. The "Silver" guys sank the boats but both planes took a hit or two. The "hits" (bullet holes) are sure picking up this last week or so and I'm glad the F-100 is such a tough old bird; it will fly with half its engine gone!

The Alert Shack is the showcase of the Wing, visited by all the dignitaries that come through, including the 4-star generals, senators, members of congress and so on. It is air-conditioned, has hi-fi tape playing equipment, a library, magazines and a TV. In the back there are beds all neatly made and a kitchen area with a refrigerator and some utensils. In the center of the front room is a card table and the walls are edged with comfortable sofas and chairs.

Some guys play cards, but often, no one really talks much at all. There are few "bull sessions" and mostly limited conversations, day or night. The pilots write letters home, read, and occasionally in the daytime (and usually always at night) go in the back and lie down. But they always wear their G-suits and gun belts, and when the red phone rings, and two guys are scrambled, they seem almost nonchalant as they move to their "survival vests" and water wings hanging on pegs, and then out the door to the their waiting aircraft.

They never look that excited, nor do they make a clumsy or inefficient move such as spilling all the cards, or dropping books or letter pages all over the floor. But they seem to be "no longer in the room" –they are already out mentally climbing the ladder and taking off. By the time the door shuts, you count to 10 and you can hear the starter cartridges explode and the engines begin to whine beneath the gigantic hiss of the "starter cartridges" gasses. About 30 seconds later, they are taxiing to the active runway.

That's "Alert," and it means we can be over almost any "target" in III or IV Corps South Vietnam in 15 to 30 minutes...or even less!

Sometimes at night, particularly when the driving monsoon rain is pelting everything in sight and the blinding, pitch-black stratus deck so seeded full of awesome thunderheads seems to have been drawn like a shroud about 50 feet above the world, I know all six of us "on alert" just pray that the red phone will not ring tonight. War aside, attempting to land that hunk of pig iron, or take it off to find the Lead and join him in tight formation, is tempting fate too much indeed.

May 26–I got one mission last night, in the clouds and rain and in the middle of terrible thunderstorms, flying on the wing at 15,000 feet, dropping our bombs under radar control. That's a tough way to make a living, Little Molly, so I want you to appreciate all the nice things your lovely Mommy buys for you; they are paid for in moments of sheer terror.

May 27–Last night on the alert pad, Jack Doub and I were scrambled at 10 p.m. and we flew for 2 hours and five minutes in immensely dense weather and thunderstorms, with most of that time spent inside the "thunderhead" towering cumulonimbus cloud cells. It was the worst mission a man could be asked to handle. Once the lightning "cooking off" almost constantly inside the cells of the thunderheads blinded me so badly that I had to break away from Jack's wing, fly instruments, and then re-join our formation in a clear area about 10 minutes later...in the pitch-black night. The lightning flashes were so bright inside the cells of those thunderheads that Jack told me later even he was blinded from time to time as he flew on instruments.

To complicate things, the clouds were so thick that I had to fly with my wing overlapped and under the tail section of his plane, with my head just six feet or less from his red wing light, just so I could see the red light. Usually, it was the only part of his plane I could see consistently because of the heavy rain–except when the lightning flashed or the "St. Elmo's Fire"–small arcs of lightening–spread blue spider webs all over our airplanes. Every three or four seconds the lightning flashing inside the cells would turn everything to bright daylight, and then pitch dark, utterly destroying my night vision. The worst part was the turbulence, which tossed us about like corks on a rough sea. All I could think of was how close my wing was to his tail section as we bobbed up and down, while the turbulence caused his wing light, which I was clinging to so desperately, to suddenly rise above me or roll down below me.

The kind of radar-controlled bomb drop we were tasked with is rarely used for F-100s, thank Heaven, because it is inaccurate, and a complete waste of bombs, not to mention a total misuse of close-air-support fighter bombers like the F-100. Jack later told me that when he walked back into the alert pad with some sweat stains on his flight suit, two guys from another squadron teased him about it. To which Jack replied, "You think I've been sweating, wait till you see Schulzie."

Jack later told the tale around the squadron about how I had stayed in formation in utterly impossible conditions, and he told me I had gained "considerable stature" by staying in formation when things were so rough.

Well, all I can say is, "There has got to be an easier way to gain a great peer reputation."

THUNDERHEAD

My Dear,
you look at clouds
    and think of them as puffy things
    that form and soar and hang
        like hummingbirds on silent wispy wings.
At times, I hear you gasp, and then
    you grab my sleeve and point,
    (wanting me to share in your delight)
at how the sun has silvered
    all the edges on the black
           and rainy,
      towering Thunderheads.
I smile, "That's lovely,"
    and try so hard not to recall
      those graying days and black, black nights
of terror.

II

"And you should see those storm clouds from the air,"
I smile,
    and my eyes lie...
"They are all snowy white.
And sometimes you can see a range of them
    stretch clear across the sky
      like giant marshmallow mountains."
And playing to the audience
    of your eyes now shining bright
I go into the boyish enthusiasm
      act
To tell you how they billow

102

and expand...
    And reach like shapeless shining living pillars
Out toward God and Black infinity...
    far beyond the limits of the engine or the art
                          within my craft.

III

I've even told you, "Never pity Icarus,
    for he and I have both gone chasing up, up,
        up those giants...
and we've twisted just in time
    to crest the rounded shining tops of those soft mountains,
falling...
    as we roll upright to increase
        both our joy and airspeed (with a roar)
racing...
    as we dart and turn and soar
to package up the mountain in a giant and imaginary ribbon...
    so to hold the memory of that wondrous
    feeling...
        evermore."

IV

But the Greeks were wrong, My Dear One,
    (and it is this that I shall always spare you)
and I know:
The waxen wings of Icarus did not melt
    from prideful soaring far to near the sun.
No.
Those mirthful wings
    were dipped for just a curious instant

103

through the edge of one small woolly,
    puffy...baby...
        harmless-looking...deadly
       Thunderhead.
His fragile, man-made wings, so streamlined,
    (more a work of art than science,
fashioned by his father stealthily at night)
    were in that unforgiving moment
      twisted, bludgeoned...
        smashed
beyond all recognition, and, more fatal...
    past all chance of e'er recalling camber, lift,
        or flight.

V

Yes, I know of clouds, their various names:
Stratus, Cumulus, Cumulonimbus, and...
      well, all about them really:
How they're born, and why they grow,
    and when they finish raining
      where they go.
So now I know it isn't true
    that you no longer fear
      the things you understand.
My knowledge increases with every flight...
myriad lessons learned from Icarus, and his followers
      who...failed to land.

VI

Then too, one learns of Thunderheads
    on night, forced flights
      in tight formation,

just you and Flight Lead.
Where having flown inside them helps...
Where having flown inside them...
Where having flown that...*special*...piece of air
where the power tries to slam you into Lead
where Saint Elmo's Fire and rain
and blinding lightning
and all that awesome turbulence
combine
to thwart your mission, which is simply:
"Keep position."
So, you stay in tight, wing overlapped, and chase
the bobbing, jerking disappearing wing light,
which is all you'll ever see .
and only intermittently...
just inches from your face.
For your job man,
and your need
is to stay in your position
Do not fail...
though you're night blind,
at high Mach
and in a racing deadly steed.
And your wingtip is just flashing past
his twisting, bouncing
tail.
Yes, where having flown inside them
for some ever-after hours on
some long forgotten missions
on some terror shredded nights,
always helps....

Yes,
it helps Fear
to one large helping of my innards,
helps to gnaw away at every bit of courage that I own;
    and grey my hair
        and line my face
           and knot my guts
                and screw my eyes
into a narrow slit of hatred...
        and of dread,
As I gaze upon your soft and puffy,
      gaze upon your light and shiny.
        gaze upon my Deadly
           Thunderhead...
                – Tokyo, 1977

May 28–Today at 10 a.m. General/Premier Nguyen Cao Ky arrives and we have an F-100, plus a bunch of other tactical aircraft, on static display near a huge stand for all the dignitaries. Guess who was assigned to stand beside the 3rd TFW F-100 from 10 to noon? Yep, your husband, proving once again that beauty will outshine brains and brawn every time.

May 28, a few hours later–When he arrived, I got to shake hands with Ky, who was a fighter pilot before becoming a political leader, and also met a nice guy who flies RF-101s over the North. I talked with Major Boddie, a black AF officer who was written up in *Time* magazine on "Blacks in Vietnam." He's the one who said that, "I'm here to protect their right to dissent." A neat guy!

Ky was impressed with the F-100 display. I think I was the only one of the four fighter jocks he stopped and chatted with. Then we shook hands. The Premier is a very cool customer and most impressive looking in his beautiful white and gold uniform. How he can be so poised and focused when he knows that with every step he is a living, breathing target for some assassin, I will never know. Call it "courage."

May 31–Been shot at hard two days in a row; it holds no terror.

June 10–I have only an hour now before the squadron party and I must get this letter done beforehand; I'm not sure what time I'll be "leaving the ball" this evening–or in what condition.

While I'm vaguely on the subject, I think I probably should explain something a little better before you begin to think your sober, clean-cut husband is turning into an alcoholic over here. Our "Pair-0-Dice Inn" is not frequented by all of us so much because we all are "juicing it up" that much, but chiefly because it is our living room and informal relaxation place each evening.

As I mentioned in an earlier letter, the Pair-O-Dice Inn is really one of the unofficial show places on the base, and we are all very proud of the way it is decorated and laid out. We, of course, think ours is the best of the fighter pilot bars/lounges on base, but the other fighter squadrons think theirs is best, too. I've actually had visiting jocks from other outfits on base say in confidential tones, begrudgingly, that ours really was a bit better than any other, but you'd never get them to admit it in front of a jury. They would die  before giving even an inch to another outfit in public.

It's really a great gathering place for all of us, and provides a venue for camaraderie and *esprit* to flourish and grow. Also, it is a great place to let off steam, and even on occasion, settle disputes, problems or business in the private of the "squadron bar."

One of our guys is a fantastic guitar player and we spend a lot of time in the evening singing various songs, both parodies adapted for

107

flying songs, and many in the original version. Four of us have formed the world's most informal quartet and suffer under the illusion that we actually sound pretty good singing the Kingston Trio, Brothers Four and other songs of the day.

June 11—Now up to 45 missions in 50 days here; sure would like to get 300. I did extremely well on my bomb runs today. I had two napalm cans that were just fine (hard to miss from about 20 feet in the air), and then dropped two bombs on two passes that hit right on the FAC's smoke marker, as directed, making the smoke disappear both times.

I should explain that a FAC controls every close air support (CAS) air strike in Vietnam, flying low and slow in his prop plane, talking on FM to the Army ground commander, and on UHF radio to direct us. He goes into a shallow dive from time to time and fires a rocket tipped with white phosphorous, which then begins to billow white smoke that is visible for miles on a clear day.

Making the "smoke disappear" won't happen every time, but none of us are off by much—just feet or a few yards away from perfect. I know that now I am back to handling my aircraft—this time the F-100, the way I could handle the T-37 and T-38: I don't have to "fly" the airplane at all anymore when I go to war. I just fight, and the Hun comes along with me wherever I want to go, and on any angle of flight from stall to 500 knots, and upside down or sideways and any angle in between. It just happens when I "think" it...really just a metal part of me as I go wherever I choose.

June 13—Tonight we had a fun and interesting diversion going on: Bob Baxter (the Rhodes Scholar) has a marble egg, which he has placed on a small pedestal, and he clearly cherishes it. He delights in leaving it out on prominent display, then watching as guys try to resist picking it up and rubbing the wonderfully smooth marble surface. They never can. One of the guys in our Hooch, Al, our Maintenance Officer, got a raw egg, painted it olive drab, placed it on the pedestal and hid the marble egg. "Bax" stayed fairly docile when he found out, but suddenly picked up the offending replacement egg to throw it at Al after he realized it was not his beautiful carved egg.

To his chagrin, he discovered that his grip for throwing a raw real egg was a little too aggressive, so he ended up with "egg on his face"–literally–and with none on Al. The fugitive miscreant departed for the Dice Bar and may soon return with his buddy, the other maintenance officer–a guy who "owes Bob a favor" because Bob spread toothpaste in his bed the other night. So, Bob has set up a little "Perimeter Defense," which includes the fire extinguisher he's placed nearby, to be prepared for all contingencies. So, now our peaceful Hootch is an armed camp...and a lot of fun!

June 15–Some news about guys who were with me in our F-100 check-out program at Cannon AFB: first, B.C., who has been stationed well north of us, at Phu Cat, since arriving in Vietnam, has just been grounded permanently after suffering a nervous breakdown. I hear he had about 20 missions. Another classmate, "Capt. B.," is up there too, and rumor has it he is about to be fired again soon. The bad attitude he's displayed ever since being passed over for promotion to Major sure gets him in hot water.

Meantime, closer to home, my squadron mate, George Riddel, who was also in my class at Cannon AFB, got "bit" by a rat and is undergoing the terrible series of 14 rabies shots in the abdomen. He says the shots are really painful and I don't doubt it a bit.

Apparently, whatever did bite him did not puncture the skin, just nibbled off one of his fingernails. George didn't wake up while this was happening because he was very wiped out that night and sleeping deeply. He had been eating cheese and crackers and had cheese on his fingernails. His new nickname is "Rats Riddel." By the way, the "jungle rats" here are no joke: they are about four or five times the size of any in the USA, bigger than our average sized cats.

Unrelated to news of Cannon classmates, my best buddy here, Gary Tompkins, has beaucoup F-100 time and some FAC experience from Europe. Tonight he got special orders to Phu Cat for four months TDY. He volunteered, and wants to be there, but I hate to see him go for four months. Our frequent conversations are always intellectually stimulating and on a wide variety of topics. He is a wonderfully well-educated guy.

109

(Note: at the time I could not say much more about that unusual assignment, but now it can be told: Gary became one of the original members of the most elite group of fighter pilots who flew in the Vietnam War: the Misty FACs. Their job was to fly at high speeds and very low altitudes for up to five hours in the most hostile air environment in history, according to military historians. They would go out over the South China Sea several times to hook up to airborne refueling tankers, then return to continue looking for targets of opportunity for our fighter bombers coming "North" from bases in Thailand and from northern South Vietnam. The Misty pilot and the Army's Tunnel Rats had what were likely the most dangerous jobs in the war.)

July 9—I'm booked out at 1:20 this afternoon on a direct flight to Bien Hoa after a sun-drenched, rain-sprinkled, drink-spiced week at Clark AB in the Philippines. I had skipped my last opportunity to go on one of these informal R&Rs after 75 missions, but Major Rook virtually ordered me to take time off and get out of 'Nam for a week. Interestingly, I seldom if ever talked about flying or about Bien Hoa while I was there, and I kept busy with golf, bar conversations with other fighter pilots here for a break, ogling the stewardesses who lunch at the Officer's Club, and most of all...sleeping. Still, I never felt the war was that far away, and indeed it's just two flying hours or so from Clark AB to Bien Hoa. It was as though I had been told not to fly or work at the office for a week, and then someone hit the slide projector and I was back at Clark and just out of Jungle School because they'd accidentally hit "reverse" on the projector.

Every night I made it a point to eat in the Club, where on-stage they featured a 1940s-style "big band" and two fabulous vocalists. The woman, who was every bit as good as any singer I ever heard, told me she was a grandmother; she looks gorgeous in her full-length formal and sings like a dream. I would never have guessed she was older than 30. I had mentioned before that the Filipinos are a very musical people, and that the latest pop songs from the USA can be heard everywhere, sung and hummed by everyday people as they go about their jobs. And they are certainly very friendly and outgoing.

110

July 13–The North Vietnamese, who are now thick as hell around here, apparently are being led by Chinese Communist and Soviet advisers we have spotted–and killed by air last week. We have recovered a couple of Caucasian bodies, and they are not French. (I wish we'd send them back to Moscow with full military honors, full pomp, ceremony and publicity--without protest or comment. Just, "Here they are, here is where we found them, and they are hereby returned--our sympathies.")

When these same elite North Vietnamese regulars, who wear cool scarves, badges, etc., catch a South Viet army regular they now give him a choice: one hand or one foot lopped off. Nice, peace-loving civil war types, huh?

The atrocities committed daily by the VC and NVA against any and all educated or pacification/conversion officials are just beyond belief. Each day they wreak terrible havoc on these poor victims, who are trying to carry out the "second front" war for men's minds. Torture, utter disgrace in death, and barbarities exactly like those mentioned in the "Green Berets" film are a daily occurrence throughout IV Corps, where many of our missions are flown. Village chiefs, teachers, soldiers on home leave and government sympathizers are primary targets and victims–up to 30 or 40 dead each day sometimes. I frankly take a sort of savage delight in hunting and killing as many of these butchers as I can after hearing the briefings on their latest atrocities. That is my response to these reports, which are conveyed to us in matter-of-fact tones, not as pep talks. The Intel officers deliver their daily briefings in factual monotone voices, just giving the information, without commentary or embellishment.

The intensity of skirmishes and battles is picking up again as the weather gets worse and the low ceilings and rain become daily conditions. That is especially true down in IV Corps, the southernmost of the four Corps in South Vietnam, a zone that begins well south of Saigon. That area is the "spilling out point" for the supplies and troops coming from North Vietnam along the Ho Chi Minh trail and it is where we generally encounter our fiercest fighting, sticky situations and most intense ground fire.

We lost another pilot and plane yesterday (four planes and three pilots now, and all from the same squadron). The guy had 23 missions and 25 days here. He was a former C-123 driver. Seems most of the guys who get it are in their first two months, or last three months here (under-skilled, and then, overconfident).

So, no matter what it may have been in the beginning, it's a savage, ugly little war that lost all pretext of being holy, "civil," or having any purity of intent quite some time back.

We are in it now for better or for worse, in sickness and in health, for richer or for poorer, 'til Truce do we quit. In a larger context, there are major consequences to a unilateral withdrawal by us now, which would not only send strong negative messages about our commitment to SEATO—the Southeast Asian Treaty Organization—but would also involve issues of "face" in a part of the world where "face" is so important. For me, our "original" reasons for involvement have become a moot point. It is a point obviated by blood, bullets, bank balance and politics; and those of us who fight each day, and each night, each year here, are chiefly involved with singular commitment and actions (which often come down to "kill or be killed").

For the privilege of perhaps having special perspectives—or special insights—we pay the price in full in a hot, grubby, lonely, uncomfortable war, where by being "dead right" in our special way, can also mean soon being dead in a very un-special, unspectacular, universal way. For me, here, now, current "reality" comes down to what Omar Khayyam said in his *Rubaiyat,* so very long ago:

> *The Moving Finger writes; and, having writ,*
> *Moves on: nor all thy Piety nor Wit,*
> *Shall lure it back to cancel half a Line,*
> *Nor all thy Tears wash out a Word of it.*

July 16—In three days we move to new quarters on the other side of the base, with air conditioned and semi-private rooms—two to a room. I don't think there are enough advantages to outweigh the disadvantages: chief among them the *esprit* engendered by living cheek-by-jowl in a situation where everyone has to get along, and does so, beautifully. But I was outvoted. Some of the guys have "hot showers" on the brain.

August 1—I lost a friend today; he only had a month to go. He isn't the first and won't be the last, but he was a highly skilled fighter jock, an absolute live wire, full of fun and charisma, and a good man. It's the first time that a loss really hit hard. I hope it's the last.

August 8—Sitting on the alert pad tonight I suddenly realized that we have a small and elite—but growing—"club" in the Wing: three of the six guys sitting alert tonight are members of what I have now dubbed the "Night Crawlers Club." They have earned this title because in the last few weeks all three of them have bailed out at night over bad-guy country during a hot mission and after a low "ground attack" pass.

One of the four Dice "Montana Marauders," Tip Clark, who is on alert with me, has a funny story to tell (even though the terror of a night or day bailout here is unimaginable). It seems he got hit over "Tiger Swamp" (that's our nickname for the Rung Sat Special Zone southeast of Saigon) and bailed out just a short distance from where the ground fire had looked like the Fourth of July each time he and his wingman flew into it.

As soon as he hit the ground, he tried to shut off the automatic homing "beeper" inside his parachute. He desperately wanted to hide quickly, but he was afraid the "Screewa, Screewa" sound that the beeper made, both on the ground and in all the radio headsets on our emergency channel, would help the NVA find where he had landed.

There was Tip, trying to shut it off by pulling on a lever he can't find in the pitch dark, so he pulled out his revolver and shot it! The only trouble was, he couldn't remember which side of the parachute pack the beeper is on, and he shot the wrong side! So, blam! blam!, he shot the other side. The beeper stopped and off he ran.

About 30 minutes later, around midnight, an Army "chopper" crew made a night landing after five tries, and two of the crewmen jumped out and found Tip in hiding (finally). The next day, three different helicopter pilots tried to land there to recover his survival gear and radio. But even in broad daylight, they couldn't fit their helicopter blades down between the numerous trees, though they tried unsuccessfully numerous times.

113

That was an awful gutsy helicopter pilot who rescued Tip. His blade tips had nicked the trees on several tries, until he barely made his chopper fit, landing in pitch darkness with many, many hostiles nearby. Our squadron commander is recommending him for the Distinguished Flying Cross, and boy do we all agree with that!

That "Montana Marauders" moniker, by the way, comes as a result of a caption under a picture that appeared in the *Great Falls* (Mont.) *Tribune* some weeks ago, showing all four of us, and noting we were all "Dice." Tip thinks that this is hilarious. He always says "Hey, Marauder" whenever he sees me, and when he and I fly together he checks in with the FAC saying, "This is Dice 21 and 22, two of the Montana Marauders, whatcha need?"

August 15–We said farewell to our dear departing squadron commander, Lt. Col. Don Hooten, last night at a party. I read some bits of shaggy doggerel (*see "Ch. 6, The Men"*) and we all had a great time, a bit of it at his expense. Today we sent him home in fine style. In a classic instance of *déjà vu*, we told the stewardesses and the airline captain that he was the winner of a bunch of top decorations for valor, implying, but not saying, that one was the Medal of Honor, and urged them to take good care of him. They did, by pulling him out of the line of 140 men departing for home, and after the stewardesses each kissed him on his cheeks, they escorted him up the steps and into the cockpit. It was the J. Fred Muggs (Frank Loftus) departure scene revisited. As his plane taxied out, the 190 guys from the Dice squadron were all in a line by the alert pad, saluting, and standing at attention as he went by. When the airliner got airborne, two of the Dice planes joined up in formation with it (with the airline captain's permission) and stayed in formation on either side all the way to the South China Sea before proceeding on their assigned mission.

September 3–We had a good target with beaucoup bad guys this time and we racked up a bunch of them who were shooting at the FAC. I was with Tip Clark again. The first FAC was shot up so badly that he had to glide home without an engine, and the second FAC spotted the two houses where all the heavy fire was coming from. So Tip and I demolished both of them with our strafe. It got a little "nitty-gritty" when we pressed in so low, strafing, but we had these cats really hosing us hard and neither of us wanted to miss. We didn't. I don't think we wasted a single round. Tip was so low on his pass as Lead that three times I was strongly tempted to call out for him to pull up before he hit the ground. He later told me he nearly did the same when he watched my strafe run.

When it was my turn, one house was already gone, and as I dived in toward it, I switched to fire all four cannons at once, hosed a long burst from in very close, and started my pull. The whole place blew sky high, with debris all around, and up so high I was in danger of ingesting some of it into my intake. Clearly, they had such a large amount of explosives and ammo in there that it caused a secondary explosion.

September 7—Okinawa, Japan, Kadena AB—I arrived here and found a very beautiful, very large base and decided to go sleep till 6 p.m. I'm here on another "permissive TDY." After dinner I left the base to look around. (No problem here, in contrast to the situation at Clark AFB in the Philippines, where there is little to see just off base except girlie bars, and not the safest place to be after dark.) A lot of the shops were still open, and I shopped for a calendar watch, which is all the rage back in RVN—we lose track of what day it is much of the time. I also looked for some travel bags I'd been asked to buy and did some scouting for an artist who might be able to paint a picture the guys wanted for the Squadron Bar.

After all this, I was thirsty, so I hit a club where the music hitting the street sounded very good; the place advertised "playgirls" and called itself the "Playboy Club," but I'm sure it's not in Hugh Hefner's empire. I was directed to a booth and in a trice an Okinawan girl was standing beside me—not dressed as one of the waitress "bunnies," but in regular clothing—and she asked if she could sit down. She spoke far better English (all the Okinawans are of Japanese descent) than anyone I'd talked to so far, so I said "yes." She was attractive in the purely Oriental sense, though very different physical characteristics and visage than the Vietnamese women, many of whom are partly French Eurasians. I have always found European and

American women far more appealing, but I bought her the usual drink, what I called "Tokyo Tea." The "bar girls" like her get 20 cents for every drink they coax from customers. I grilled her on the history of Okinawa and its population (100,000), where I could find an artist to do my assigned task--getting a Snoopy dog painted for the Dice bar-- how she liked her work, what education was required in Okinawa (12 years), how big the Island was (four miles wide, 12 miles long), and a number of other things. She was interested to know about airplanes, so I had a good time and an educational one talking with her.

I guess the gal, whose name escapes me totally—something like Kimeko or Emiko—took some liking to me, so she filled me in on what her life was like and also told me about the kickback system for the hostess-girls like her, as well as the wages on the island for various jobs. (I think she made 55 cents an hour; waitresses made 70 cents an hour, and the stripper/dance girls who hit the dozen or so strip joints on a half-hour-per place basis, moving down the line each night to perform at each one, make $7 per show, per place!

That's at least $60 or $70 a night—about four times more than a relatively new Captain in the USAF on flight status with combat pay, and that's using very conservative numbers.

Anyway, I got a great education for about $10 total. (Drinks were 75 cents per person per round, and we both had about eight rounds in a four-hour period.) Mostly, I learned an immense amount about night club girls the world over and the tempo of life in Okinawa, as well.

Finally found an artist who could paint Snoopy-dog tap dancing beside his dog house. The caption will read, "Anybody that can't tap dance is queer," which has become a standard gag line for the pilots over here, even over the radio, in formation, after some missions.

September 16—This year, except for missing you, more and more, and loving you to a greater degree each day, has not been bad at all, really. In fact it is one of the most fulfilling and rewarding years of my life. In a way I'm sorry that things aren't rougher here so that it would not be very enjoyable. As it is, it is good duty much of the time, due in no small part to the highly spirited squadron I'm in and this gives me some guilt feelings. But I know it isn't all roses over here; as you likely read, we lost another Hun yesterday. The pilot got out OK. There are only 65 of us or so (on a base of about 6,000 Americans) flying fighter combat missions in the Hun on a daily basis (we also have some "attached" pilots who spend much of their time on other jobs and fly sometimes). But because we know each other so well we all take it personally when we hear there's an ongoing pilot rescue operation. The biggest, and almost only real hardship for me is not being with you.

September 21—Well, it finally happened. The 90th lost a guy today. He was on his 301st and last mission and was coming over the field fast and fairly low on his farewell fly-by (we'd already had his farewell party) when his plane began to rock and pitch up and down and then just started coming apart almost right over our heads. One of his wings fell off, spun down and killed one of the crew chiefs in the 510th TFS aircraft parking area next to ours.

We are all very stunned and deeply saddened, but the war goes on and tomorrow it's business as usual.

I guess we just have to log it as a "freak accident" and let it go at that. *(Note: See "Three Bad Weeks in the Hun," in Ch. VIII, "The War," pp. 181 to 187 for full details.)*

September 22—One of our alert pad missions today was really a ball.

We destroyed 35 sampans and damaged 20 more, all belonging to the VC or the NVA, who were having some sort of big meeting or gathering from up and down the Mekong River, somewhere in the jungle nearby. Those are really extraordinary results for two F-100s, and a rather unusual target to say the least. On our second scramble for the day we surprised a company of VC unloading supplies. Results: eight military structures destroyed, six damaged, three killed-by-air (KBA), three

117

large sampans destroyed, six damaged, and 150 pounds of rice destroyed. It was a good day for me and my roommate, Pete Robinson.

I hope you don't think I've turned into some sort of monster, exulting over the havoc we wreak, but this is our way of keeping score, and also settling the score for our guys and the Vietnamese people who get zapped by darling Charlie and his NVA friends.

September 23–I noticed you closed saying you pray for me. Please continue to do so, because I have little time for God here. If I wrote a book on the machinations of my mind this year, it would be titled, *A Timeout From Heaven,* because sometimes I get into very hot situations that have bad guys shooting at me, every bit as determined to "get" me as I am to get them, and I then tend to make as many passes as I can to get *all* of them. But I can't very well go to church that same day or week and pray; I don't really feel bad or guilty about the way I fight, and thus can't ask for forgiveness, but after killing god's creatures, I also don't feel I can ask him any favors. Thus, pray for me, as I am not doing much of it except to thank Him from time to time for getting me back alive from some of the missions where I sometimes scare myself by going it too low, or pressing to close in, especially on my nape and strafe runs.

Note: *On September 24, all the pilots received a "special" briefing where we learned that every F-100 in the Air Force was being examined with spectrographic equipment. Clearly, my comment on September 21st that we would have to log the death of Clyde Carter "as a freak accident and let it go at that" was completely wrong. There were cracks in the wing root of almost every plane we were flying, and the wings could snap off at any time.* (See "Pre-Flight, just below.)

PRE-FLIGHT AIRCRAFT INSPECTION

There are over 200 items in the checklist for almost all modern fighters. The average fighter pilot can complete the entire inspection in less than five minutes outside the aircraft, and check the maze of switches within the cockpit, go through the post-start checks with the crew chief, and be ready for takeoff (assuming there are no weapons to be armed at the end of the runway) in about seven more minutes.

On the alert pad, he can "scramble start" the pre-armed and inspected aircraft in about 10 to 20 seconds, and taxi to the runway while strapping in.

A supersonic fighter is a complex thing. And, as with all machines whose complexity is far beyond the layman (and somewhat beyond the pilot), any one of several hundred things can go wrong.

Something very definitely did go wrong with our entire fleet of F-100s throughout the world, as was revealed when several fatal accidents at Bien Hoa and others elsewhere across the globe in a very short time led the experts to a chilling conclusion: our birds were developing metal fatigue at the wing roots, and the wings were coming off, especially in the pull-outs from high-G dives.

But at Bien Hoa, despite six pilots lost in nine days, we still had to fly our regular combat dive bomb sorties, rolling in at 7,000 feet or less and pulling out of some shallow-angle runs as low as 30 to 50 feet above ground. Each time we pulled out of the dives, using up to six Gs or more, we wondered if the wings would hold...or would we join Clyde Carter, who died before 1,000 witnesses or more, right above our base?

After three weeks of intensive repair work on most of the Bien Hoa fleet, with all the planes continuing to fly combat until their turn for "the temporary fix," the problem was solved, as were numerous other deadly problems that cropped up during the nearly two-decade history of the Hun. Indeed, deadly mechanical problems have appeared from time to time in the history of almost every fighter in the world, and too often they've been solved at the expense of many pilots' lives.

Basically, all aircraft have the same pre-flight, checking first the items visible outside the cockpit: the engine, the wings and landing gear, control surfaces, etc. Then, inside the cockpit, we check the warning lights, the switch settings, various power systems and the movement of the control surfaces after the engine is started.

It was relatively easy to accept the normal, very ornery and dangerous characteristics of that incredible hunk of metal and technology that became a part of a man's soul and body as the two of you melded into one and together experienced "flight."

But under these new circumstances, and during that "special time," it was as though very undesirable, un-bargained-for and new conditions had been imposed on a very special love affair. And this change came just at the time when the conditions are most difficult to circumvent or handle them: while we were fighting, together, in a war that called for 15 or 20 pullouts from attack almost every mission, and especially with "troops in contact."

I often wondered, in the aftermath, what was going through the minds of my fellow Super Sabre pilots as they went through their pre-flight inspections before heading off on another mission....

PRE-FLIGHT

Hello, you brute!
Good Lord, you're big!
Don't kill me today −

Metal heart, don't skip one beat,
I don't have time to worry about you,
So,
Don't quit breathing fire through this hollow soul.
Wings, don't fold and snap off; wings −
I'll treat you very gently in my pullouts.

Tires, don't explode!
  You'll just destroy
      yourself in flames by getting me
In seconds....

Your "FIRE" lights work...
Don't blink them again today.

How can one man control so much power?
How can so many tons of steel dare
      to float on top of clouds?

I do not trust you:
So many of your Brothers
Have killed so many of mine....
But I won't have time to watch you,
So, please come with me
As I think of where I next shall be:
Down, down, down–then UP!
Straight up the sky....

Today we must go fly,
Just you and I.
Don't let me die.
–RAF Lakenheath, UK, 1971

October 26–I am going to Tainan, Taiwan, to deliver a Hun and pick up one that has been through IRAN (Inspect and Repair as Necessary) at the big plant there. I'll be returning with an F-model (the two-seat version) that has been through "heavy maintenance" and is now in compliance with all recent technical orders. We take turns getting these trips, and each man gets one while he's here. My turn! And our Operations Officer, Dale Rook, will be flying up to Tainan in another D-model and returning with me in the front or back seat of the "F."

November 14–Been out of country all this time due to a typhoon that settled in between Taiwan and Vietnam. The guys in Dice Squadron had a couple of surprises waiting for us when we returned. *(See Ch. VI, The Men, Major Dale Rook.)*

November 20–I have 180 missions now, should have 200 by Christmas. The weather here the last few weeks has really been great–low humidity and never a cloud in the sky. It does get pretty blistering hot, but the lack of high humidity (so prevalent during the six months of Monsoon rainy season) makes it quite bearable. It's also much easier to fly in this weather, to the point of almost being routine and even somewhat boring on the "scheduled" day missions.

Before, we were always "between a rock and a hard place" on each mission due to the very low clouds, ubiquitous rain showers and poor visibility. Here in the South, we must keep the target and the FAC in sight as we circle the target area, setting up for "our turn" to commence the next attack, to be sure we are positive of our target. To do this in bad weather, we have to stay below the cloud ceilings and keep a tight turn going in order to stay close in. But that's ol' "Catch 22" again, because as soon as we tighten up our turns, we lose airspeed. So, here we are on a bomb run, low and slow as we commence our dives to begin with, and we don't have enough altitude to pick up the required speed in the dives. The kicker is that the plane doesn't recover well at slow speeds and tends to mush right on toward the ground. I guess you'd say the trick is to walk the tightrope between staying loose enough in our turns to keep speed, and tight enough to keep the target in sight.

A lot of times as we set up around the circle to go in, we also popped in and out of rainstorms all around the target area, which meant transition from instrument flying to "contact flying" (using outside references), and back again—even when we're in the middle of an attack run.

Sometimes you'd start diving at the ground "in the blind" from 1,500 to 2,500 feet, pop out of the rainstorm, make a quick correction on the target, "pickle off" the weapon, and then pop back into another rainstorm. It got a bit "dicey," (Ok, excuse the pun) sometimes, but that's all over now for three or four months and I may have seen the last of monsoon season before it's time to go home.

It really is amazing how quickly you adapt to a situation like that, though. You get so you can really "bulls-eye" the target (or, despite the "bad weather excuse," you aren't a member of the 3rd TAC Fighter Wing very long). I have a lot better perspective now on why and how I had such a terrible start here on my sixth mission. And now you understand why I said it seems almost too easy in this good day weather...as long as I heed the lessons 180 missions have taught me.

November 22—I guess I was wrong a few weeks ago when I voted against moving from our old hooches to the new "Pilot's Quarters" on the other side of the base.

Despite the highly tempting offer of hot-water showers, semi-private and air-conditioned rooms, etc., I voted against the move for one reason: I figured that a good portion of the wonderful *esprit* and camaraderie so evident in the squadron was due to our all being "roommates" in one of three hooches, causing us to work a bit harder to ensure that we all got along well together.

Well, I underestimated the men of Dice. When we moved into the new quarters they were like a fairy tale: GRIM! But everyone pitched in and after getting all the individual rooms squared away and decorated in our spare time, and we set aside three adjoining rooms with connecting doors, making it into the new "Pair-O-Dice Inn." And wow, have miracles been wrought!

One room is for drinks, has the tape deck set up, and Mai Ling, our little Vietnamese barmaid, works behind the bar from 5 to 10 p.m. every night but Sunday. The barroom is lit by indirect lighting coming through two Plexiglas-covered openings in our lowered panel ceiling. The two panels are sprayed with red paint and shaped and marked with the two big dice that make up our Squadron Patch and Symbol. If you walk on into this room with your hat on you have to "buy everybody a round of drinks," and that allows you to ring the famous "J. Fred Muggs Bell" suspended from the ceiling. One of our engineers in the squadron designed the indirect lighting and lowered ceiling system, and about 10 of our amateur carpenters put it all together.

The adjoining room on one side is the "TV Room," and it is decked out in comfortable new rattan chairs and sofas, and has acoustical tile on the walls and ceilings. (Thus, the TV doesn't interfere with the tape music in the next room, or vice-versa.) Pictures of each of the guys, framed in bamboo, adorn the walls. In one corner is the TV, and in the new tiled floor is the centerpiece, with two red tiles with white dice markings that conform to our Squadron patch and flag. The rest of the floor is tiled in green, so the squadron symbol stands out beautifully. We have a tradition now that anyone who steps on the tile pieces with the "Dice" on them *also* "buys the bar."

The third room, adjoining the bar on the other side, is the library, and has all the books set up along one wall; (I've categorized them by type, and it is certainly a wide-ranging collection, reflecting the varied interests and eclectic minds of the guys in this outfit).

That same room also has the poker table set up and we have rigged a nose piece from a napalm can and turned it into a nice overhead light right above the poker table...which is used every night for "nickel, dime, quarter poker." If you win the whole pot in a poker game, you "buy the bar" then, too.

Our jack-of-all-trades, "Willy" Williamson, is just beginning to do his preliminary sketches for what will be a gigantic mural on one wall in the TV room.

Some squadron, huh?

December 13–Well, it is terribly late and I'm so exhausted I feel like I'll fall down dead if I don't get some sleep. I can only say this: I deeply regret that I am unable to unlock with this pen and writing hand the things I wish to say to you, to tell you in the million ways how much a I love and appreciate you, and how guilty I feel for not writing you at least one, if not two or three letters a day–all of which SAY something. Always, though, I must do my various jobs first, and it is said by some, including both the Wing Commanders I have worked for that I have "the toughest job in the Wing." It is gratifying to know that they appreciate the many hours each and every night that I spend going through these immense piles of paperwork, examining and carefully editing each. Then I must make sure that my administrative assistant in Wing HQ retypes each one so it is flawless and ready for signature by the Wing CO, or ready for forwarding directly to higher headquarters. The great advantage is that the time flies by in what could be a very long year otherwise. The second advantage, as I see it, and one that others might dread, is that for most of the year I have gotten to fly a very high percentage of my missions off the Alert Pad, where things are hot, immediate, exciting and for a very evident purpose. By flying up to three missions in one day or night tour of duty at "the pad," I can spend all those many hours with the paperwork, and also stay caught up with my peers on the number of missions flown for the year

The one downside to having this inordinately time-consuming job, and this unusual privilege of getting so much time on alert (and direct access to the Wing Commander), is that by sleep time, be that day or night, I am then so exhausted, spent and burned out that all that's left is a charred mass of protoplasm who has only one other task worth accomplishing: a few minutes of peaceful communication with you. And yet the brain reels, the eyes burn and my hand is cramped from all the editing, and also some writing that I do for hours most days. I'm sorry.

One goal emerges day to day more solidly and builds into a bit of a monomania as the weeks stretch from here to April, and that is now to live through this year so I can return to you and try to then give you all the "presents" I've stored—the stories, the thoughts, the adventures, the humor, and the sorrow of loss that affects me and all my fellow Hun drivers here at Bien Hoa. If I can give you all that, and express this pent-up love as well, the year will have been more than just "worthwhile."

December 23—We are all swept up now, in this 90-plus-degree climate where we bestow eternal peace on fellow men each day, with the spirit of Christmas. Part of it comes from the small, artificial Christmas trees here and there around the base and the many decorations that bedeck our buildings. But each of us resists the holiday feeling to some degree because there is too much pain in thinking about what we are missing. I was on a mission yesterday afternoon and listening simultaneously to our U.S. Forces Saigon radio station, en route to the target areas, when the announcer read a message from the governor of Florida (himself a veteran of two wars). It was a simple message, trite perhaps in some ways, saying thank you quite skillfully, more meaningfully than most "thank you's" of this kind ever do. I had to lift my visor to wipe away tears twice before I went back to the war.

December 30—This squadron is a unique entity, as I have indicated in the past. The whole truly is greater than the sum of all its parts, and unique even here within the Wing. Every man I have heard give his farewell speech as he departs the 90th—none of them overly emotional types of guys—has said that they will never again see or experience anything like this squadron and the people in it. The thing that is most gratifying is to see how each of the newcomers rises to meet the challenge of replacing the amiable, energetic and accomplished men who came before them.

January 14—Today was grim. We lost a new guy in our squadron (he had only seven missions, and was on his second "D" model ride as a solo pilot). He was flying the number Two position in a flight led by Gary Tompkins, with me as the "chase pilot" (and sort of "other supervisor") in the number Three position. Gary and I had flown each mission with him to help "check him out," i.e. get acclimated and up-to-speed on doing things right. Needless to say, we had taken extra hours of our time on the ground to brief him on all sorts of stuff before and after each flight.

But this flight turned into chaos only seconds after Gary lifted off on takeoff. Fifteen seconds after Gary started his roll, Number Two lit his afterburners and started his takeoff run. Fifteen seconds later I started mine, and noted that the kid in front of me was doing fine. Then all Hell broke loose. I hadn't yet reached takeoff speed when I heard Gary calling a "mayday" and saying in a calm voice that he had a fire light in the cockpit and would be making an emergency landing.

I pulled the plane off the ground the second I could feel it would fly, well under the normal rotation and lift-off speed, and immediately started into a quite steep turn so I could start climbing the sky 90 degrees to the runway and head up toward where Gary was circling back—about 1,000 feet above—to set up for an emergency landing. (Two former Thunderbird pilots, "Buster" McGee and Hank Canterberry, were getting ready to take the active runway as all this happened, and Buster told me later my right wing wasn't much more than 10 feet in the air all the way around my turn). As I was turning, I took one last glance at the kid who had just lifted off well down the runway in front of me, and though it barely registered at the time, he had raised his gear and was starting into a left hand turn, which is standard at Luke AFB, where he trained, but takes you right into the outgoing firing of the Army artillery batteries at Bien Hoa. In that half second or so, I saw him start to roll back to the right, having realized his mistake, and then returned to the sky in front of me to locate Gary, so as to confirm whether he had any smoke or fire emanating from his airplane. I abandoned all "call-sign" procedures and just radioed to him, "Gary, this is John, negative smoke, negative fire!" (If I had spotted either, he would have had to bail out immediately.) He calmly replied, "Roger."

Not two seconds later, Bien Hoa Tower came on to the all-channel emergency frequency to warn all airborne aircraft that there was a "Base emergency, with an aircraft down off the end of the runway." I thought the tower had messed up, so I immediately replied on "tower channel" that they were wrong: I told them that Dice One (Gary), was on downwind leg for an emergency landing. They replied on the same more discrete channel that they were talking about "Dice Two." Apparently, when he rolled to the right to correct his mistake, he turned too hard and too quickly at slow speed, with a fully fueled Hun that was loaded with "garbage" (all the bombs, which affect aerodynamic streamlining and flight).

He likely forgot to apply a heavy dose of right rudder *before* moving his stick into the right turn. The Hun is the only supersonic aircraft where rudder is necessary, most especially when we are slow or pulling heavy Gs. The result was exactly what they warn us about: adverse yaw, followed almost instantly by a snap-roll to the inverted. As a result, he spun into the Tak Hahn River right off the end of the runway. They say it all started and ended in an instant, but I never saw any of it. The bank on my turn was so steep that by then, that looking left, all I could see was sky.

Gary got back to the runway okay, and I then circled briefly to direct the start of the recovery operation for our Dice 22 from my vantage point above the end of the runway. I burned off fuel (we aren't allowed to go out solo on any missions), landed and went into the Ops Office to schedule another flight for as soon as possible that afternoon, just to get the whole thing out of my system. I was pretty depressed.

I'm sad that the whole mess happened, but I don't blame myself (though I second-guessed myself for quite a while today before concluding there wasn't a single thing I could have done to prevent it). He was newly married, and had only been here about six days—just not long enough to never forget it's the F-100, fully loaded with garbage, that he's flying, and that even when "clean," the Hun flies differently from every other plane built. He left a lesson for us all. And, too, he died doing what he lived and dreamed of doing, and how many of us can say that? Few, except jet pilots and Formula 1 race car drivers.

January 22–Two guys are leaving the squadron and we're really going to miss them. Clifton "Tip" Clark and Jack "Scoobie" Doub were wonderful characters–charismatic, full of life and fun; and they made tremendous contributions that improved the squadron and quality-of-life in general. They were two of our several "clown princes," and could have everyone in a wild and wacky mood at the drop of a hat or with a wisecrack, and it kept our morale and esprit high all the time.

They both believed firmly that this is the most fantastic and special squadron in the entire Air Force, and they worked long, long hours on extremely tangible projects to make it true. Tip has relatives in the nightclub/casino business in Reno, and it was he who arranged with his uncle for our "adoption" by his club in Reno that sent us the red dice--each in pairs looped through a chain that we all then loop through the zipper on our flight suits. We have a tradition about those dice now: you wear one die for your first six months, then two for the rest of your tour (the second is presented with appropriate pomp and ceremony when the time comes). All of our 200 or so enlisted troops wear them also, looped through a button hole on their fatigue collars. Tip was also responsible for getting the beautiful rattan sofas and lounge chairs in the Pair-O-Dice Inn, and down at the squadron building on the flight line.

And of course "Scoobie," our "Golden G-Suit," is the biggest character I ever met in the Air Force. Besides being a very hard worker, he is an outstanding writer who does all the written nominations for Awards and Decorations in the squadron. That job is a man-killer, because you are always writing and researching records to prepare the nominations signed by the squadron commander.

He got the nickname "the Golden G-Suit" because of all the really hot missions he's been on. Getting medals over here is luck to a degree, being in the right place at the right time on a very unusual mission, but once you are there, it takes a special breed of cat to really make the most of those situations and Scoobie is just that person.

Because we fly missions together from time to time, randomly paired for flights or the alert pad, we all know how each guy flies and fights in the target area. Everyone in our outfit knows what a tiger Jack turns into when he has a fight he can sink his teeth into. He was a real hunter, a man with a very quick wit, and we are going to miss him—and Tip, who is much the same when the mission is hot, and always full of fun.

January 23—Last night at the farewell party for Jack Doub and Tip Clark, Jack made a big deal out of "willing" his golden G-suit to what he called a "worthy successor," and then called me up to head table and gave it to me. The guys all cheered. I was surprised when he did that. (But I remembered then that before he left, our ops officer, Major Rook, once confided in me that any number of the guys had come to him with scheduling requests, half of them saying they wanted to be "scheduled with Schulz whenever possible, because he flies on so many hot missions," and the other half saying "never schedule me with Schulz"...and for the very same reason.) Hmmmmm.

January 31—The dirty little war that ebbs and flows throughout this pitiful, bomb-pitted land came home to roost last night and stayed awhile. It left in its wake a bunch of very tired, haunted men and boys, and snuffed out the lives of five unlucky people. Throughout the

Chinese made .81mm

murderous morning, the helicopters here have been in a constant gunfight with more than 200 VC and NVA who have captured one end of our runway and infiltrated other parts of the base. And all that terrible concussive noise that sent over 100 pilots to the bunkers in the middle of the living quarters has borne its fruit this morning.

Besides the very few killed and wounded, there was an A-37 totally destroyed, leaving a smoking hole in the parking revetment where once there had been a plane. Beside it, in six other well-fortified revetments are six crippled and perhaps destroyed A-37s as well. Here and there on this huge, sprawling base, there is a singular attraction: a building, a trailer or a bunker specially picked by God and a lucky mortar man for death or destruction, transformed into now-mangled and twisted wood and buckled walls.

But for all the noise and terror and unbelievably concussive force the explosions caused, there are only a pitiful few signs of destruction, really, just a pitiful few.

We all thought that a small unit of guerrillas had caused the big fuss at the end of the runway, and at a few other places on the base perimeter,  so we were all very surprised when a long, long parade of POWs came by us later.

Down by one of the revetments are stacks of bodies piled up to five or six high, ten yards wide. It is a grim, hauntingly ugly, awful sight.

So the war stopped here at Bien Hoa for a few hours and left a calling card or two of what war is supposed to be like, really, and of what destruction can be wreaked by even a single small bomb we drop (in comparison with the 122 mm rockets that struck us). And it left its terrible mark on those many of the more than six thousand men who live and work here who didn't know what it was like, except in their mind's eye, to be in a war zone. And a not-so-gentle reminder of the terrible night is sprinkled here and there on some landmark that won't be repaired overnight, just as when a scar takes some time to disappear from our bodies.

And the day will be referred to as a landmark in questions among the base's inhabitants: "Were you here for the mortar attack during the first night of Tet? Or did you get here later?"

And for most, it will be good, because they can feel like they've been "to hell and back" and they'll feel like real "he-men" who've been at war. Yet for all but the few of us on the base who fly various types of planes in combat for a living, it will be their only taste of war and violence and concussion (unlike what our Army and Marine troops endure here "for a living"). And they will long remember.

As for me, it was a terrible succession of concussive sounds cutting away the blanket of sleep, then a wait until there was a few seconds of

pause and then a quick run out to the bunker and safety, and that was all. It was really not all that much more than a large inconvenience, and actually not too much of that, even.

And at the time, I didn't think it was that impressive. Even when a hundred or more VC and North Vietnamese prisoners in trucks began riding by us here at the alert pad around noon, it was a curiosity, just as was the four-and-a-half hour battle of guns and rockets and the smoke and flames and explosives that "put on a show" 4,000 feet away at the end of our own runway. Meantime we watched as the Army helicopters attacked over and over and the troops inched in from all around. After a while, all the novelty wore off and I went to bed here at the alert pad and slept for two hours.

By the time you get this letter, the newspaper reports of this action, in what they are now calling the "Tet Offensive," will already be three or four days old.

But I am fine, and was not "shook up" by it all, and am slightly amused, if not bemused, by my own reactions. I'm only worried that

131

with those news reports you will be worried about me. While I lay in bed with the explosion breaking all the glass in my light bulbs, and the noise causing the walls to shake, I had pondered alternative courses of action: 1.) get up and run in the middle of flying shrapnel? No!; 2.) Roll off the bed and pull the mattress over me? Nope, broken glass on the floor now; so, 3.) Wait for a pause and then go? Yup! Now! Although I realized I'd taken no direct hits and might be OK in bed, I reasoned that the sheets here on the bed were not much protection. So, "oh well, find your shower clogs and let's go. Now, body!" And thence to the bunker and safety with half a hundred friends, smoking, sitting and waiting. I joked a little with the guys and then went back to bed when the noise stopped. After all, my job was to be rested for alert duty in the morning...and I was.

February 1 to February 15—No excerpts from letters to Linda pertained to the Vietnam conflict during this period, despite the fact that the 1968 Tet Offensive was in full swing—and later viewed as perhaps the most famous and intense combat on the ground and in the air in all the time of American involvement in Vietnam. There were two reasons for this: first, I was to join Linda in Hawaii from the 15th through the 21st of February, and our correspondence dealt chiefly with details pertaining to our planned reunion. Second, as with all the most "nitty-gritty" fighting I experienced throughout the year, I purposely avoided mentioning in letters what I was doing during those 15 days and nights.

(Throughout the year, I would not have mentioned pilot or aircraft losses either, but I decided to mention a few of them because I knew Linda would read and hear about them in the news, and I didn't want her to think I was "holding back" the bad news.)

o-0-o

As for what *WAS* happening then...

One of the gutsiest, most skilled, and most intelligent men I've ever met, Captain Gary Tompkins, was asked by our squadron commander to volunteer for a special night alert set-up that would be based in each of the three squadron buildings, involving two pilots in each squadron who would supplement the overburdened regular alert force. Because the NVA and VC night activity throughout South Vietnam was unprecedented and intense during that period, the 7th Air Force Command Post would often "scramble" two of the pilots on standby alert at one of the three squadron buildings when the primary alert force was supersaturated.

He was back from his TDY assignment, where he flew long missions over North Vietnam in the original Misty Squadron. He eventually won the Silver Star, two Distinguished Flying Crosses and the Vietnamese Cross of Gallantry for his valor and extraordinary aerial achievements. He was by this time the most experienced and respected member of the squadron and a natural choice for the job.

I was asked to join Gary, and readily agreed. We had flown at least 40 missions together already, and thought so much alike in the air that the barest minimum of radio conversation was needed between us. And we had both developed a technique at the end of attack runs that allowed us to pull up into near stalling speeds, swap ends with the airplane, and swiftly re-engage and attack just as the other guy was pulling off his attack run. Although I had only experienced this strange "ESP" with two other pilots in my first 2,000 hours and six-and-a-half years of flying, the results were sometime phenomenal, instinctively using tactics that were sheer ballet and almost poetry in motion, and we both recognized it when we began to "click" in such a freakish manner.

For 10 straight nights, we flew that special night alert, most often sent on missions three times a night in what were by then terrible weather conditions: low ceilings, heavy rain and terrible visibility. For one night, Gary called it quits from sheer exhaustion, and the next night I had to stop for the same reason, and I slept for 15 hours. (We were only getting about four to six hours sleep each day; it's tough to sleep in the daytime.)

On 12 February, we were assigned to the main alert pad together, and were again on alert in the squadron building the next night. On the night of the 14th, I "stayed home" to pack and get some sleep before my trip to Hawaii the next day, and learned in the morning that the guy who had replaced me the night before to join Gary on the *special squadron alert was killed instantly when a "quad-50" (which is a .50 caliber machine gun with four barrels firing simultaneously) stitched his plane to ribbons when he was on a low-angle night strafe pass. Three days later, Gary completed his tour and returned home. I missed his farewell party: I was on my R&R in Hawaii. Two months later we had a special two-man squadron reunion in California with our wives there!*

Many members of the "Dice" Squadron at Bien Hoa during that brief period will probably well remember their "special squadron night alert" experiences during the 30 or 40 nights that commenced right after the Tet Offensive began. Everyone began taking turns until things quieted down completely. But I know for sure that neither Gary nor I will forget the 15 or 20 most intense "under the flare" night ground attack missions we flew together...and especially the five without flares.

("Under the flares" was an expression used often to refer to night missions, because they were supposed to be conducted under the lights provided by the powerful flares-with-parachutes dropped by "flare ship" cargo planes circling overhead. During Tet, our several missions without them violated every regulation in 7th Air Force, but at the time, Gary and I thought that while doing so was absurdly beyond "dangerous," those few situations seemed to us to be pretty darned "operationally necessary" at the time. Suffice to say that ground attack to as low as 50 or 100 feet, without flares, and with as much as an 800-foot lag in the readings on the altimeter in the steeper dive attacks was "a considerable departure from 'Standard Operating Procedures," and would be deemed preposterous by anyone with an ounce of sense. Suffice it also to say the Marine Division trapped on three sides in the pitch dark 170 miles south of our base were "mighty grateful" for our three missions over them on February 2nd.)

o-0-o

Dear Linda: March 13—At this point, all I want to do is get home alive in one piece. With just 21 days to go, I don't care if all of my missions are boring daytime "tree busters" until I leave. I'm awfully tired of a lot over here: long, long hours writing and editing until 2:30

134

in the morning too often,; bullets going by my face and head; friends crashing and jumping out; rockets, and bad food, etc ... wa wa wa!

LEAVING VIETNAM BEHIND, SPRING, 1968

On April 5th, 1968, I looked forward to seeing my beautiful wife and my little baby daughter. On the very long flight from Bien Hoa to San Francisco, many thoughts and emotions came and lingered for long minutes, or flitted quickly on stage and then off again.

At some point, in contrast to the near certainty, which had become fully absorbed in my psyche with several months to go, a fatalistic sense that I would not survive the war, or many more of those very close calls, I realized as I sat, homeward bound, that I was going to live, and perhaps for quite some time. This new "lease on life" prompted me to anticipate reunion with the beautiful woman I had married. I began to write, recalling the rigors of the many sonnets we had studied in rigorous high school English classes for two years.

A PEACEFUL KINGDOM, DEAR AND TRUE

Soft dreams of stardust fill the air
And etch the face that I see there.
Sweet dreams and silvery moonbeams float
Within the Milky Way-flecked moat
That guards our castle near the moon
Where once again I'll kiss you soon.
For there, beyond the thunderous roar
Of jets, and crowded worlds--and war,
Beyond deaf ears, and blind who see
There is, in dreams, a place for me.
A peaceful kingdom, dear and true,
In which I'll swell when I'm with you.
For when you're near, I float above
The earth, cloaked in your wondrous love.

--Flight to San Francisco, April 5, '68

135

CHAPTER VII

THE MEN
(April 12, 1967 - April 5, 1968)

The following is engraved on a stone over the library at
Maxwell AFB, Alabama, home of the Air Force War College:

> *"And most of them are gone –*
> *The gay, the bright ones*
> *Whose laughter was too spiral for the earth*
> *Who sought above the clouds a swifter mirth*
> *And found a strange peace there–*
> *The winged, the fleet ones."*

o-0-o

This chapter is dedicated
to the men of the Dice, Buzzard and Ramrod squadrons of the 3rd
Tactical Fighter Wing at Bien Hoa and all the other "in country" F-
100 pilots who faced extreme danger almost every day in defense of
the helpless or hard pressed in a faraway land in 1967 and 1968.

And for those who did not return home,
may this serve as a lasting salute.

"INSTANT POETRY"

It was a very hot and bright Sunday morning, and my Cannon Air Base classmates and I from the F-100 checkout course had spent our first night in Vietnam sleeping to the lullaby of 8-inch howitzer guns. We were outside the Wing Commander's office, waiting for our fates to be decided and/or to be assigned to one of the then-four squadrons of the Third Tactical Fighter Wing, Bien Hoa Air Base, Republic of Vietnam (RVN).

It was then that King Henry VIII reincarnate walked through the door, into the meeting. He was rather tall, slightly potbellied, darkly suntanned, a bit grey and balding, and terribly, terribly hung over. Within a few minutes it was decided that Doug Spencer, George Riddel and I would be under his command, and this book was born of that decision because of all that transpired in that remarkable squadron during my year as a member of it.

There are a lot things you could attribute to Lt. Colonel Don Hooten, because he was a leader, a fine speaker, an outstanding pilot and an exceptional athlete. He was a man of superhuman capacities for work and for play, and he could outwork us all and drink us all under the table...either or both! His raucous, roaring laughter and Texas plains accent belied the fact that he had a master's degree. Stud among studs, "Hot Stick" in a squadron full of gifted, top-of-their-flight-class pilots, and fun-lover among the wildest "kids" in the world; all this and much more could be said about our "Colonel Hoot," all without exaggeration. But, simply, he was the leader—always the leader—of a squadron of fighter pilots. And in that role, he was never found wanting.

Between Colonel Hooten and Major Dale Rook, our diminutive Operations Officer, there existed a rapport and mutual admiration society that helped create a kind of 20th century Camelot, a legendary squadron with more than 50 years of tradition behind it–the 90th Tactical Fighter Squadron, "Pair-O-Dice"–the second oldest Squadron in the Air Force.

With their leadership, and with the abundance of talent available under their command, they developed a tight-knit band of warriors, composed of the hardest working, wackiest fighter pilots you'd ever run across. Within the 90th at that time was a Rhodes Scholar, an Olmsted Scholar, a doctoral graduate of Heidelberg University, several guys with Masters degrees, often in aerodynamic engineering, several Instructor Pilots, a Fighter Weapons School Grad (Top Gun school for the AF), a card sharp, two wonderful guitar players, and superabundance of former class clowns.

To get assigned to the F-100, virtually all of them had graduated in the top handful in their flight school classes. The vast majority of all flight school graduates are assigned to multi-engine aircraft; the handpicked few got the top choices at graduation, and generally chose fighter pilot training or instructor slots.

As each man prepared to leave Vietnam, the "Dice men" threw a steak and champagne banquet in their honor, complete with an honor guards convoy of pilots on their motorcycles from the flight line to the Officer's Club, and two wobbly lines of slightly inebriated, saluting pilots waiting at the Officers' Club entrance. It was quite moving to see these departing warriors, with as many as 300 combat missions and years of playing the "crusty old fighter pilot" role, suddenly stopping in the middle of their farewell speeches because they had tears in their eyes and "frogs" in their throats.

Among the traditions that developed at these Dice banquets was the "Poet's Hour" (late in the program), featuring yours truly standing to read a bit of newly composed rhyme-with-meter designed to "roast" the "victim" and bring a laugh.

There was one catch, though: it was tacitly understood that I could not begin "creating" until the beginning of the first course; but being lazy anyway, this suited me fine.

What follows, then, are a handful of 15-minute-compositions of shaggy doggerel that were part of the farewell party for these wonderful squadron mates, to be taken with a grain of salt, and served with dessert.

LT. COL. DON HOOTEN: The Leader of the Pack

It is only appropriate that the first of these is about "Hoot," our departing Squadron Commander; it was written to commemorate his then-infamous attempt to make a gear-up landing, which was prevented that day by the head's-up pilot at Mobile Control, situated abeam the landing zone.

HOOT GETS TO "GO AROUND"

Now Old Colonel Hoot was a very fine Lead,
And a very fine lead was he,
He called for his pressure*
And he called for his flaps*
And he called for his little gear three.*

Now please excuse the meter change,
And yes, the change in rhyme,
It's something that I just must do
To get this done in time.

We left this story with Dice Lead,
A-turning final there
When suddenly from "Mobile"**
There came a big red flare.

Then Mobile says, "Please go around,
I'm sorry, sir, your gear,
It is not there, but mum's the word,
Your tale no one will hear."

139

I'm sorry too, Sir, I must say,
Your little secret sorrow
Has been discovered, now been told...
I'll be a FAC tomorrow.***

-----

*   *After checking hydraulic pressure, gear and flap handles in the proper position, the standard call to the tower or Mobile as we start the base-to-final turn is, "Dice 21, Base, gear down and checked, pressure up."*
** *"Mobile," the "Runway Supervisory Unit" is always manned by a pilot whose job is to "wave off" an unsafe approach by radio call or firing a red flare.*
***   *"FAC" is a Forward Air Controller, stationed with the Army units all over South Vietnam, flying a low-level light plane to direct each battlefield fighter-bomber attack.*

SORRY, SIR, THERE IS MORE...
(Before you reassign me to the Aleutian Islands)

But that's not the end of it, because we "nailed" Hoot with another bit of doggerel to commemorate the day he went out over the South China Sea to release his empty rocket pods from the outboard wing stations.

There are three pylon stations per wing, which hold and release our weapons, but the middle pylon on each wing of our F-100s held a 330-gallon fuel tank. Although both fuel tanks could also be released by hitting the middle "Aux (auxiliary) Release" button, which activated an explosive charge that unlocked the clamp bolts, that "middle" button was covered by a "hood" to prevented accidental release of the "permanent" auxiliary fuel tanks.

The problem was that when he hit the Aux Release button on the dashboard in his cockpit, his finger strayed to the middle Aux button, which should have had a protective plastic cover on it. But sadly, someone in maintenance "goofed" and it wasn't covered.

As the fuel tanks departed the wings, spiraling down to the watery depths, Captain Frank Loftus (AKA "J. Fred Muggs"), flying formation as Number Three, called, "There go the big ones!"

A moment later the rocket pods departed, and I radioed, "And there go the little ones!"

"Gee, it's a pretty bird when the wings are clean," roared J. Fred. At this point, it might be said, "his Majesty was not amused...."

THE DAY OF HOOT'S DISASTER

Sunlight sheen on his green machine
As we skimmed the ocean blue.
And in the Lead, yet to do the deed,
Was our squadron commander true.

The other lad in this trio bad
Was "J. Fred Muggs," stout fellow
It was time, you see, for me and Three
To watch our leader bellow.

The mission was o'er, so we went "full blower"
To watch Lead drop his rockets.
The sight we saw was our Lead's first flaw,
And it bulged our eyes in their sockets.

The "Aux" he mashed, and the pylons' blast
Sent the huge old gas tanks flying
He hadn't done what he wanted to do
But we knew he was still trying.

Then the rocket pods, to the old sea gods
Were the next to follow suit,
O'er the ocean's sheen, 'twas a clean machine*
Now flown by Colonel Hoot.

141

It's nice to know, Sir, you can goof,

I didn't think you could,

But you shan't forget, nor can I yet,

'Cause the middle button...had...no...hood!

----

*   *Any aircraft whose wings were free of under-hanging drag devices, whether landing gear, flaps or anything on the six pylons, was a "clean machine."*

o-0-o

DALE ROOK: "Mister Operations"

The second half of the fabulous "Dice" command structure was our diminutive Operations Officer, Major Dale Rook. "Diminutive" was the diplomatic word to describe this dedicated and extraordinary officer at normal times, but he seemed to double in size if you were "on the carpet" for anything, and to us, he was a mighty, mighty man anytime.

Possessed of a wonderful sense of humor and great talents as a leader of men, he was the usual voice of authority and discipline to the squadron pilots, and thus the target for near-constant jokes and pranks by the Dice men, most notably, the irrepressible ringleader, Jack Doub, fighter pilot extraordinaire and prankster without peer.

One of the running gags was that "the little fat Major who works in Ops" had never actually been through a formal Air Force flying school, having been a pilot since before there were such things. The often embellished-upon narrative had it that "Major Dale," (who was actually a highly skilled pilot who'd begun his career flying fighters in Korea) was a graduate of the "Wilbur Wright Correspondence School for Flying" who had, according to Doub, gotten his wings in a box of cornflakes and had been given his diploma "conditionally" for failing to pass "Lesson 13" on aircraft landings.

Much fuel was fed to this little fire when our beloved Ops Officer scraped the bottom of his tailskid while landing his F-100 on a night mission. Although he insisted that the tailskid was there for that purpose (it will barely touch on perfect landings), he was kidded every

142

now and again on this subject, especially when Doub would go into one of his "shticks" about the "Little Fat Major who works in Ops," while Rook would sip his drink and shake his head, grinning the whole time.

Despite his atrocious backhand, he was a half decent tennis player, with quick moves and a vicious forehand shot, and he was a ringleader of the squadron's revolving "Bien Hoa Wimbledon" tourneys. At times, those were more a running comedy in three sets because of the presence of Major Jack Doub, master prankster, who, third drink in hand, would find a slightly elevated chair beside the net and "umpire" the matches, sometimes with a running commentary or "ruling" explanation that defied sanity, or any rules of tennis.

As mentioned earlier, Major Rook and I were targets of one of the best pranks the Dice men ever pulled. Dale had only a few weeks left "in country" when the two of us were given the opportunity to fly two F-100s up to Taiwan, where we would turn them in and pick up a two-seated "F" model from the "IRAN" shops, where each plane is pulled apart, updated and cleaned in the "Inspection and Repair as Necessary" process.

But because there were delays at the shop and then a typhoon that lingered between us and "home," we were 13 days returning to Bien Hoa. When we arrived, the guys had us all "fixed up": Rook had orders extending his tour in Vietnam for a month, and I was reassigned to the A-37 "Tweety Birds,: a squadron recently sent to Bien Hoa to test whether the plane used for primary jet training could be adopted for combat. Its unofficial nickname came from the high pitched whine of its twin engines. I'd flown the T-37 for over two years as an instructor pilot in Training Command.

The orders were clearly "official"; they were neatly typed on proper forms and even signed by the Wing Commander! Clearly everyone in the chain of command, from the top down, was in on the gag. Well, we both hollered and yelled and carried on like a couple of kids who'd been told Christmas was cancelled. Meantime, our squadron mates all nodded sympathetically, mumbling words of condolence while suppressing the impulse to laugh hysterically.

143

I went outside to smoke a cigarette and blow off some steam, and told my friend, the Chief NCO (Non-commissioned Officer), Jim Nelson, the bad news.

He listened for a minute and then said, "John, it's a joke!" Apparently even the 200-plus enlisted guys in the squadron were in on the gag. I walked in and roared, "OK, you guys, VERY FUNNY!!!" And at that point the dam burst and the whole building erupted in the longest, loudest laugh you could imagine. At the bar that night, Rook and I took more ribbing, with "hey, welcome back to the squadron, that was a close one" as the usual theme of the sarcasm.

A potential fighter squadron commander without peer was lost to Tactical Air Command when his education caught up with Dale Rook. Because he had the appropriate Master's Degree, his new assignment took him to Air Force Systems Command to do safety research for future fighter planes. Thus, he would be "flying a desk" instead of his beloved fighters.

But the discipline, *esprit* and flying know-how he instilled in his men would be in fighter cockpits for years afterward.

On a personal note, he learned soon after I had joined the squadron that I had spent six months after college as a wire service reporter in San Francisco.

"So you were a mild-mannered reporter for a large metropolitan daily?" he asked, quoting exactly the description for Billy Batson, the fictional reporter, who would then say, "*Shazam!*" and be transformed into Captain Marvel of comic book fame.

"Yes, sir," I said, "but you can just call me 'Captain Marvel.'"

That was not to be. Every time I entered his office, it was, "There are a million stories in the Naked City, what's yours today, Batson?"

Not long after our lengthy TDY, and as Thanksgiving approached, it was time to say farewell to Major Dale Rook, our LFM.

A fun Post Script: thanks to the moniker Maj. Rook gave me, mine became the only F-100 in the wing with a special extra marking. The crew chiefs painted "Capt. Marvel" on the little front gear door, which also had the usual "Dice" squadron symbol. On days when my plane had a cartridge start, I would stand up in the cockpit, point skyward and yell "Shazam!" as I hit the start button and the smoke billowed all around me.

L.F.M. (Little Fat Major)

You may talk of tough wars here
When the weather is quite clear
And you're sent to petty fights and still get shook.
But when it comes to Ops men,
I guess I've known the tops, men,
So sit back and hear the tale of Dale Rook.

He was blue-eyed and well-browned,
And, well, built close to the ground,
And his backhand was the toughest on the court.
And he ran Dice Operations
In between his "short" vacations,
And we'd kid him 'cause we loved to hear him snort.
With a rudder and a stick,
He surely was no hick--
Though his landings weren't the best you've ever seen.
For a "Wilbur Wright" flying grad
He didn't do too bad
Though he ne'er completed "Landings: Part Thirteen"

Though 'tis sad, a desk of wood
Is what he flies now, yet that's good,
'cause "Mahogany Messerschmitts" don't land at night,
And so you'll hear no tailskid sound
When your tires hit the ground
Whoosh! There goes his desk in supersonic flight!
So we'll meet him later on
In the place where he has gone,

Where it even gets "quite warm" when you're not shook,
He'll be "Ops" for Satan's crew
And be bossing me and you
And we'll have more wondrous times with Dale Rook.

o-0-o

DALE SISSEL: Our Master Parachutist

Shortly after my arrival in early April of 1967, a pair of characters showed up to help fill the ranks of the Dice; they added immeasurably to the legend of the 90th in Vietnam. Dale Sissell and Roger "Willy" Williamson had been Air Training Command instructors and both made life more pleasurable for all during the long and wacky nights around the Pair O' Dice Inn. Dale was a short, quiet Texan who managed to maintain his decorum at all times, except when he had an evening martini at our bar...an event of fair frequency. At that point he became one of the most uninhibited guys in the outfit. By the second drink, every formal noun he uttered ended with "a-roon-a-rinski." No wonder, then, that he quickly became known as "Dale-a-Roon-a-rinski."

He was only two weeks from reassignment and had over 250 missions on a fateful day when we were out together at the alert pad, waiting for the red phone to ring and "scramble" us on another mission in support of troops somewhere in III or IV Corps. We had already flown twice that day, and it was my turn to lead when we were scrambled again. Seventeen miles west of Bien Thuey, the remarkably brave and able Vietnamese IV Corps Rangers, as tough a fighting unit as existed in Vietnam, were in an intense fight and a tight situation. Pinned down by very heavy .30 and .50 caliber automatic weapons, they had already called us in over them once before that day, and on each pass on that first mission, the ground commander had relayed through the Forward Air Controller that we were taking heavy ground fire.

On this mission, the same message was relayed, and on his second low-angle strafe run, down between the trees and right in the mix of battle, Dale was hit as he started his pullout, and immediately the fire warning light in his cockpit came on.

I abandoned my attack and joined up on his wing and confirmed he was on fire. We headed for the Bien Thuey runway–the longest 17 miles I'd ever flown.

En route, his controls began to burn through and the plane began pitching up; he would immediately re-level the nose–the strangest flight pattern you could imagine. I had radioed ahead to the Bien Thuey Tower, and to Saigon Control, so when he bailed out right over the runway, one of the several helicopters that had responded to our "Mayday" call quickly swooped in and picked him up when he landed a mile from the runway.

Ten days later, Dale was shot down again. This time, he broke his leg, and he was on the ground 50 minutes before a chopper got to him. It was in the same area, down in IV Corps, the southernmost of the four "Corps" of South Vietnam, where a pilot's life expectancy on the ground is only about 25 minutes. When the helicopter arrived, Dale ran 50 yards or more from his hiding place on his broken leg.

He got out of the hospital just in time for his farewell party, and we threw him a real wingding. He not only was alive and well, and headed for an instructor pilot job at Williams AFB in Arizona, but he needed only three more jumps to qualify for Army Jump Wings. Dale and his pal, Willy Williamson left the same day, also to be a Williams AFB instructor.

DALE-A-ROON-A-RINSKI

Dale-a-roon-a-rinski's going where
There are no bullets in the air.
Instead, in Williams Airstrip's clime
There's other danger all the time:
Not only is Williamson going there,
But idiot students fill the air.

Now, going at your present rate,
Your chances, Dale are somewhat great

That you'll soon wear some Jumper's wings
From three more rides in those "parachute" things.
Now since that's true, Dice man renowned,
Consider what grows on the ground.

In Arizona, you'll recall,
You land in cactus when you fall.
So I'd advise that when you fly,
Your flying suits you modify
With padding, for your future practice,
'Cause, babe, you're gonna land in cactus!

o-0-o

ROGER WILLIAMSON, Our Artist-in-residence

The day Dale Sissel showed up, another Texan arrived with him. As mentioned, they also departed on the same airliner, headed back to Air Training Command (ATC). The interesting "back story" is that both of them were originally assigned to Ton Son Nhut in Saigon, the Command Headquarters for Vietnam, to be Command Post duty officers.

They were to spend a year answering phones and scrambling alert pad fighters throughout South Vietnam. Well, that lasted about a week, as they tell it, until they had bugged some colonel so many times they were granted their request for a temporary duty transfer just to get them out of his hair.

By sunset that same day they were 13 miles up the road at Bien Hoa AB, and soon after that became permanent fixtures in the Pair O' Dice Inn, and on the combat flying schedule.

Captain Roger Williamson already had a colorful and interesting career in a number of fields and myriad talents that were put to good use. Among other things, he had sold and flown many civilian airplanes. After he retired he built one of his own, as well as a beautiful big fishing boat. He also dabbled in inventions, design, and finally, in oil painting. The latter, his first attempt in oils, resulted in a mural covering a full wall in the library portion of the Pair-O-Dice Inn. It was a beautifully executed piece, portraying three F-100s "out at work" on a ground attack mission.

"Willie," as he was called, began sporting a mustache part way through his tour. I encouraged him to continue to persevere through those first scraggly days of growth, and convinced him that eventually, he would look exactly like Clark Gable, only with smaller ears! He quickly got into the spirit of this and began sprinkling his conversations with, "Frankly, Scarlett, I don't give a damn." And by Jove, he really *did* look like Gable.

Willie's carefully trimmed 'stache went with him on his seven-day R&R rendezvous in Hawaii with his wife; everyone in Vietnam got one such R&R. But he returned without the 'stache, admitting sheepishly that it had lasted about an hour after he got to Hawaii. His wife didn't like it.

Personal tragedy, as he viewed it, nearly struck Willie when he received an assignment to the F-111, but he got that assignment changed to an instructor pilot (IP) job in Air Training Command (ATC) again, just days before leaving He celebrated his "escape" by going to a tailor in Bien Hoa City, where he bought a custom-made flight suit, complete with fancy pockets and a white neck scarf; the suit was a flashy fire-engine red!

"FRANKLY, HO CHI MINH, I DON'T GIVE A DAMN"

Our Willie babe is going to be
At Williams, back in ATC.
Sans mustache, and sans cannons four
Instructing will be quite a bore.

From an F-One-Eleven to Phoenix land,
He really has things quite well planned:
For, since he's shaved that mustache silly,
(It drove his poor wife willy-nilly)
He's junked that old Clark Gable role

149

To be number one in the Students' poll,
By being the kindest and sweetest IP
Who ever flew in A.T.C.
Giving real high check scores every day
While dressed up in his Santa Clause way.

o-0-o

BILL ELLISON: Sing, Boy, Sing!

Often in the evening, we sang in loud and enthusiastic groups in the Pair O' Dice Inn, and a few of us even got serious about making "The Good Sounds," particularly while Ed Clarke, a fine guitar player, was with us. In the squadron sing-alongs, our tone-deaf basso profundo was Bill Ellison, an Annapolis graduate and an outstanding young officer and fighter pilot in every way but one...

"BASSO BILL PROFUNDO"

Big Bad Bill has a long, long stride,
And it's well known both far and wide
That he left the Navy, and his "boat,"
As well as that smelly Annapolis goat,*
To join the Air Force—we knew he would:
'Cause the Mach on battleships ain't too good.
But where he really earned his name
Was as the Dice Choir Boy—THAT'S his game!
And he's earned a reputation proud:
He doesn't sing well, but Man! He's loud!

----
* *The Naval Academy mascot.*

o-0-o

JOE NEELY: "Football Joe," Command Post Chief

Among the members of the Wing Staff who were attached to the 90th for flying missions periodically was a former professional football player, Joe Neely. Several years before, Joe had published a book on football and was working on another during quiet times at "Hawk Control," the Command Post, where he spent many hours, day and night.

Joe saw to it that the Alert Pilots at the "pad" received "launch" orders, via the red "Scramble" phone" the minute there was a need for fighter support anywhere in the III or IV Corps area. He also insured that his staff kept close tabs on the weather—especially critical during the six-month-long monsoon season, to be sure returning fighters were diverted to Phu Cat or another suitable landing strip when the weather got too bad. Many a black and stormy night, the pilots at the alert pad would dread the ringing of that phone and the ominous words, "Scramble Dice, (or Ramrod, or Buzzard)" that sent them into the fury of a monsoon night.

"ANSWER THE PHONE, JOE

Good old Joe heads up the C.P.
And works real hard, as we all can see:
With telephones ringing all around,
Plus "Hawk Control,* we're on the ground."

With "scramble this" and "scramble that,"
And, "You guys must land at Phu Cat."**
And at night, how the pilots moan
When Joe plays with his damn red phone.
It seems he cannot talk at all
Without a phone on which to call.
So, pity his wife at the breakfast nook
When she wants to know what chow to cook:
On his toy red phone, as in days past,
"Now scramble eggs, and make it fast!"

----
*   *Our Wing Command Post call sign was "Hawk Control."*
**   *Phu Cat was another F-100 fighter base, but a long ways north.*

PETE ROBINSON—Major General to be

My roommate for several months when we moved to new quarters was Captain Pete Robinson, an Air Force Academy graduate who then went to Heidelberg University on an Olmsted Fellowship. He graduated very high in his Academy class and was very thoughtful, bright and neat—an impeccable officer. He was also the Dice Squadron's Weapons Officer and a graduate of the prestigious Fighter Weapons School, the AF version of "Top Gun School." He was witty, observant, studious, very conscientious, and rather distant from everyone, yet somehow never in a stuck-up or noticeably aloof way. Finding a chink in his armor was difficult, but on "Farewell Night," I tried.

"SAINT PETE"

And now, old Roomie, comes the time

To nail you for your every crime,

At last expose your every flaw

That, day or night, I ever saw.

(Good Grief! I've used up half the verse,

So comments now had best be terse.)

I guess, St. Peter, your only flaw

Is quite apparent, they all saw,

Yes, all the Dice men always knew it:

When you picked a roommate, Man, you blew it!

As a post script: it was many years before I saw my old roommate again. Things had changed for both of us: it was the early 90s, and I was by then a civilian graduate of our National War College in Washington, DC with years as an international journalist and news executive behind me.

After spending two years covering the Soviet-Afghan war from my base in Islamabad, Pakistan, I had joined the NWC faculty for two years. A year or so later, I was asked to come to Maxwell AFB, Alabama, to look at a job as civilian Dean for Academic Affairs for the

Air Command and Staff College, part of "Air University," which included the Air Force War College. I was invited to meet with the Commandant of the University, and when I walked in to his office, there, behind the desk, with two stars on his shoulders, was Major General Pete Robinson. I had left the Air Force after eight and a half years; Pete had stayed, and done "rather well."

JACK DOUB: "Our Golden G-suit"

As mentioned before, of all the colorful, crazy, hilarious guys who ever flew for Dice, or in any other F-100 squadron for that matter, then-Major Jack Doub, from Georgia, probably tops the list. Possessed of brilliant flying skill, steel nerves and an omnipresent sense of humor, he was the ringleader of many spur-of-the moment pranks, parties and acts of outright skullduggery that were great for morale. He prided himself on being spokesmen for his fictional "Senior Advisory Council,"–a group composed of the four flight commanders. He would explain that the Council's sole purpose was to keep the Commander and Ops Officers "squared away" and well informed of any (usually fictitious) goofs or wrong decisions they might have made. The four Majors, with Jack in the lead, would storm into the poor harassed Ops Officer's office grinning from ear to ear to demand some new concession "for the men." The other three would nod in happy assent while Jack explained that if the demands weren't met, they would hold out for "better job, higher wages," and lead all the pilots out on strike for a week in Bangkok.

True to form, good old Major Rook or his deputy, Major Al DeGroote would throw them bodily out of the Ops office as Jack yelled, "But, sir, you're becoming too short with the men. You need a rest, you're becoming nasty...the war has hardened you."

Jack was not only a natural wit and tireless mischief maker, but an energetic, talented writer as well. He stole the whole show one night at the Officer's Club, where, in front of almost every officer in the Wing, he played the part of our departing Deputy Wing Commander for Operations, Col. Bob Coury. He was on stage for nearly 15 minutes "warming up the audience" for the other skits, and he brought the house down with his "tap dance routine" and his Col.

Coury impersonation, complete with grey temples he acquired with some cooking flour he patted into his hair. That touch completed a rather remarkable resemblance to the departing, highly respected Wing flying leader. All of it was completely unrehearsed and adlibbed, but his one-liners, delivered sternly to a room full of fighter pilots, were in perfect "pitch." It was a wonderful impersonation.

Jack had been an excellent athlete, and had athletic scholarship offers from several of the Southeast Conference schools of football fame. Unfortunately, he never graduated from Georgia Tech, nor did old snake-hips get a chance to star at halfback, due to a recurring misunderstanding with school dormitory officials as to the occupancy of his dorm room. (Near mid-career, he *did* complete his college degree at Nebraska, and then got an MA from the Army's Command and Staff College while on the faculty there.)

Of all Jack's many adventures and feats of derring-do, the one thing he prided himself on most was his ability to scrounge up excuses for getting to other ports of call for few days of R&R. He said he was planning a book titled, *See Bangkok on $100 a Day*. A bachelor, he was equally adept at charming every woman of every age that he had the great pleasure to meet. The pleasure was soon mutual. This is not to imply for a moment that he shirked his duties. It was widely known that he was a brilliant pilot, almost at the level of "magic," and before he was reassigned at the end of his tour to be a briefing officer to the PACAF (Pacific Air Forces) General Staff in Hawaii, Jack had become one of the most decorated fighter bomber/close air support pilots of the Vietnam War. Flying quite often in combat with him, I quickly realized he was one of those rare "hunters," who earned his every decoration and deserved more. He loved combat, and wanted to be on all the hottest missions, day or night, where he could do the most damage and give the most help to our "kids on the ground."

He and I had many wonderful flying adventures together through most of my combat tour, and just as with his pranks in the bar, or his joy in harassing the two Dice ops officers, he approached the most dangerous battle situations with enthusiastic *joie d' vivre* was infectious At some point, the more than 200 enlisted men in Dice, having heard from time to time about Jack's fierce fighting skills, and the growing accumulation of combat decorations, put gold spray paint all over a spare G-suit–a piece of gear we all wore as extra "pants" to prevent blackout during high G maneuvers–and they awarded it to Jack, dubbing him "the Golden G Suit."

As indicated earlier, after his tour in Hawaii, Jack volunteered for another Vietnam assignment, became a Misty Pilot, flying low level for many hours each mission over North Vietnam searching for targets for Navy, Marine and Air Force fighter bombers to attack. As a result, Jack Doub holds the record for the most combat missions of any F-100 pilot in Southeast Asia (more than 500).

But before that, in early January, 1968, it was time for the "life of every party" to depart. His farewell banquet was a rollicking affair. During his farewell speech, he took a moment I shall always treasure, telling folks it was time to "will" his golden G suit to someone, and that he could think of no more worthy a successor than yours truly, mild-mannered Billy Batson, a.k.a. Capt. Marvel.

Some 40 years on, Jack and I remain dear friends, and when I send him e-mails, I sign off "GG II,"–short for "Golden G-Suit Two." He signs off with a simple "GG"...and the added admonition: "Check 6," which is "fighter pilot speak" indicating that in any dogfight, he will be in gun range, directly behind any foe, "at six 'o clock,"–the perfect shoot-" kill" position. He ain't braggin', he's just sayin'....

"SCOOBIE-DOOBIE DOO"

With magic hands and gleaming eye
Ol' Scoobie Doo goes off to fly.
He bends his bird around the blue,
And 'round his finger, every "Stew."
And every road but Mandalay
Ol' Jack's been on at least a day.

But in between his TDYs
He sticks around, and yeah, he flies!
(Enough to win a "rag or two"
That will look good on Air Force blue.)

Now soon he joins the General's Staff,

Gives General Ryan* a daily laugh

Each daily briefing starts with his cheer:

"Hey! Anybody can't tap dance is queer!"

*   *General Ryan, then "CINCPACAF"–Commander-in-Chief, Pacific AF.*

GARY TOMPKINS: "Tops at all he ever did"

While I was on R&R in Hawaii, the Dice men said farewell to my closest friend, Gary Tompkins. Like Jack Doub, and a handful of others, he was a brilliant, gifted pilot, a fierce but utterly cool warrior, and, even compared with the Oxford Dons I studied under later, the smartest guy I ever encountered. During the year, he and I had flown at least 50 missions together, a number of them a bit "sporting."

Most sporting of all were the often three-per-night missions we flew during the Tet Offensive of early 1968. Fighting was so intense for a month or so then that the three sets of pilots on the Wing Alert Pad faced demands that exceeded the "supply" of close air support alert pilots and planes available.

Thus, Wing Commander George MacLaughlin, later a major general, asked Gary and me to sit nightly in additional alert, from the Dice squadron building, with two planes "hot cocked" for immediate takeoff. For about two weeks altogether, quite often in dreadful weather and with minimum visibility...or worse, we found ourselves in some awful fights.

Our second night we flew three times over the beleaguered 9th Marine Infantry Division. They were trapped, with water on three sides, and pinned down by a vastly superior North Vietnamese Army force that had ambushed them at the shoreline as they attempted a massive landing.

The "required" flare ship could not get down through the weather, which was very low ceilings and bloody awful, so, ignoring every regulation in PACAF, we elected to attack anyway, making 15 or more passes each on every mission, not knowing exactly where the ground was, not able to get up to proper attack speeds because of the low ceilings, and never sure whether the next pass would be our last. Two guys from another 3rd AF squadron did the same that night.

156

It's worth noting that during the steeper ground attack dives, the altimeter reads lags by up to 800 feet, so reading it as a guide to how close we were coming to plowing into the ground was a useless exercise. After each sortie, we raced north almost 100 miles, calling ahead to Dice maintenance to load up another two aircraft so we could land, swiftly run through the pre-flight inspection, and race back down to the battle. Subsequently, after the Marines surveyed the battle area the next day, we learned that well over a thousand, and closer to two thousand NVA were "killed by air." Two sets of "scrambled" Bien Hoa flights had done that. We also learned that all six of our Dice aircraft used that night had "battle damage," a nice euphemism meaning they were shot to hell.

Gary and I had, in the past, devised a tactic where, if either of us ran out of bullets on our strafe runs, the one without bullets would turn on his "running lights" and make low passes as a "target," because all the muzzle flashes as "target lead" was being shot at, betrayed the positions of the "bad guys" who were then subjected to strafe by the incoming plane.

Some months later we learned that the Marine commander had recommended all four of the pilots for the Silver Star. That was Gary's second one. In 53,500 sorties flown by our Wing during my year from Bien Hoa, only six were awarded, and four of them came from that night.

While the recollection of that night (above) was written just a few years later, I find, reviewing my manuscript and that passage 45 years later, it remains as vivid as if it happened yesterday evening and night. And some nights, infrequently, that night's missions have returned in not-so-pleasant dreams.

Gary was used to situations that were even more "hairy"; he had been one of the original handful of F-100 pilots tasked with setting up that subsequently legendary group known by the call sign "Misty." He had flown 50 "Misty" missions, which meant flying 50 different times in and out of North Vietnam, where the mission profile called for two F-100 pilots in a two-seat "Hun" to troll and search at extremely low for up to five or more hours at a time. The Misty mission was to find targets for the F-105 Thunder Chiefs and F-4

Phantoms out of Thailand, and Navy and Marine fighter bombers off the carriers. During the air strikes, the Misty guys were the Forward Air Controllers directing each strike pass.

In jets, the lower the altitude, the faster the fuel tanks go empty, so the Misty pilots would rendezvous at sea with refueling tanker aircraft, fill up, and go right back into the most dangerous airspace in aerial warfare history.

To this day, guys like Gary, and Jack Doub, and all the 157 Misty pilots who did that job over time, remain heroes to all other F-100 pilots. That's no mean feat: guys who flew "the Hun" normally take second seat to no man...no matter how old and creaky we've become!

When he returned to Bien Hoa from his "Misty" tour as one of the "originals," stationed at our northernmost F-100 base in South Vietnam, he became the Dice squadron's "Standardization and Evaluation Officer." His job was to insure that safe and proper procedures were followed on each mission, so that we didn't get any bad "surprises" from a formation flight mate. Needless to say, he did "not sweat the small stuff" very much, and indeed, ignoring regulations, flew with his sleeves rolled up and, when not at high altitude or in the battle zone, with his mask dangling to one side–a common practice for many.

His next assignment was to the Air Force Academy as an Air Officer Commanding (AOC), supervising some of the "Zoomies," as the Air Academy students and graduates are called.

But there is more to tell about Gary Tompkins, and it underscores what I meant in my opening paragraph: he was subsequently promoted to Major three years "below the zone," ditto to Lt. Colonel, and subsequently became either the youngest–or part of a tiny handful who could say they were among the "youngest colonels in the Air Force." A standout student at UCLA, then first in his flight school class and again in gunnery school, he retired after 20 years to become a high school teacher in California, where some mighty lucky teenagers were exposed to such a brilliant teacher that he won the "Teacher of the Year" two or three times.

Although I could not be present to give him a little rhymed grief at his farewell party, I made sure that he heard from me anyway, in absentia.

"GARY, ROLL UP YOUR SLEEVES AND GO TO WORK!"

Now buddy mine, I can't be here
To join the gang for one last cheer,
Despite this fact, now it is time
For you to suffer through my rhyme

It's time now for old "Gar" to go--
Our Stan-Eval troop, as you know.
He's headed east to "Zoomie Land"
To take his kaydets by the hand
And feed their dreams of general's stars,
Then hand them all their new brown bars.

Now Gary baby, I can see
The kind of A.O.C you'll be.
Just like when you roamed Dice's sky
Gloves in 'G'-suit, sleeves rolled high,
You did things just like every guy,
EXCEPT the way you dressed to fly.

Yes, I can see you, Leader mighty,
With shining shoes and hair all tidy
In your "beautiful blues," just oozing charms
But with your sleeves rolled up your arms!

Gary's Revenge

In early March, 1968, soon after he arrived home, I received a letter from Gary in which he responded in kind, alluding to my former days as a college quarterback, and in verse, gave me some "fatherly advice." Gary is only two years my elder, but he had 1,000 more hours

159

than I did in the F-100, and given both that extra time in "the Widow-maker" and, most impressive of all, his time as one of the original "Misty" pilots, he was worth listening to!

TIME TO "COOL IT, DUDE!"
As College Back you must desist,
But hero's notions oft persist,
And give a brave and headstrong man
Fear of age and lost élan.

But now, as in those ages past,
War has set his grim repast
For those of courage, strength and wit
Who must, to live, with heroes sit.

The weapons borne are not the same;
Their purpose still: to kill and maim.
And death, to those who wage the war,
Is still as swift as e'er before.

So when they shoot the steel that's cold
Think of us, Knight Errant bold!
Yes hit the foe at whom you aim,
But keep your cool that won the game.
  --Gary Tompkins, Capt. USAF

My Reply: "Careful am I."
The message was clear. I had stuck my neck out pretty far whenever I encountered a hot target, especially when there were "troops in contact," without any serious consideration of the potential dire consequences. I realized I was fighting very, very aggressively, "with fire in my belly and ice in my brain." Toward the end of my tour, that burning anger increased, and was reflected in how, and how often, I would "press the attack." Gary knew this perfectly well,

160

because he or Jack Doub were the two guys I flew with most often, day or night, off the alert pad, where the hottest missions came, and Gary was certainly "hunting" right with me whenever the FAC reported "heavy ground fire" or "automatic weapons fire"—and most of all, with our "troops in contact."

But, it was almost time to go home to my wife and a new child, now nearing a year old, that I hadn't seen until the month before, on my R&R to Hawaii. Little Melinda Marie had been born two weeks after I left for Vietnam. So I responded to Gary, kiddingly reassuring him that I was pressuring our operations officer to give me nothing but day missions on "V.C. Base Camps" located way out in the quiet jungles. These were safe, incredibly boring flights by that stage in the year-long, eventful war-zone tour of any fighter pilot. With curled lips, and great disdain, we called such missions "Tree Busters."

"SAFETY FIRST"
(A reply to Gary's cautionary advice)

Do not fret, old Buddy mine,
My head is down when bullets whine.
So timid since my R and R
That I won't even drive a car
Much less a nasty combat jet—
I wouldn't ride one on a bet.

With twelve days left, it's time, I think
To talk about it, and to drink.
But, if I do fly, Ops men, please
Just schedule me to bust some trees.

FAREWELL TO BILLY BATSON, AKA Capt. Marvel

One evening in early April, it was my turn to say farewell. It had been an exciting, educational and highly rewarding tour, and as I enjoyed my "end of tour banquet" along with two other departing Dice men, some unexpected guest got into the act. First, the full colonel in

161

charge of Wing Maintenance, who never attended any of these farewell parties, stood and informed the group that ours was not the only farewell celebration in progress tonight.

He said his Sheet Metal Shop team was also celebrating my end of tour and reassignment. He was alluding to the fact that my "hit ratio per sorties flown" was sort of off the charts. I had thought it was, oh, perhaps three or four times the average, because, working so much of the time on paperwork for the Wing Commander, I purposely sat many extra days and nights on Alert to "catch up" with my contemporaries, so we all had an equal number of missions when we were reassigned. Sometimes, it was possible to get three missions in one shift.

Sometime in December, found out I was pretty far off in my estimated "hit rate" when Dice Squadron Commander Lt. Col. Bill Haynes called me into his office and, with our Ops officer sitting beside him, confronted me with a letter from 7th Air Force Headquarters. It said I had more "damaged aircraft" (read that: shot up planes) than any F-100 pilot in Southeast Asia.

The letter then suggested that they review safe flying procedures with me, and perhaps consider a formal reprimand. To both my bosses, it was a concern, but also a bit humorous; they knew that so much time "scrambling" to hot situations and ongoing battles from the alert pad would invariably increase the chances of getting shot at with vigor and great frequency.

By the end of tour, I had brought back "damaged aircraft" 107 times in 275 missions. I felt lucky to be alive.

The night of the farewell banquet, several guys rose to pay tribute to all three of us who were departing, or singled out one of us for a bit of "roasting" fun.

But the icing on the cake, for me, was provided by Dice Squadron Commander Lt. Colonel Bill Haynes. With a wicked gleam in his eye, a big smile and a fist full of paper, he rose to deliver this ode of his own creation. (Clearly it was time for even-handed justice to return the ingredients of my poison pen to my own lips--to paraphrase Shakespeare's *Macbeth*).

See footnotes, p. 165, to "decode" the acronyms and jargon in this poem.

"SCHULZIE'S DONE IT AGAIN"

When Dice men gathered to say adieu
To yet another whose year was through,
They'd join together to raise a glass
And drink a toast to all that passed
Between them, and perhaps recall
That one most fabulous mission of all.
But as the evening drew to a close,
A lanky figure, who slowly rose,
Would wave a paper and clearly speak:
"Hey, Mr. Vice, the floor I seek""
The conversation would suddenly hush;
Those who were standing would sit with a rush,
Anticipation would build, and then
"It's Schulzie; Schulzie's done it again!"

Then followed a poem of doggerel rhyme
That kidded he who had run out of time,
And sent him merrily on his way
With a poem to help him recall the day.
But now the shoe's on the other foot.
The time has come for us to put
Our poet laureate on the spot
And let him sit in the seat that's hot!
I well recall the incident that,
Dale Rook reported in accents flat,
Soon after the Dice were given to me,
'He's taken a hit? Well that makes three
This week, and seven this month," and then:
"It's Schulzie, Schulzie's done it again!"

163

So Schulzie, here's a toast to you,
Though magnet-assed, you made it though!
Another occasion comes to mind
When paperwork was to PACAF signed–
Though lacking in proper coordination,
Resulting in Wing-level agitation.*
The Wing Commander was heard to exclaim,
"It's Schulzie; Schulzie's done it again!"

The last example is classified,
A story intelligence tried to hide
For fear all other pilots would be
Filled with professional jealousy!
It seems a *Chieu Hoi*** reported in,
His weapons were gone, his body thin,
The last survivor, he claimed to be,
Of two full companies of VC.
They'd struck a hamlet one murky night,
The "PF*** compound" put up a fight
And held the inner perimeter there
Until the "ALO"**** could call for "Air,"
The duty officer's sage advice:
"It's troops in contact, so scramble Dice!"
By now the Commies were through the wire
And laying down a withering fire.
Their ultimate triumph lay in sight
When "Spooky's"***** flares rolled back the night.
And out of a lowering overcast
Two Dice men roared their cannon's blast.
Their engines screaming, they clove the air
And filled the attackers with black despair!

164

The *Chieu Hoi's* body still shook with fear
Of CBU pellets and napalms' sear
But as he recalled that awful night,
It wasn't the bombs filled him with fright,
But the icy precision of element Lead
As he deftly rode his titanium steed...
This man the VC had known of yore,
His deadly technique was part of their lore,
They cursed as their dying rattle began:
"It's Schulzie; Schulzie's done it again!"
-- *Lt. Colonel Bill Haynes, "Dice" (90th TFS) Commander*

----

* *In an effort to expedite a piece of important paperwork for the Wing Commander, I had bypassed proper channels in Saigon and sent it straight to Pacific Air Force Headquarters in Hawaii.... Fingers burned, lesson learned!*

** Chieu Hoi: *A Vietcong fighter who surrenders. Occasionally, as with Dice's Abe Tanaka (as he'd claimed after a drink or so), the* Chieu Hoi then fought on our side.

*** PF Compound: *A South Vietnamese Provincial Force Unit living area and fort (compound).*

**** ALO: Air Liaison Officer. *Boss of the FAC's in a given area.*

***** *"Spooky" was the call sign for the flare ships—Air Force C-130s, used in night ground attack missions.*

CHAPTER VIII

THE WAR
(April 1967 - April 1968)

FIGHTER PILOT'S
NURSERY RHYME

Sing a song of combat, and cockpits full of wry.
Four and twenty fighter jocks screaming down the sky.
When the cockpits open, they all climb down to drink
To wash the taste of death away, and try hard not to think.

-- Hong Kong, 1974

EPITAPH: "MY WAR"

When you come upon the place
  where, after so many "sales" nearly made,
I finally "bought the farm" at last,
    and now am laid...
Warrior, Poet, Scholar and much more...
  the thing that even now
    I must explain is still...
    My War.

For all that time we fought
  and killed and grieved,
  and found out soon or later
    that we had been deceived,
It did not make less true
  our sacrifice, or courage or great skill;
Somehow the thought is lost (and long has been, I fear):
  The simple answer to "What are we doing here?"
    was given long ago, and by another:
"Amen I say to you that greater love hath no man,
  than that he'll lay down his life for his brother."

    – Cape Charles, VA, 1999

166

I'VE SEEN THE WAR FROM BOTH SIDES NOW, FROM UP ABOVE AND DOWN BELOW....

From what I could deduce at the time, from the narrowed perspectives of a pilot in 1967-1968 participating in a far broader war in the southern two Corps of South Vietnam (north of Saigon to the southern tip of the country), and from what I saw from far broader perspectives as a foreign correspondent reporting from various places in South Vietnam, 1972-1975, there were three fighting wars involving U.S. combat forces there. For the most part, they could have been fought on different planets for all they had in common.

The first of these was the war fought on the ground, chiefly by our Marines and Army troops, who comprised the vast majority of U.S. combat personnel in South Vietnam. This ground war was, in many ways, similar to those fought by soldiers the world over for at least 250 centuries. It was a war of boredom, sweat, blood, blisters, thirst, fear, constant dust or rain and the inevitable mud. It was a war of long hikes or short, tense helicopter rides with 60-pound packs, a war of searching, destroying, shooting and being shot at occasionally, and sometimes being destroyed in return.

The second of these wars was fought in the skies over North Vietnam. It was quite similar to the air battles of World War II in some ways, combining flak much like that faced during WW II bombing raids over Ploiesti with the terrifying prospect of "bandits" screaming down out of the sun, shooting guns and missiles. And there were similar long stretches of hostile airspace to and from the combat areas.

167

What was added, in this war, were the paralyzing sights of modern technology like supersonic planes disintegrating at near supersonic speeds, surface-to-air guided missiles rising to kill and moving nine times the speed of sound, Fan Song radar tracking and guidance for these missiles, and then mandatory air-refueling once each way just outside Hell. Like Korea, it was a war where the pilots were based mostly in another country or on ships offshore, hitting frustrating targets at high personal expense, and with the horrifying prospect of an Asian Communist prison camp for the unlucky ones who didn't finish their "100 counters"–the 100 missions over the North that signaled the end of a tour for them. For quite some time after that war, the greatest status symbol in the Air Force was a small shoulder patch that said, "100 Missions, North Vietnam, 196_." It was a justly deserved status.

The third war is quite different from the other two that have been written about fairly extensively; only a handful of books of recent vintage have touched on it. That is the war of the close air support fighter pilots and the Army gunships, whose pullout from each of many attacks on any mission was often at treetop level or below. It was a war that was very close to home because in Vietnam, the enemy could and sometimes did set up mortar and rocket sites just outside the main gate of the Base or Post where pilots were living. Thus, these pilots based "in country" were exposed on the ground to hostile fire–a circumstance for which they were ill-trained and found distasteful, to put it mildly. In the air, they faced the same challenges as pilots coming in from aircraft carriers or from Thailand whenever those units flew missions in South Vietnam, but then returned "home" to places out of immediate danger.

While their friends elsewhere might fly one or perhaps two passes over Northern targets most of the time, and only in at least marginally favorable weather conditions, these "in country" pilots sometimes found themselves being launched from alert pads at any time of day or night in some of the worst flying weather in the history of aerial warfare. They would then make multiple low altitude, low angle passes at buzzing enemy concentrations. Often, they repeated runs from the same positions and headings to parallel the very close-by friendly forces. Their one advantage was that the ground fire was generally smaller caliber bullets, and there were no surface-to-air missile sites set up in the South, nor any MiG threat from the several MiG bases in the North. Thus, in the South, ours was a "permissive air environment," where the threats involved target fixation, difficult terrain, split second timing to avoid the trees, "walls" of ground fire at times...and the challenges posed by delivering ordnance very close to friendly troops in near-prohibitive weather at times, day and night.

While the massive bombers often got headlines for their air strikes from thirty thousand feet or so against targets in the south, the fighter and helicopter pilots collectively flew hundreds of sorties each day, delivering their bombs, rockets and strafe with what was often near surgical precision. Visiting NATO generals described it as "unprecedented accuracy in unprecedented bad weather."

Prior to each pass, the attacking pilots received clearance for delivery from a Forward Air Controller (FAC). He had cleared the air strikes in that area with the Tactical Air Control Center in Saigon. On pre-planned air strikes, the Province Chief, and the Army commander with specific Tactical Area Responsibility were also involved in the decision. In the many pitched battles that went on, the FAC was in radio contact with the besieged ground unit commander on FM radio while "managing" the incoming fighters that he directed on a UHF radio frequency. Thus, the FAC was a very busy man in a very slow, light, propeller-driven airplane, driving around at near treetop level in dangerous places. What should also be clear is how much care and effort was being taken to prevent killing civilians or destroying real estate that had nothing to do with the battle zone.

Each year for several years, the four Air Force Tactical Fighter Wings based in South Vietnam flew between 40,000 and 50,000 combat sorties a year, making what amounted to tens of thousands of passes over what were, in many cases, difficult targets. Yet with all that, each of the wings had no more than two or three "short round" incidents per year, where the target was missed badly, or the wrong target was hit. There was little or no excuse for those incidents, the pilots responsible were punished, and sadly, it was those incidents that were most focused upon by reporters, with too little attention paid to the day-to-day heroics of close air support pilots all over the country, including the highly experienced and extremely accurate South Vietnamese Air Force fighter pilots.

They flew WW II-vintage A-1E propeller-driven fighter bombers and often had five or more years of steady combat flying; and some of us considered them the world's best and most accurate ground-attack pilots.

All the preceding is, of course, a gross oversimplification. Certainly it is a cliché to say that the war was complex, and made even more so, just from a military standpoint, by the myriad roles and missions of ground forces, and by the terrain, weather, enemy concentration points, and the different tactics and weapons employed in each of the four Corps. While pilots in the 3rd Tactical Wing at Bien Hoa, just 16 miles north of Saigon, were very familiar with the terrain, weather and troop concentrations in III and IV Corps, we seldom flew in the mountains of II Corps and never reached I Corps.

As a result, I subsequently found that in discussing the war with other fighter pilots, I always asked where they were based in Vietnam, because their experiences were generally somewhat different if they did all their flying in the two northernmost Corps of South Vietnam.

Inevitably, then, veterans returning from Vietnam could be considered reliable sources of information on what happened in their little corner of the war, but their expertise and perspectives are severely limited due to the amount of territory they covered, the fights they got into, how much responsibility they had in the command structure, and which of the "three wars" they were in. And most of all, the war itself ebbed and flowed in its intensity, and the question of "when" U.S. veterans were in Vietnam is one of the biggest variables of all.

Perhaps the only people who acquired sufficient information, insights and perspectives to be able to "tell it all" with some decent degree of accuracy were the Theatre Commanders and their senior staff members, who were briefed daily, read constantly, traveled virtually everywhere and usually stayed at their duties for two or three years or more.

170

As for the rest of us, even the two or three of us who fought in Vietnam and later returned as journalists to report on the war, we were blind men describing Aesop's inscrutable Oriental elephant.

ECHOES OF ANOTHER TIME AND PLACE

In an effort to eulogize the unknown dead who were buried by an impersonal artillery shell in a forest in France called the Rouge Bouquet, Joyce Kilmer wrote an intricately metered poem that has lived long after his own death in WW I.

Perhaps at the time, the tragedy went mostly unnoticed by anyone but the sensitive and talented Kilmer. In contrast, an intense and terror-laden night mission by two of the pilots from my own "Dice" squadron over the Special Forces Camp at Tong Le Chon was the talk of the entire base for days afterward.

The pilots, who were later awarded the Silver Star for their "gallantry in action," were credited with over 300 killed by air (KBA). They were later told by the Special Forces camp commander they had personally saved the camp. He said he had already given up any hope of survival when this flight of two F-100s swept down over the isolated compound and began their multiple attack passes along the camp walls. Agents later confirmed that the attacking force had been between 1,200 and 1,400 men. No reliable tally was ever given on the actual KBA, but the attackers left over 300 dead on the field of battle as they beat a hasty retreat.

Although the pilots had, between them, flown more than 500 missions, they were still pretty shook up and feeling lucky to be alive as they tried to describe their experience to me the next day. Not only had they faced a lead curtain of bullets and a fireworks display of tracers on each of their 20-odd passes on the first mission, but they were also in constant danger of hitting the nearby trees, or even the ground, as they flew through the area at 200 feet and below. Moreover, they were faced with the problem of insuring that their accuracy was "surgical" because they had to drop much of their ordnance and do their strafing on the outside edge of the poorly lit perimeter of the camp and just inside it, scant feet from the camp defenders. In addition, they had to make a number of dry passes because the ground

171

fire was sometimes just too intense, and sometimes they weren't exactly sure their attack would be accurate enough.

When they returned to base, almost out of fuel, they assisted the load crew as much as they could to make the fastest possible turnaround. An hour and forty minutes later they were back over the camp. In all, they made 42 "hot" passes that night, often straight and level at 300 feet above the ground, as was required for the particular type of ordnance they were delivering. According to a subsequent report in *Time* magazine, the attacking force was the largest ever committed until then to come across the border from nearby Cambodia. The report cited intelligence sources as saying an estimated 14,000 North Vietnamese troops were involved in a plan to start at the entry point, and using Tong Le Chong as a first objective, they would then be moving to take other objectives on a track to eventually take Saigon. About one-tenth of that total force was involved in the attack on that Special Forces Camp.

In the weeks and months after that awful August night in 1967, we all came to learn how they must have felt out there alone in those non-bulletproof Plexiglas-covered cockpits in the middle of the night. As the war heated up, beginning about November, and especially during the month-long Tet Offensive of the following February, I sometimes wondered what those attackers thoughts and feelings were as they exulted over certain victory just ahead in their bid to take a lonely piece of real estate. But then so suddenly found the tables turned as they faced thundering death raining from the night skies, delivered by just two brave, sometimes near terrified, but very skillful pilots whose job it was to provide "close air support."

ROUGE BOQUET REVISITED

In the grass outside of Tong Le Chon
One hundred and eighty men are gone,
And in the woods that stretch away,
Two hundred more are dead today.
These were guerrilla fighting men
Killed on a monsoon night,

Fighting with odds of one to ten...
Now, nevermore to fight.
For death was dealt by just a pair
Whose Sabers sliced forbidding air
Again and again like they didn't care
If they survived.

Though tracers laced the midnight sky,
They knew that they must make a try,
So, in they dived.

At dawn the grass and clay will all
Be damp and still.
While sleeping these two got the call
To fight and kill.
Scramble Dice!
Scramble Dice!
Though your bed may, instead, be with the dead,
Brave the clouds, and the flares, and hungry lead.
Special Forces men are dead
Those alive
Cannot survive
Fight and dive.

"Green Berets" and Montagnards
Ordered here as frontier guards,
In this jungle no-man's-land,
Dug in for a last-ditch stand.
Suddenly, through inky skies
Their last prayers are heard.
O'er the guns and dying sighs
Roars a thundering bird.

Shells and bomblets fill the air,
Hit beside defenders' lair,
Kill attackers swarming there,
And stun good friends.
Do not fear,
Dice is near....

Hiding there, in your lair, attack with care,
Or you shall be where your friends have gone,
In the grass outside of Tong Le Chon.
And beware
The deadly air
Treetop high.
They delivered airborne Hell
All around you, comrades fell.
Then it stopped and they were gone!
"Now we can take Tong Le Chon...!"
But they returned.
Spreading Death with every pass
Underneath the bright night flare
Then silence; they were gone.

By dawn's light men highly trained
Lay in silence as it rained
Nevermore to laugh, or fight,
Killed in instants on that night
As death came flying through the air
Touched them each and left them there
Unwakened by the morning light.
Mark the name of Tong Le Chon,
Mark how many now are gone—
"Killed by air."

Swiftly gone as swift they came,
Later we may learn the name:
"Dice" was there.   *-- Bien Hoa, November, 1967*

JOKERS IN THE SKY

*"A hundred thousand comedians starving to death,
and you clowns get paid to fly airplanes."*

As a collective group, I think that many of the funniest and often most witty people I have ever been around are fighter pilots. It is almost axiomatic that next to nothing is serious or completely sacred to them. Consequently, there is little or nothing they don't joke about.

This seems to be especially true when fighter pilots return to the squadron or walk into the bar after a particularly "hairy" flight, where for seconds or longer, they weren't sure if they were going to "buy the farm," or walk away safe and sound.

Somehow, they would then weave the tale of horror and disaster into a very humorous yarn, leaving us laughing instead of sympathetic or fearful. But we were also learning something more to "look out for" as we flew that sometimes ornery beast, the F-100.

o-0-o

It was almost three in the afternoon, and Norm Thouvenelle and I were running low on gas. Bien Hoa Air Base was fairly "socked in" with bad weather and we were trapped above the undercast about 15 miles from home when up ahead I saw an opening in the clouds.

In pilot's jargon, these are called "sucker holes," because they lure in the pilots who are flying under "visual flight rules" (VFR)–the other kind of flying is "instrument flight rules" (IFR), done occasionally under radar control. The trouble with these openings in the clouds is that every pilot in the area who is flying VFR will head for that bit of air where they can avoid going into clouds, and Bien Hoa was a busy, busy airbase every day.

Norm was flying off my wing in "route formation," which means he was out about two ship-widths away from me instead of in close with his wing overlapping mine. When I turned into him, he was

175

expected to dive down a bit to stay in position in perfect line off my wing. On turns away, he was expected to turn when I did, but to stay in "echelon position" at the same altitude as mine, keeping the fuselage of my plane "on the horizon" as we moved through the turn.

When I spotted the opening in the clouds, I made a steep-banked turn away from him so I could keep an eye on the opening. Because we were still on a "discrete" radio frequency where our conversations would not be broadcast to others, I called to Norm, "Hang on, buddy!"

I led him in a high G turn once around the hole in the clouds, searching for any signs of aircraft just below the cloud deck that might be headed toward the same opening.

Then, still turning, I released some back pressure on the stick, allowing the nose of my aircraft to drop so that we would descend fairly rapidly below the clouds. To avoid building up our speed as we dropped down, I called for "speed brakes out."

Just as we dropped underneath the cloud deck, an F-100 from our home base suddenly was placed where Norm would be if he had been in tight formation. That pilot's plane was overlapping my right wing, and perfectly parallel to my own F-100 *but going the other way!*

The near head-on collision happened so quickly that I never saw where the plane had come from or where it went, but clearly he was climbing out at the same angle I was descending. While I knew that Norm was level to me in my turn and descent, out in echelon and about two ship widths away, I didn't see how that other plane could fit between us without colliding with Norm, nor did I know where the other ship in that formation was, and there was every likelihood that it, instead, could be the one that might have collided head-on with Norm.

In the micro-second that the other aircraft had been on my right wing in tight formation, the image of that plane just beside me in formation and just a few feet away burned itself indelibly in my memory. For an awful split second, I was certain there had been a two or three-ship collision on my blind side, away from my turn.

I held the turn for the longest two or three seconds of my life, looking about frantically to find another F-100 in that oncoming flight. Seeing nothing, I continued my descending turn for several more seconds, dreading the thought that Norm was probably scattered in a million pieces a mile behind me somewhere.

As I rolled out of my banking turn, I looked to my right, and sure enough, there was Norm, grinning at me with his oxygen mask unlatched and pretending to mop his brow in mock terror.

He grinned even more broadly and nodded enthusiastically as I fastened my own mask for a moment and called over to him, "It's a cute little war, if you survive it."

JOKERS IN THE SKY

Why are those who love life best
Always put to death's grim test?
No one with more *joie de vivre*.
What men laugh more easily?

There's mirth and joy where eagles soar,
They're men kept young forevermore.
Boundless humor fills the sky
Silenced only when they die.

Yes laughter, and great talent too,
Bubbles through each thing they do.
Zooming high or bound below,
With twinkling eyes where e'er they go.

They've eagles' grace, and verve, and style,
They're always quick to quip and smile.
The "Brotherhood" of men who soar,
Is Sky, and Laughter—nothing more.

Do you want to join this band?
Then, supersonic, sweep the land,
And roll and zoom straight up the sky
In craft that sleek as arrows fly.

Then, when that constant specter, Death,
Once more nearly snuffs your breath...
Then, quickly, come up with a quip,
For one is on each pale white lip.

– September, 1967

.

o-0-o

CALL IT COURAGE: THREE BAD WEEKS IN THE HUN
By John J. Schulz
(First published in The Intake *magazine, Issue 18, Spring, 2012)*

PROLOGUE: In the winter of 431-430 B.C., with the Peloponnesian War begun, Pericles, the Golden Greek who presided over Athens' finest era, gave a funeral oration so profound and eloquent that it is widely read and quoted to this day. In addition to summarizing perfectly the value of meritocracies and full citizen participation in

politics, he provided what I consider the best of the various definitions of "courage." This passage was translated by Rex Warner, a scholar on ancient Greece.

And this is another point where we differ from other people. We are capable at the same time of taking risks and of estimating them beforehand. Others are brave out of ignorance; and, when they stop to think, they begin to fear. But the man who can most truly be accounted brave is he who best knows the meaning of what is sweet in life and of what is terrible, and then goes out undeterred to meet what is to come."

Pericles in the Golden Age

For 13 years at Boston University, the last of my three-hour lectures each semester—to every class—included this and a previous passage that said, *"Here each individual is interested not only in his own affairs but in the affairs of the state as well...we do not say that a man who takes no interest in politics is a man who minds his own business; we say that he has no business here at all."* My two "life lesson points" from Pericles were that each individual must become informed of the "affairs of state," using several reliable sources, and then vote. The larger point being that the rarest and most valuable thing on this earth is not some rare metal, gem or other substance. Rather it is "courage," that virtue without which all other virtues are blunted or rendered useless. In my now 70 years and more, I have seen it very seldom.

o-0-o

But long before coming across that wonderful passage from Pericles in later, more scholarly pursuits, I had learned all I would ever need to know about courage and how to best define it. That "life lesson" or demonstration came at a special time and in a special place with some very special, gifted, extremely courageous men.

The place was Bien Hoa, RVN, and the time was a three week period that began on the afternoon of September 19, 1967, when Capt. Clyde Carter of the 90th TFS "Dice" flew the last, the terrible and tragic last, of his 301 combat missions. We must begin there.

In the two or three days preceding Clyde's last flight, we had lost two planes and two pilots at low altitude as they began their pullouts. One or two of the men who had been on those same missions reported seeing white smoke or vapor running from the wing root, down the fuselage, and moments later, swore the planes had exploded. Those reports were, from what I saw and heard, rejected out of hand by the more experienced Hun drivers among us. I recall one former Luke instructor saying, when he heard this rendition, "That can't be right. The F-100 just does not explode in flight, never has, never will."

On September 19th, Clyde Carter went out on his final mission with plans all prepared for his post-mission flyby over the base and a bit of an air show for us all. That was the word that had gotten around, and everyone in Dice was alerted to keep an eye out for whenever Clyde and his wingman returned. He had alerted Major Jack Doub the night before about his plans, and no one was more capable of getting the word around at the speed of light, and widely, than Jack, who became an eye witness to an unexpected and numbing tragedy. As was I.

That day, on the only mission of its kind I ever flew, I was to lead a flight of four on some routine tree buster, hard load, dive-bombing mission in IV Corps. What was unusual was that two of the pilots were to be from the Dice Squadron, and two from the "Ramrods" of the 531st TFS, headquartered just about 100 yards down the flight line from our own "squadron shack." My briefing there, was unremarkable, at least until "Ramrod," the squadron's pet nine-foot python decided to join my briefing, arriving without warning from the rafters and plonking himself down on the middle of the briefing table. I can't say I was terrified, and "surprised" is too mild a word. That lovely British understatement "non-plussed" comes to mind. Lucky for me, Ramrod arrived near the end of my briefing, and we headed out a bit early to preflight because the taxiway rendezvous would be a bit more complicated.

My squadron mate and I had not gone more than 30 yards up the ramp toward our own part of the flight line when I noticed a single Hun nearing the break for landing. Too often, that was a very bad sign that someone wasn't coming back. But then I remembered Clyde's promise of a final mission air show, and scanning up and left of the ramp, there he came. He was at about 500 or 600 feet, and descending, smoking along at what seemed close to 500 knots. At about that same time, Jack Doub, riding on his motorcycle to the flight line, saw from further distance, at a different angle, that Clyde was headed inbound, so he dismounted and grabbed his camera.

What we both saw, and have collaborated to verify all these many years later, was that just a few hundred feet before he would have been above the Dice Squadron building, parallel to the runway and a couple of hundred yards to the side, his plane began to bob slightly up and down. I thought it strange because Clyde had a velvet touch, was a deft, outstanding pilot and one of the very few in the Wing who had won a Silver Star during his tour (for actions on March 13, 1967). I remember thinking that he must have some very unusual maneuver in mind, for surely, he otherwise would never be so ham-fisted as to cause the plane to porpoise like that.

Then, all Hell broke loose in a terrible, freeze-framed matter of seconds now indelible on the minds of everyone who might have witnessed what happened next.

I saw a stream of white vapor suddenly appear along the left of the fuselage visible from my vantage point (upon reflection, perhaps a stream of fuel). Then, too fast to separate that vapor from what came next, the left wing snapped off and fluttered down toward where we were standing, spinning on a longitudinal axis the whole way down. But that was almost peripheral, because at virtually the same moment, the canopy flew up past the tail section, followed swiftly by what appeared to be Clyde's helmet.

But it was not just the helmet; in that terrible instant Clyde was beheaded and, as subsequently reported by Jack Doub, the head and helmet thudded down through the roof of the big maintenance hangar to the west of the 90th squadron shack. Jack added that a couple of the young airmen working on the flight line were so traumatized by it all that one was relieved of duties for awhile and the other was "sent away" for psychiatric treatment.

Then, as the F-100 went into a spiraling dive that took it just off the base, I became aware of an incredible crashing sound less than 100 feet away; that disconnected wing had come down on the edge of the Ramrod flight line, literally slicing in two Airman First Class Victor Negron of the 510th TFS, killing him instantly. On the Vietnam Memorial Wall, he and Clyde are listed as dying on the same day.

Captain Clyde Carter was easily 6'4", a superior pilot, wonderful photographer who knew much about cameras, and was (at least) as a

On a happier day, en route to tennis in the 90th TAC Fighter Squadron's "Vietnamese Sports Car" Clyde in back with (L-R) Al DeGroote, Jack Doub and Dale Rook.

tennis player, with a deadly drop shot, from the accounts of his equally mediocre tennis mates in the group. This sad tale gets even worse: his wife and child were already on their way to San Francisco, driving to meet him there when he flew home; as a result, they could not be reached for notification until more than two days after the fatal accident.

But that is only the beginning of the fuller story: While the two or three eyewitnesses from the two other, earlier mission fatalities might have felt vindicated, things had happened so fast, and parts of the Dice F-100 with serial number 56-3330 were so scattered, it was likely to be weeks before any scientific findings could be verified.

182

Fortunately, vital information came much sooner. Because that wing had come off before many witnesses, our maintenance teams set right to work with spectrographic equipment to determine the cause. So, by the next day (or the day after—recall is imperfect on this), word came down from our own Wing HQ to all the Hun pilots.

To paraphrase: "The cause of Clyde Carter's accident, and possibly one or two of the most recent ones preceding his, was metal fatigue, that is indicated by a crack in the wing, along the wing root area, visible with spectrographic examination. We have checked every plane in the fleet (*about 65 planes total, -jjs*) and have identified 54 of the planes with these cracks. We are not going to tell you which ones. We are working day and night to put riveted metal reinforcing straps along the wing roots of every plane in the fleet. But meanwhile, we have our mission to fulfill, and we recommend that during pullouts, you plan ahead so as to stay below 4 G's in the pullout." And, indeed, in something under three weeks, the entire 3rd TFW had a stopgap measure in place on the wings.

Our Wing shared these findings immediately with all F-100 units, but it was *another* accident that prompted more comprehensive measures to fix the problem. On October 21, 1967, at Laughlin AFB, the Thunderbird team, and specifically future AF Chief of Staff "Tony" McPeak, had pulled vertical to initiate the "up the middle" solo part of the famous Thunderbird Bomb Burst maneuver when, without warning, his "wing box" failed. He bailed out safely from a decomposing Super Sabre just seconds later.

That his accident happened *where* it did, may have saved many F-100s and the lives of those who flew them, for years after that.

Because all the aircraft parts could be recovered quickly on the barren Texas plains, close examination made it clear that a much larger, more comprehensive fix would be needed on the wing boxes of every F-100 in the inventory. Within weeks, every plane in the fleet was *scheduled* for IRAN, where this was subsequently done.

But this fact remains. During a nine day period, the 3rd TFW lost six planes and six pilots—two before Clyde and three after, as day and night we continued to do the job, most often having to pull more than 4 G's to do so.

I am certain this awareness–and amazing courage—was on display in each of the F-100 Wings in Vietnam during that brief, terrible period. The guys in the wings at Phan Rang, Tuy Hoa and Phu Cat faced the same Damocles' Sword each time they lit up their Huns and taxied out to War. Simply stated, of all definitions of "courage" that I know, and all the many inspiring examples, nothing exceeds the experience I had of being around a whole wing full of warriors in the 3rd TFW who, every day and night for about three weeks, climbed without hesitation into those cockpits, then launched on missions, knowing full well that most of the planes were, literally, flying coffins.

"Courage," demonstrated by the jocks in all the SEA squadrons, was going forth to fly and fight, undeterred by this knowledge of wing root failures and the desperate race to fix every plane before even more of us died with terrible suddenness.

I never heard a single murmur of fear…but I'll bet I heard at least 10 good wisecracks filled with gallows humor or marvelous irony during that period. Not a single man refused to fly, or even hinted at such a thought.

As I think again about what went on, and try to put it into perspective, I am ever mindful of some terrible facts that confronted us, and all our "brother men" who flew in other wars or in other airplanes. First of all, the F-100 Super Saber had the highest accident and fatality rate in fighter flying history, peacetime or wartime; number two was the WWI Sopwith Camel, and number

Clyde Carter's mangled canopy amid the debris field in the 510th TFS ramp area where Victor Negron became a collateral casualty of the jaws of war. Greg Norwood photo, © 510th FS Photo Archives.

three was the F-104. Second, the life expectancy of a WW I fighter pilot was just five combat hours. And, in WW II, the grim statistics for the bomber pilots on runs over Ploiesti, and some of the other targets, underscore the need to "toast the host of brother men who fly" and did so with such terrible odds against them. What, in my mind, is different about those three weeks and our experience is that pilots have always known their own lack of skill in combat or airmanship against a better enemy pilot, or pure bad luck amidst terrible flak could spell death. But I am not aware of design deficiencies in the Sopwiths or other WW I "crates," or the Allied fighters and bombers of WW II or Korea, that meant we could become a fatality because the plane itself betrayed us as we skillfully did our jobs...to fly and fight. Uniquely, and for that brief and terrible time, we, the Hun drivers were, to quote Pericles, "in the hands of the gods."

(-- *End of* The Intake *article, Issue 18, Spring, 2012 --)*

o-0-o

THE SMELL OF LOSS AND CORDITE

It was some weeks after that horrific period when we lost Clyde Carter and then five more pilots–all in nine days. The intensity of fighting and numbers of heavy battles had increased noticeably, especially in IV Corps, where the size and activity of North Vietnamese forces seemed to be growing every day, as was the amount of ground fire headed our way.

I came into our squadron bar late in the afternoon from some day mission, only to learn that another good friend of mine had gone down that day. Gin and tonic in hand, I went out into the soft evening rain alone to smoke. I came back in, got a notepad from behind the bar, sat down at our vacant poker table and began to scribble. Checking with the guys, some 30 minutes later when it was done, I asked if this captured the way they sometimes felt and what they experienced. The universal response was, "Yeah, that's got it right."

185

NEWS ITEM:
"TODAY AN F-100 WENT DOWN IN THE DELTA"

My soul is ravaged and tattered and shorn,
My senses bombarded, my mind is untidy,
My body's been driven, my nerve endings worn;
I'm not a young man, I'm old, and not mighty.

The moon is all bloody—I no longer dream
And my conscience is beaten and shred.
Things are no longer quite what they seem,
And my country's hand-picked are now dead.

I used to weep when a friend of mine died,
His spiraling laughter transcended the earth.
But the salt has now turned to steel inside,
For, who cares what our talents are worth?

I know I'm a hundred years older than most,
And quicker, and skilled more by far.
The eagles I fly with are similar ken
And they soar above men like a star.

Today a jet pilot went down in a dive
To destroy a nest full of hot lead,
He was a close friend—while he was alive,
And now, one more friend of mine's dead.

And eight thousand miles away in the night,
A star falls from out of the sky;
Unknowing, a child, with all of his might,
Makes a wish...that some day...he will fly.
                    – Bien Hoa, November, 1967

WITHIN A FIGHTER PILOT'S EYES

My friend and I then began discussing our profession, and I said, "You know, it's amazing when you stop and think about it. Four of my former students have now been killed or captured while flying missions over North Vietnam, and I've been good friends with all but a couple of the guys we've lost this last nine months in our Wing."

Gary smiled sadly and said, "Yes, I've been flying fighters for seven years now, and that death yesterday makes my personal tally 38 guys I've been in the same wing with. It's really terrifying if you keep track. And you know, given the tremendous numbers of accidents and losses in peacetime and wartime fighter flying, imagine how many friends and acquaintances a senior officer in Fighter (Tactical Air) Command has lost over the years. And imagine what that does to him, subconsciously."

20-20 VISION

Within a fighter pilot's eyes
A tiny hint of terror lies
Unseen and seldom ever bare,
Hidden deep, but lurking there.

But bold and cocky as he goes
So no one ever sees or knows
How much the swagger and the boast
Veil the dangers he fears most.

For in that tiny cockpit high,
In microseconds, speeding by,
Terrible instant Death ... almost!
Comes calling, and it leaves a ghost:

The ghost of all the reasons why
He should have been the next to die.
And ghosts of friends who are not there,
Who've died a dozen ways each year.

Yet still, there is a challenge there,
That keeps him slicing through the air.
And knowledge that those few who live
Have much they've seen, and much to give.
For those same eyes have seen from high
Vast beauties that transcend the sky.
And for such beauty, and each belief,
They face the terror, loss and grief.

– Bien Hoa, February, 1968

o-0-o

It was late November, and Linda and I had to postpone our planned seven-day R&R in Hawaii, where I would meet my new baby daughter and be reunited with Linda after so many very eventful months. I was very disappointed, and very, very tired from several days and nights of intense flying, much of it from the alert pad, and from huge loads of paperwork to edit and process as well. One night, after an earlier mission launched from the alert pad again, I had some time alone. The other guys were in back resting or sleeping, and given that I had originally planned to be in Hawaii in just a few more days, I had a touch of the blues.

THREE MISSIONS OFF THE ALERT PAD

It's late, and every inch of marrow
Deep within me screams in pain.
Ah, the insights cause such sorrow,
And I think of you again.

Here, alone, late, late at night,
I've been awake a million years,
And thoughts are dressed in different light
(Are my eyes tired, or are those tears?)

188

I'm now too old, no time exists
(Or very little–how time races!)
To enter all the jousting lists
And take each of my pre-planned paces.

So I'd best choose with care those few
Things that I think are "well worthwhile."
And best is being just with you,
Refreshed and reborn in your smile.
                    – November, 1967

o-0-o

HOW TO WALK AWAY FROM A THING
YOU LOVE SO MUCH

It was a quiet early December night on the alert pad and, not for the first time, my thoughts turned to a tough decision I had to make, and make soon. Those of us who were commissioned and went through flight school had a total active duty commitment of five years in those days, and by the end of my combat tour I would be very close to that decision point.

The real problem I faced was to decide whether I should continue a career in the Air Force, or leave and begin to take the next step in a previously established "schedule" of things I wanted to do with my life. Perhaps it was time to pursue my earlier dream to be a foreign correspondent.

All well and good, but I had fallen deeply in love for the second time in my life, this time with the F-100 and with its mission and the type of flying we did in it, and this prompted lengthy discussions by mail with my first love, Linda, as to whether I should stay in the Air Force or resign my commission or move on to a peacetime assignment in the F-100. I knew that it was important to separate my love of flying the F-100 from my love of flying it in combat. Growing inside me for many months was the realization that I loved more than just the excitement of combat; rather it was a kind of

189

hunter's instinct to do something very good–save the lives of our ground troops, while doing something very challenging, fly and fight and yes, kill, in a dangerous, lethal fighting machine. I had also come to know that such enthusiasm was not universally shared. And I recalled an earlier conversation with my friend, Gary Tompkins, about my approach to combat.

"Don't be too hard on the guy, John," he said to me that night as we sat waiting for another possible launch for a night mission from the alert pad. "You know, this may sound strange to you and a handful of other guys around the base, but most people are a little afraid of getting killed in this war."

He was more insightful than I was about that. I had not thought about it in months and it was sufficiently obvious to most who flew missions with me that on a couple of occasions as we rushed out the door on the second or third scramble for the day, my wingmen had grabbed me by the arm, or stopped me for a second to say, "Hey, take it a little easier on this one will ya, I want to go home someday, ok?" That attitude had disturbed me, and I wasn't sure what to think of the guys who said it, and that is what prompted Gary's comment.

Mine was neither a heroic stance nor a form of bravery; it was merely a mindset, an attitude based on preconditioning during nine years of disregarding dangers on football fields and hyper-extended to a form of unreality by the pressures of combat, cordite and loss–and more than a little anger.

Later that night, weighing the pros and cons of "staying in or getting out" of the Air Force, I realized something else to consider.

The most compelling attractions of the F-100 related to its mission, and to the fact that for all its terrible down sides, I loved being in combat, and loved to join with my metal partner as we roared down into the hottest battles we could find. But how would that translate to peacetime flying?

Before I knew it, I was writing a love song to an inanimate piece of machinery. But oh how addictive the "blend" with that machine could be!

o-0-o

190

ONCE AND EVER AFTER

Something there is
Seductive
    flying fighters in a war.
At least for some.
And for those few
    who hunt,
      there is no other anymore.

The comradeship, the danger
    the sense its
      "all for real"
(no dives with little practice bombs)
    the taste, the sound, the feel....
The awesome sense of Mission,
    sense of Purpose
      and the Love,
combined with all that awesome skill
      in fighting from above.

For almost any man alive
    this so-addictive "thing"–
    this movement just beyond ballet
    this blend of man and wing
    this wild freedom of the heart,
    this sense of conquered fear
      will steal his heart
        his soul
        his mind
no other "ride" comes near.

191

No other "bird"
    with passengers
    no other beast of prey
will be a "nice alternative"
    when he calls it a day.

No words can ever get it right
    (explains why so few try)
when speed, precision, grace and art
    combine with "live or die."
So
call it "fighter combat,"
    "speed addiction"
        or, "a thrill."
I'll merely say
    "Seductive"
    as when fear combines with skill.
*   – December, 1967*

    As Christmas approached, I had the feeling that I was a bit of a failure when it came to finding and then sending, on time, a suitable Christmas present to the lovely lady anxiously waiting at home. I had scoured the Base Exchange, but found nothing all that appropriate that couldn't be found in most department stores in the USA, and I had no real time to shop in other countries in recent times, nor did I know what might be available in Bien Hoa City; at that point, I had never been there. And worst of all, I had let the early mailing deadline pass for packages to home and whatever I then sent would not get there in time. I had given thought to what would be "unique and wonderful," a fine pair of adjectives to describe Linda. But we both knew that war meant "delayed gratification, and so instead, I sent her this heartfelt poem about what I was thinking and feeling about the whole task of "gift giving.'

192

THE CHRISTMAS GIFT

What can I give as a Christmas gift
To one as fair as thee?
What do I offer to one so sweet
And place beneath your tree?
I cannot offer the soft south wind,
For you own each breeze, I know.
For everywhere I hear your voice
Whispering sweet and low.

What can I offer the Queen of the Stars
Whose face is etched in the skies?
How do I offer the moon to you,
When the moon is in your eyes?

How do I choose the finest gift,
Or pick the dearest stone,
When the beauty of each jewel fades
When placed beside your own?

I cannot give you the finest rose,
For never a flower was there
That had the subtle, soft, warm hue
Which glows in your lips so fair.
I own not stars, nor wind, nor moon;
No precious jewels are mine.
But I've two loving and gentle lips,
So I'll press them close to thine.

– Christmas, 1967

o-0-o

SORRY TO INTERRUPT, BUT I BEG TO DIFFER

I was in my office, working with my administrative clerk, Airman First Class Wayne Clutter from West Virginia, who did all the final typing on tons of my paperwork for the Wing. Sitting at my desk nearby, I couldn't help but overhear the comments of a newcomer, a sergeant with about 50 hours of light plane flying experience, relating to several listeners how unimpressive the student pilots were at the Undergraduate Pilot Training base where he had last served. He talked about how many mistakes they made while learning to fly jet airplanes, how awkward they were just taxiing the planes when they first arrived, and much more. Then he said, "It's gotten so just about anyone can fly, you know."

My year in Vietnam was winding down; I had flown over 260 combat missions by then, and with all the time on the Alert Pad and with the exhausting fighting during the Tet Offensive, I was worn down and tired, which perhaps helps explain my undoubtedly impolite response to what I'd heard.

With anger masked, I asked the self-appointed expert if I could borrow his pencil and notepad for a moment. About fifteen minutes later I handed it back to him with this poem written on it.

A DIFFERENT LANGUAGE

Don't talk to me of glory,
And the romance of the blue,
Of jet jocks slipping surly bonds
Of earth in flights of two.

The little toys in which you play,
And all those metal clouds
In which you ride from place to place
In stewardess-serviced crowds,

Have just two things in common
With the war birds that we fly:

194

They get you up above the earth...
And when they fall, you die!

But there all similarity,
My airplane-loving friends,
Between the world in which you fly
And my world, quickly ends.

Inside my small cramped cockpit
The comforts that are there
Are just to keep me warm and safe
While striking from the air.

For everything about my craft,
Each switch and each sleek line,
Is built for wrenching, grinding flight.
There's death in each design.

I know the blue in which you fly
Is full of peace and beauty.
You do it 'cause it's fun and sport,
Or as a well-paid duty.

My blue is full of blackout grey,
And pounds of sweat, and terror,
A million rules control each move,
And Death greets each small error.

Yet, there's delight in what we do,
Fierce pride and awesome grace,
And many dead friends that we knew
That none of you can e'er replace.

> *– Bien Hoa, Late February, 1968*

195

"GENTLEMEN, THE COMMANDER..."

There is one job that senior officers actively seek, but which incurs, along with its privileges, the awesome burdens of responsibility and loneliness. In the U.S. Air Force, it is the job of Wing Commander, the last "test" and gateway for that handful of officers who will then be considered for "flag rank," where their title becomes "General."

The men who sit in that big office at Wing Headquarters are not only responsible for every one of the billions of dollars-worth of equipment on their base, but for the safety, welfare and deportment of every one of the thousands of people under his command (and their dependents).

Not only is he ultimately responsible for the discharge of the mission of his wing, (which may be as vital as the task of unleashing his combat aircraft and crews on missions to deliver nuclear weapons if, heaven forbid, orders were to come to launch into WWIII). The wing commander must also insure that his wing is capable of performing any and all secondary missions, and he must answer for how well these tasks are executed, down to the minutest detail.

Above each wing commander there are all the planners, all the staff and headquarters officers, and in his direct chain of command, several generals who continually press those under them to execute the myriad plans, policies and missions with which each wing is tasked. Because, it is here, at the wing level, that the "greasy coverall and sweaty flight suit" Air Force begins, and where the job is to get those planes airborne.

A wing commander's days are spent coordinating (from time-to time) with the one- to-four-starred bosses above him, and in meetings, conferences with his wing staff, and each of his three or more squadron commanders and the heads of many sections and units on the base. He is suggesting, hinting, questioning, giving orders, and then insuring that these orders are executed properly. The moment any flaw is noted by his boss, the one-star general who supervises several wing commanders, he is "on the carpet." At any time, throughout the year, the commander, and his entire wing, can suddenly find that swooping down without notice is an Operational Readiness Team, which will stay on the base for four or five days or longer putting everyone in the wing through their paces, and grading every aspect of every operation and mission execution. Any number of wing commanders have been known to be fired on the spot if their wing fails an Operational Readiness Inspection (ORI). Indeed, in the 1950s, one Inspector General, in charge of these operations, was nicknamed "Sundown Wells," because General Wells would tell the failing wing commander that he "had until sundown to be off the base."

In normal times, the wing commander's nights are taken up with a constant round of social obligations. And wherever he goes, 24 hours a day, he carries with him the "Talking Brick"–a walkie-talkie that is also used by key personnel on his staff to keep him advised of everything important that is going on at any hour. And their jobs have yet another facet: they must stay current in the front-line, mission aircraft of the wing, and if the commander wants to keep the respect of his pilots, he'll do more than just stay current, he'll draw upon his years of flying experience and take the time necessary to stay proficient in the bird.

He has been in the flying game long enough to know that a lack of knowledge and proficiency can quickly prove fatal in a fighter airplane. And unlike other forms of flying, the gunnery range in particular has a rigorous measuring standard: the number of bullets through each strafe panel, the distance from center of every practice bomb, is measured to the foot and reported back to each squadron after every flight of four returns from the gunnery range. Indeed, pilots tend to lay a standard wager ahead of time that can reward, or cost, the pilots in the flight "a nickel a hole" and "a quarter per bomb."

But this flying duty is a task that most wing commanders enjoy best, because they are most at home in the company of pilots, having spent the majority of their careers in this milieu, and they often form warm relationships with some of "the youngsters," who occasionally kid them about taking it easy on "the old man" when they fly together.

Moreover, just prior to getting airborne, they can relinquish their burdens until they land, by delegating their authority to the Vice Wing Commander, via the walkie-talkie. I wonder how many 50-year-olds in this world would view an hour and a half or more in a

197

dangerous high performance single-seat jet fighter—perhaps on a combat mission—as a form of "rest and relaxation"?

During my year at Bien Hoa, I had the privilege of working on the wing staff for two of these gentlemen, with direct access to meet with them at any hour of day or night. Both were truly remarkable individuals and it was easy to see why they had been picked over so many other candidates to be wing commanders. And on more than one occasion, I was moved to wonder what went on inside them when they learned of the death of one of the pilots who was a special friend, not to mention the loss of another aircraft, for which they had to answer directly to a four-star general. The following, then, is respectfully dedicated to those two men, who both became generals themselves, and who used to have one of the two most underpaid jobs in the world.

THE OLD MAN

"Another loss...? No, not again!
(My God, please why?
How many fine young men
Must I have die
Because I fly?)

"Who, Bob, who? Not "Woody!"'
(He was smart and quick.
My heart
Can only take so much
Of dead young men...
And he was like a son to me.)

"Listen...there, you hear that sound?
That is another pair, just airborne,
Going, (I would guess) to where
They just shot "Woody" down."

198

"I wish, somehow, that I could go
Right now, and fly."
(But no,
My first job is this office
Full
Of paper and command,
And now,
Of that sad letter, too,
That I must write....

No
Those two letters:
The "boss" will need "preliminary notes"
That he can read
To his boss...
And they'll both be howling mad...)
"That's the third one lost this month
From off 'the pad.'"

"I still just can't believe
That it was him."
(And yet, I have no time
To grieve...
There is so much to do
Before my day is through
That's not all...)
"Well, Bob, I may have lost my job
Before nightfall."

— Tokyo, 1975

o-0-o

JIMMY

.30 caliber and 20mm Cannon

He was on a low-angle run covering pinned down troops when he was shot down. Killed instantly. There's just no way to get out at 50 feet and almost 500 miles an hour. In my year's tour, he was the last of the more-than-twenty pilots (out of 60+ in our Wing) to "buy the farm."

It happened just three days before I was to go home, and when I heard it, I wasn't as steeled for it as usual, and I remember that I could barely see the steel locker I was smashing my fist into—until I realized how stupid that was.

It was just one friend too many.

He was small, and quick, and very good looking, and extremely witty. I was a close friend in a place where friendships come quickly and are based on mutual respect.

He was wild as a hawk, and his many elaborate, crazy stunts belied his disciplined Air Academy training. And he was a genius, and a talented musician, an excellent artist and a writer of prose and poetry.

He was to be married in December, after five years as a bachelor fighter pilot. Jimmy was 27.

And he was a damn good pilot. And now, Jimmy's gone....

JIMMY'S GONE, ONE MORE ROUND...

Sittin' on the pad, he said
"Ain't the "hero bit" for me;
Heroes always end up dead:
A general's what I'm gonna be."
But Jimmy's gone, one more round,
One more round, Jimmy's gone,
Jimmy's gone, Jimmy's gone, one more round.

200

Stood and sang in daily showers
Sang the Ode to Billy Joe
Sang the bloody thing for hours
Better'n anyone I know.
But Jimmy's gone, one more round,
One more round, Jimmy's gone,
Jimmy's gone, Jimmy's gone, one more round.

"Squadron needs a bar," he said,
"And we need more booze here, too."
So he built one, and he stocked it,
Then got drunk and queered the do.
Now Jimmy's gone, one more round,
One more round, Jimmy's gone,
Jimmy's gone, Jimmy's gone, one more round.

Pick a subject, pick a gag,
Start a party, do a "bit,"
Guaranteed, things never lag
'Cause Jim's in the midst of it.
Now Jimmy's gone, one more round,
One more round, Jimmy's gone,
Jimmy's gone, Jimmy's gone, one more round.

Fly like tigers all the way
Tigers always know their kind.
Don't pick up no lead today–
That'll really blow your mind.
A Tiger's gone, one more round,
One more round, a Tiger's gone,
Jimmy's gone, Jimmy's gone, one more round.

"Scramble 'Buzzards'–troops in trouble!"
Go in low, the troops are near.
Hot lead through the plastic bubble...
"Jimmy's bought it...have a beer".
Yeah, Jimmy's gone, one more round,
One more round, Jimmy's gone,
Jimmy's gone, Jimmy's gone...one more round.
                    – *Bien Hoa, April, 1968*

FAREWELL TO YOU...AND TO ALL OUR ABSENT FRIENDS

It was a clear, warm and moonlit night, and the air moistly warned of the coming monsoon season. As I stood before the suntanned, eager faces, warmed by the glow of wine and just-spent laughter, I took a deep breath to clear the emotions that kept welling in my throat and pulling at the edges of my eyes as I prepared to say farewell.

Behind me were the desperate early days of trying to carve myself a place within the ranks of men like these after my disastrous beginning, and to adapt at rapid pace to the very different skills and requirements needed to become an effective pilot in a close air support combat fighter. Behind me were the exhilarating tastes of fear, joy, excitement and pride that blended so well with anger, frustration and conquest into the delicious flavor airborne hunters can extract only from combat flying. Behind, too, were those occasional terrifying and unspeakable moments that the mind refuses to accept and so buries forever in the unexplorable recesses of the subconscious. And too, this would be my last day or so with men who had shared many combat experiences with me, a sense of brotherhood which cannot be duplicated, and which, in a matter of hours, would become a thing of the past.

Now, in those very moments, as I stood before my fellow Dice men, all the myriad magic hours of mirth and humor and good fellowship, and yes, the love and mutual admiration and respect exemplified by such things as the poem my squadron commander had composed and read about me just a minute before--all these things and more were about to slip away, never to be recaptured, never to be relived.

I knew then, as I know now, that volunteering to stay on for an extended tour of six more months would not and could not maintain for me the magic glow of life in this 20th Century Camelot squadron. Even as I looked out over the table at the 30-odd men gathered to pay tribute to the three of us departing the war zone, I could see the less tanned faces of newcomers I barely knew, and the ghosts of many long-departed, or dead, stared back at me as well between the rows of vibrant, attentive listeners.

And yes, there was ahead of me the wonderful prospect of reunion with my stunningly beautiful wife, my family and friends. Ahead also was the prospect of becoming acquainted with, and father to, a lovely little one-year-old girl about whom I felt perhaps more curiosity than acquired emotion. Ahead, too, was the prospect of seeing England and Europe during my three-year assignment, of learning much more about "dog-fighting," the skill of air-to-air combat, and the chance to continue my love affair with the F-100.

So, as I began to speak, I promised the group assembled in the back room of the Officer's Club at Bien Hoa that if they would promise to listen, and give me no "assistance" with what I had to say, then I, in turn, would try to say things they had not heard expressed that way before.

They held beautifully to their end of the bargain. How well I held to my end I can only judge from the warmth of their smiles, the length of their applause, the firmness of their handshakes and the kind comments as each, in turn, spoke of lasting friendship and good fortune in the days and years ahead.

I had worked to prepare for those minutes "on stage," and worked especially hard on the poem that would conclude the things I wanted to say before departing. In the many years since writing it, I have had occasion to re-read it, and each time am struck by the prescience of the last four lines, and just how true they were.

REQUIEM FOR A FIGHTER PILOT

I've reaped the harvest of the moon,
Skimmed silver fields of clouds at night,
And in the terror rain monsoon
I've dived too low in deadly fight.

In a beauteous brute that takes your breath
I've roamed the pagan sky,
And danced a pirouette of death
To strafe those next to die.

How often have my Lead and I
Seen beauty that bombards our senses!
The battle nears...who's next to die?
The beauty's gone, the work commences.

There's no time now for God's distractions,
There are a million things to do.
We've previewed Heaven's vast attractions,
Now many guns await just two.

But we are skilled, work in an office
In kingdoms where there is no air.
Our great war-birds would kill a novice,
So few e'er rock in my high chair.

Yes, now the long commute is done,
And cordite mixed with blurry fear
Combines with lasting color dreams
While War thuds loud within the ear.

Thuds...erupts...blurs past in inches,
Hangs on moments stalled, undone.

Precision slammed, by will, on chaos
Till something near to flight is won.

Then, too soon, it all is o'er
The great excitements all subside.
Too soon the fight, and yes, the War,
And slowly...we each die inside.

We few who hunt will soon roam skies
Where we must search, or teach or train.
Then we must veil our Hunter's Eyes,
But life...will never...be the same.

— The close to a farewell speech to the 90th TFS,
Bien Hoa, April, 1968

o-0-o

CHAPTER IX

LIFE AT LAKENHEATH
(1968-1971)

"For you, the War is over...."

(But 18 planes lost in 18 months at Lakenheath does keep you focused)

THREE INTERESTING YEARS
WITH A DIFFERENT MISSION IN MIND

In May, 1968, we began an exciting new chapter of "Life in the Air Force," this time in that marvelous nationwide wall-to-wall museum known as the United Kingdom. It was time to give the peacetime Air Force the opportunity to show me that life in the fighter business could be the right choice for a full career for me and a good and interesting lifestyle for Linda and our family. Those three years were, in many ways wonderful and difficult at the same time. Wonderful because the chance to live in a foreign country was, for both of us, mind expanding, and wonderfully educational. We were, after all, living not far from Cambridge, in Norfolk County, north of London, and all around us and throughout the country was the opportunity to wander through a vast outdoor museum, one of the few countries in Western and Central

Europe that was mostly undamaged, despite the terrible ravages of WW II and all the devastation in London from the German bombing raids and rocket attacks.

We took full advantage of every opportunity to learn more about the long and colorful history of the county and of many of its centuries-old towns and villages, castles and churches. Many weekends, and with other chances to take a few days of leave, we at the same time could enjoy quality time with our toddler, Melinda Marie, our "Molly" and her little sister, Ariel Ann, who arrived at Lakenheath Hospital in September of 1969. On some weekends, Linda and I would drive down to London, attend an evening play, and then a Saturday matinee at another theatre, and return home. We also took advantage of the fact that in the late '60s, the cost of goods and

207

services was considerably less than in the United States, and we were able to collect some fine antique furniture at very low prices, not least because foreigners had not yet discovered the "wonderfully good deals" to be had in the UK in the antique-buying business.

On one occasion, Linda and several of the other wives in the 493rd Tactical Fighter Squadron drove down to northern Italy, where we were on temporary duty at Aviano Air Base, in the northeastern part of the country. Together, we explored Venice, Florence and the warm and friendly hospitality of the northern Italians, whose restaurant menus were full of delicious foods.

At RAF Lakenheath, and at all the other Air Force Fighter Wings in United States Air Force Europe (USAFE), the main mission was distinctly different from that of flying close air support over beleaguered troops in combat. In Europe, at the height of the cold war, the F-100 played a role in the over-bridging strategic standoff known as "nuclear deterrence," and "mutual assured destruction," which ultimately kept the peace and avoided WW III during those years. Because the versatile F-100 could fulfill the close air support role wonderfully, and was capable of air-to-air combat and nuclear strike delivery, each F-100 wing in Europe kept six pilots on "Victor Alert," at special alert compounds where the six planes were armed and ready with nuclear weapons and could be launched in under 15 minutes to strike at military targets deep inside the Soviet Union and some of the other Warsaw Pact countries.

As part of the U.S. NATO commitment, one squadron in most of the wings was away from home for a month at a time on temporary duty to another base in Italy or Turkey, complicating Soviet defenses and providing another "angle of attack" in the event of nuclear war. Thus, every third month, in rotation with the other two squadrons in the 48th Tactical Fighter Wing, we deployed to either Aviano Air Base, Italy, or to a base along the coast of Turkey. There, we continued our frequent practice to perfect our low-level navigation and map reading skills, and, when in Turkey, re-deployed for a week to Wheelus Air Base near Tripoli, Libya (before Gadhafi's revolution), to practice our gunnery and bombing skills at a range set up in the desert not far away from the base. This cyclical absence from our families was somewhat difficult; most of us had young children at home and wives who had to cope alone with all normal duties and family emergencies. At home, we were also away on alert duty several days and nights for a month, meaning that our actual time away from home was at least 40 days out of every 90.

At Lakenheath, the flying itself focused on things far different from our rather singular mission in Vietnam. Moreover, the weather in England posed challenges quite often, turning all of us into excellent instrument pilots, and making the simple task of returning to base at the end of a flight an often somewhat challenging event. We also got to see many parts of England, Scotland, Wales, the Netherlands and northern France at high speed from 500 feet above the ground (or lower) as we spent many hours practicing the "high- low- high" flight profile that would be used, God forbid, in the event of WW III. A portion of most of the low-level navigation missions involved cruising at high altitude until we were 100 to 200 miles from our "target," because jet engines burn far less fuel at high altitude, and this greatly extended the range of our navigation practice.

We did have at least two to three gunnery range missions or more each three months either at the range not far north of Lakenheath or elsewhere if we were TDY. At the bombing and gunnery range in the UK, in addition to four dive bomb runs, two very low altitude skip bomb passes and several low-angle runs at canvas panels set up as strafe targets, we sometimes had the added challenge of delivering a dummy nuclear weapon to the same target we used for the 25-pound dummy dive bombs. That delivery was challenging to complete, and involved use of a special instrument in the cockpit to guide us through the maneuver. I was very familiar with the other maneuvers, thanks to a year of doing them almost daily in Vietnam. This new maneuver was not my strong suit. There was also a gunnery and bombing range near Aviano, Italy, and when we were not on alert or out practicing low level missions in the lush Italian countryside, we were enjoying the famously beautiful range at Aviano, where there was seldom any wind to affect our weapons-delivery accuracy, and where the weather was clear and sunny every day.

One thing that kept these "range missions" interesting was the fact that the Range Officers sat in a tower next to the action and were able to triangulate and grade how far every practice bomb landed from dead center on the intended target. It was customary to place a bet among the pilots headed out to the range in the flights of four. The stakes were a quarter per bomb, with the guy who hit closest on each pass collecting a quarter from his three flight mates. The other fun part of these range missions was that each of us carried one hundred 20mm rounds of ammunition in our cannon bays, and each bullet was painted with a color that would leave a stain on the canvas as it went through. After every flight of four left the range, those strafe panels were taken down, and the four different colors left by the bullets were counted and reported back to the squadron by telephone. At the debriefing after each flight landed, pilots tallied up the strafe scores, along with the bomb scores, and the strafing winner collected a nickel a hole from each of his mates, based on his score differential. For example, if one pilot had put 70 bullets in the target, the one who had 55 would owe him 75 cents (15 bullets difference times 5 cents each bullet). Each of the others would owe more or less, depending on their scores. Woe be the lad who had only scored 25 the day the best shooter scored 75; he would owe the winner a whopping $2.50.

Then again, no one said we'd ever get rich by joining the Air Force.

o-0-o

THE MYSTICAL BLEND OF MAN AND MACHINE
The Strong Reason to "Stay."

From the time we began as neophyte students in flight school until the day of my last formation flight in an F-100 eight-and-a-half years later, pre-flight briefings involving everyone in the formation went through a rather standardized pre-flight briefing where every portion of the flight was discussed by the flight leader. And, after every flight, from our first flights in the Air Force, there was a post-flight debriefing, where every small thing that might have gone wrong, or could have been done more perfectly was also discussed.

That notion of "debriefing" was central to one of the poems, which was inspired by one of those really great days in the air. It came to me at a time when I had spent months struggling with the "stay or go" notions about a career in the Air Force.

One of the strongest impulses toward staying in for a full career was the flying itself, and the knowledge that I had the talent and ability to fly airplanes precisely most of the time and to fly formation exceptionally well. Sometimes, on the wing in formation, I could remain in position, absolutely motionless for extended periods.

That flirtation with perfection was so satisfying it would almost take my breath away. And at other times, free from the shackles of formation, on the gunnery range or elsewhere, it was sometimes possible to go an entire flight feeling as though the aircraft was melded with me, simply a piece of me as I willed where I would next want to be in space, and the machine would come along for the ride, instead of the other way around.

I first discovered that feeling quite early in flight training, and in each of the planes I flew, after a short time, that feeling of "one" would come, and stay. That sense of mastery came while out alone, pushing to the very edges of the plane's capabilities, and my own, and in his wonderful 1970 book, *Jonathan Livingston Seagull*, the F-100 pilot-turned-author Richard Bach, took his mythical seagull through all those very stages of the exploration of flight, sometimes to the edge of disaster.

I was certainly not alone in any of this exploring, nor in the resulting sense of extreme confidence in my time in the Hun. These were, after all, F-100 pilots all around me, and they had been some of the top flyers in all of their training classes en route to that special and very unforgiving piece of machinery, and most of them had surely "gone exploring" too. But that special feeling, or, to use the cliché, that "mystical blend of man and machine," was part of the bargain in my love affair with that plane.

211

DEBRIEFING

S
  L
   O
    W
     I
      N
       G
and taxiing
and shutting down
and taking off the binding light-spun harness...
You decompose
and decompress
into a disassembled pair:
A man
and a machine.
And now you've time to
shake away the harness...
and remembrance of the thing
that happens up there--
Up......where
You take a man imperfect
in an imperfect machine...
and you send that Pair
s l i c i n g
through a vast, imperfect
c h a n g i n g
mass of air....

And for ever-after moments
try to force away
how
tugging at the edges of P e r f e c t i o n
felt
    and looked
        and smelled
…and even tasted,
When,
up in tight formation
for sixty breathless seconds, sometimes more,
nothing moves.
Yet every formulation
And each physics calculation
Shows this simply can't be done:
Two fighter planes now locked as one,
Screaming down the sky, or up to thinner air.
(Oh how pale is recollection!)
That special You together
joined up with another One.
How close you came up there
In formation, as a pair,
And,
in other ways that only fighter pilots
ever
even get a chance to measure (in oblique
and so unsatisfactory ways)
by totting scores back from
the Practice Range, for nickels
and for fun…
        and praise.

II

But each one senses,
none of them ignores,
Because from closer or
from further, and for
longer or for shorter...
they've been tugging at it too,
as they scratched for frozen moments
microseconds — maybe more —
at a mystical,
impossible,
Reality they know within their hearts...
when a blend of all such
obvious, and deadly imperfections
reaches (oh, how far it reaches)
to a whole that equals
something far — so far
beyond the sum of all its parts.
(Can you D R E A M what it is l i k e
to work so hard and come so close to all that beauty
...and so close to perfect F l i g h t?)

III

It is good we that we have taxi time
and shut-down ceremonies.
And harness straps and all
that gear to free our bodies from...
and a ladder
that so helps us plant
our feet so squarely once again

on solid ground....
(Well planned, and such a logical sequence to go
    through:
first our three round,
rubber feet–
    and then our two.)
And more:
there is "Debrief" when we all land,
where language,
with all its glorious limits,
r e d e f i n e s this madness
and illusion—
in terms we Earthmen understand...
and limit
and can grasp
and dissect
into components that had flaws
and imperfections,
and confusion...
and procedures that weren't followed
and...it's good.
We're no longer men from
Outer Space
with visions
that could be misunderstood.

    IV
And...
Except for unbid moments,
floating moments ever-after
for a Lifetime,

it all goes away…
'till that sudden Sense of Laughter
merges you and your machine
when both of you are up at play
some other…imperfect
day.

     V

Eventually, (they say)
perhaps with work,
You can
Taxi
Park
Unstrap
and shut it down…
Debrief,
(as I am now)
and walk away…
         But not today….
         – RAF Lakenheath, 1971

o-0-o

"NOW, GET OUT YOUR NOTEBOOKS"

The portion of the atmosphere in which "earthmen" live and work each day is called the "troposphere," and just above it, at 25,000 to 40,000 feet (its height depends on temperature and season), the second layer, the stratosphere begins. It's there that the 3.56-degree-farenheidt-temperature-drop-per-thousand-feet-of-altitude also ceases, changing to a constant temperature of minus 55 degrees Celsius. And it is there that the instant formation of ice crystals occurs, caused by condensation from the heat of our engines.

There, at the "tropopause," all jet planes begin "pulling contrails" (condensation trails) across the sky behind them. And there, eight miles or so above your back yard, the sky above us begins to get darker and darker as we go higher.

There, slicing through the thinned-out molecules of air, the aircraft must be handled delicately, because our airspeed indicators reflect very slow speeds, even though we may be going close to 1,000 miles per hour.

And there also, the most minute black dot and the tiniest hint of slashing white contrail far across the sky can be instantly upon you, gigantic, blurred, and terrifying.

The closure rate is often close to 2,000 miles per hour. At that speed, human reaction time is such that the following will occur: in the first fractions of a second you will spot the tiny, threatening speck.

In the next few microseconds, the message will be transmitted from your eyes to your brain. In the twinkling of a few more flashes, your brain will sort out the material, translate it into the pertinent data that includes the information that it is an aircraft you see; it is approaching, and it is a danger. Prior to further consideration the brain sends a red alert to the reflexes, which will begin reacting almost immediately.

Unfortunately, your time was up somewhere in the midst of the digestion process and just about the time the red alert was sounded, so your only consolation lies in realizing that you'll know what killed you.

But, dear reader, before you abandon the idea of ever flying again and rush to the nearest train station, let me hasten to add that this terrifying process would only occur if two aircraft are coming exactly head-on, and at exactly the same altitude. Any angle off produces increased visibility and reaction time. Moreover, each plane flying at high altitude, all across the world (and outside small pockets of highly restricted acrobatic airspace), is assigned a separate altitude 1,000 feet apart or more from any other planes in vicinity to preclude the threat of any danger whatsoever. And up there, I always assumed that "other guy" was on his altitude. Be assured that unlike the barely discernible madhouse highways below, "the other guy" is a safe, skilled professional, and that he would almost invariably be in his designated portion of the assigned "highways in the sky." And "almost" is almost good enough.

o-0-o

ADDED NOTE: A Remarkable Coincidence

The picture that is the backdrop for "Scratches on the Sky," which graces the back cover of this book (and is repeated below), was selected by Medley Gatewood, editor of The Intake, a thrice-yearly journal for the Super Sabre Society (SSS), whose members are all former F-100 pilots. He was looking for the right picture to accompany the poem when he decided to make it the back cover of Issue 19, 2012. His search resulted in a perfect match for the poem, plus a story-within-the story, and an amazing coincidence. First, it shows how, at high altitude, the horizon does, indeed, "stretch away in white-blue sky along the seams" and does turn "blue-black" directly overhead. Second, it perfectly depicts the "boiling, billowing contrail(s)"; but the story within the story is that it shows an actual combat intercept with two F-15E Eagles moving into position in the skies off the coast of Alaska as two incoming Russian MiG-29s are inbound, planning to spend the night at a USAF base in Alaska before flying down to Canada for an international air show the next day. As for the "amazing coincidence," it turns out the photo was taken in 1997 by my dear friend and former combat squadron mate and SSS member Jack Doub, with whom I flew many day and night combat missions in Vietnam. It was later, while assigned to an AF base in Alaska that he was flying "chase" in a passenger-carrying T-39 and took the picture of two F-15s on a high altitude intercept mission

The poem itself was inspired by the many high altitude flights I took in four-ship formation from Lakenheath to our temporary bases in Italy or Turkey, where we would then spend most of a month on nuclear alert. Crossing from England into France, I was always struck by the large amount of high altitude jet traffic on that portion of the route, a place where it often seemed, the contrail "scratches" were all over the place.

218

SCRATCHES ON THE SKY

High
sometimes I fly
where a million square miles of air
stretch away in white-blue sky
along the seams of Earth,
but up here, galvanize, blue-black
an inch or two above my head.

Occasionally, I
see scratches on the sky
at every angle:
going away from me into forever...
or coming closer,
                    closer
until,
ahead of the now-gigantic rent,
a slicing sliver of shimmering steel,
pulling the boiling, billowing contrail
along to God-knows-where
from God-knows-whence
          appears...
               and runs an icy shudder to the marrow of my
     bones.

Sometimes,
   the far-off contrails cross,
          and even...
          COLLIDE
with the trailing scratches I slash across the sky...
          but not with me...
                    so far.... – *RAF Lakenheath, 1970*

DOWN IN THE WEEDS

This poem by an anonymous F-100 pilot derives its rhyme scheme from the famous poem, "High Flight," by Pilot Officer John Gillespie Magee, Jr., an American who joined the Canadian Air Force shortly after the outbreak of WW II. His famous poem is known to just about every military pilot since soon after he wrote it, shortly before he died in an airborne aircraft collision in 1941

> *Oh, I have slipped the surly bonds of earth*
> *And danced the sky on laughter-silvered wings,*
> *Sunward I've climbed and joined the tumbling mirth*
> *Of sunsplit clouds--and done a hundred things*
> *You have not dreamed of....*

"Low flight" captures in a lighthearted but wonderful fashion the type of flying I did whenever possible, and loved most, and which was just plain stupid, really, because it was often way, way too low. During my three years at Lakenheath, I always volunteered to be "Three" in the three-ship practice navigation flights we often took, where Lead would practice his low level map reading skills, Two would fly in extended trail, 800 feet back, with Three trailing Two by another 800 feet. Flying way back behind the other two, they couldn't see that instead of staying 500 feet above ground level as regulations required, I was down low, "racing through the tulip patches," having a wonderful time, and avoiding the utter boredom of straight and level flight. At one point, the risk taking to prevent boredom started to get out of hand, and I found myself flying my own special "slalom course," doing knife-edged, steep-banked, high-G rolls as I weaved between the masts of boats strung out one behind another along a canal in the Netherlands. Landing after that one, I said to myself, "What the hell are you doing? D'ya have a Death Wish?"

We did a lot of low level navigation practice because we had to pass an annual test where we were required to fly over the designated target around 450 miles from home base within two minutes either side of the assigned time. It was an unusual way to play tourist in parts of the UK. But, as this poem by the anonymous F-100 pilot shows, I was far from being the only one who decided to get some added thrills by flying far, far closer to the ground than 500 feet whenever possible. My guess is that there isn't an F-100 pilot who didn't find occasional fun in roaring along "down in the weeds" a few feet off the ground at 470 miles per hour or more. It certainly satisfied any "need for speed."

LOW FLIGHT

Oh, I have slipped through swirling clouds of dust.
A few feet from the dirt,
I've flown the F-100 low enough
To make my bottom hurt!
I've flown in the desert hills and valleys—mountains too!
Frolicked in the trees where only flying squirrels flew.

Chased the frightened cows along; disturbed the ram and ewe,
And done a hundred other things that you'd not care to do.
I've smacked the tiny sparrow, bluebird, robin--all the rest,
I've ingested baby eagles: simply sucked them from their nest!

I've streaked through total darkness, just the other guys and me,
And spent the night in terror of things I could not see.
I turned my eyes to heaven as I sweated through the flight...
Put out my hand, and touched the Fire Warning Light.

−Anon.

o-0-o

LAUGHTER-SILVERED WINGS
Humor Even in the Worst of Times

I was leading a flight of four from RAF Lakenheath to our TDY base for the next 30 days at Aviano, in northeast Italy, and my call sign, "Yellowtail 21" indicated that the four of us were from the 493rd "Yellow Tail" squadron at Lakenheath. The other two squadrons in the 48th TAC Fighter Wing were the "Red Tails" and the "Blue Tails."

After flying over France, I turned the flight left and into Italian airspace, and directed the other three to change radio channels so we

221

could talk with "Jerry Control," the radar station controlling traffic in that airspace.

"Jerry Control, this is Yellowtail 21, a flight of four, at flight level Two Nine Zero (29,000 feet)," and I told him where we were, when we expected to hit our next reporting point, and our ultimate destination at Aviano."

He acknowledged in a slightly Italian accent, telling me to maintain that altitude.

We were flying in to relieve the "Blue Tail" squadron, and each time they heard one of our flights check in, it was a signal to them that they could launch the next flight of four and head home. Sure enough, not two minutes later, I heard Blue Tail 21 call in with a flight of four, saying he was climbing out, headed directly in the opposite direction from us. But then I heard something that sounded like a grave error, when Jerry Control responded to assign them an altitude.

"Roger, Blue-a-Tail Two-a-One, you climb to flight-a-level Two Nine Zero."

I jumped on the radio. "Jerry, this is Yellowtail Two One, WE are at Flight Level Two Nine Zero." (Usually, flights going different directions were assigned to altitudes at least 1,000 feet higher or lower than ours. Instead, Jerry had a different safety solution:

"A-Roger, Yellow-a-Tail Two One, You keep a sharpa look out!"

I think there were guys in the other three cockpits, and maybe in all the other cockpits where that command was heard who started roaring with laughter at the crazy directions. But I also know there were three other sets of eyeballs besides mine scanning every inch of sky ahead of us, up, down and off to the sides.

About 10 minutes later, here came the four Bluetails, slightly to the left and a couple of hundred feet below us, with closing speeds that were near twice the speed of sound. They saw us, and we saw them, but I know for certain there were funny anecdotes told at the Officers Club at both bases for a couple of days after that, and often we would say before going to fly, *"Hey, you keep a sharpa look out!"*

o-0-o

222

Sometimes, guys in our squadron experienced first-hand what George Bernard Shaw meant when he said, "England and America are two countries divided by the same language." Some of the funniest were told by guys whose conversations came with "natives" on the ground soon after they had bailed out of ailing F-100s. Bob Riggs, for example, had to use his parachute one afternoon and he landed in a small, fenced-in back garden of a semi-detached house in the suburbs of one of the bigger cities in north central England.

He was still untangling from the parachute that was spread all over the rose garden, and still in his helmet, making him look like a man from outer space, when he spied a little boy about four years old, wide-eyed and peering at him through the slide door to the patio. The astonished youngster turned and ran away to find his mother, a young matron who came to the door, opened it, and took in the sight of this uninvited guest, who by this time was un-helmeted, untangled, and looking more human.

Her opening words prompted much laughter later, as the story was retold: "I don't believe we've been introduced, actually."

No doubt she then offered him a cup of tea, the all-purpose, for-every-occasion drink of choice in England.

o-0-o

Former Thunderbird Demonstration Team pilot Buster McGee, now a squadron mate, had a very different exchange when it was his turn for a "nylon letdown." Flying chase behind me as I led on a two-ship low level mission over northeastern England near the Scottish border, Buster suddenly alerted me that his engine oil boost pump had failed, his engine was seizing up, and as he spoke, he zoomed the aircraft as high as possible, trading airspeed for altitude that would allow him a safe exit.

He landed in a farm field, bordered on all sides by a low rock "fence." His plane descended and then crashed with a huge bang into the side of a nearby hill, creating a big black hole and a small fire that lasted a few minutes. As he gathered himself and his parachute, he noticed a farmer and his twenty-something son climbing over the neighbor's fence to come and speak to him.

"Is this some sort of exercise?" the farmer asked?

"No sir," Buster respectfully replied, "that's my plane burning there on the side of the hill. We never do crashes or destroy those very expensive airplanes for practice."

"Roight, then. Are ye all roight?," the sunburned farmer asked solicitously.

"I'm just fine, thank you."

"D'ya need any help gettin' back 'ome?"

"No sir," Buster replied, "that plane circling overhead is calling for help now, so some helicopter will pick me up pretty soon."

"Roight, then." He replied, and, no doubt uncomfortable with the notion of trespassing on his neighbor's property, he turned, muttered "Come along," to his son, and headed back across the fence.

That was it. In that part of England, known for breeding men of few words, that much conversation was "sufficient unto the day."

o-0-o

We were all very aware that the penalties for Driving While Intoxicated (DWI) were far stiffer in the UK than in the United States at that time. Six months suspended license for the first offense, and permanent suspension for the second. That was clearly on the mind of one of our squadron bachelors, after a night of drinking at the Officers Club, was headed back to the lovely country home some miles from the base that he shared with several other bachelor pilots. That night, as happened often in the Autumn, the lowland areas of the road were full of mist and fog, and the fear of getting caught while driving with a snoot-full of alcohol, and the fog, were very much sources of restraint as he drove, ever-so-slowly, along the two-lane road.

At some point, driving with intense focus, he heard a tap on his side window. When he rolled down the window, there was a local police patrolman *WALKING* beside his car, asking him to pull over.

Yes, he was being a careful driver. But driving with intense concentration at three or four miles per hour was a bit curious as far as that patrolman was concerned.

For the next six months, our careful driver had to carpool each day to and from work. And we all had a laugh at his expense.

HERE AGAIN, GONE AGAIN DAD

England, November, 1968–A United States Air Force pilot in Europe during the Cold War years, and perhaps still today, was away on TDY (Temporary Duty) about 40 of every 90 days. That's a bit difficult for an 18 month-old toddler to understand or cope with. And this toddler was a year old before she met ever her dad, who had been away at war.

TO MOLLY THE TODDLER

Listen, little girl, I know
That we have barely met,
But Daddy has to go again
And fly his Sabre jet.

No, I won't be gone that long,
Please, now, don't you cry.
It's only twenty-nine short days
That I'll be T.D.Y.

Mind your Mommy while I'm gone
And don't forget my name.
When I come home, we'll play again
Our "horsie-riding game."

Be gentle with the kitty-cat
And don't pull Doggie's ears,
(Just wait a minute, baby,
While I wipe away these tears).

Now kiss your Daddy "night-night"
And take your teddy bear,

When you wake in the morning
Daddy won't be there.

I know you only understood
A few words that I've said,
But they help me, a little bit,
And now...it's time for bed.
– RAF Lakenheath, 1970

TO STAY, OR NOT TO STAY–
THE TOUGHEST DECISION I EVER MADE

After all the conversations with other pilots while sitting on alert, and in long talks with Linda as well, the very difficult decision to resign my commission and move on to a civilian career was becoming more solidified in my mind. It hadn't taken all that long to realize that the biggest factor in taking too many crazy chances in the plane was because of boredom. I wasn't learning anything new anymore, nor was the challenge really there. And, in the Air Force at that time, I knew I would have to be in my 16th–or even 18th year or more in service before perhaps getting my first squadron command. In the meantime, regardless of what airplane I might fly next (and the choices at that time were very limited for those of us who wanted nothing but a single-seat, single engine fighter plane), I would simply be "moving two sticks around the sky" (the control stick and the throttle).

To me, learning, and facing the challenges while doing that learning, meant that I was still growing. But when I reached a point, doing anything in life, where I was merely repeating myself, I was no longer growing, I was dying. While some of the poetry and prose, designed to convey the realities of flying what was often called "the most dangerous plane ever built"–in peacetime and in war, may leave the impression that the risks and constant dangers were a factor in my deciding to choose another career.

But in reality, every fighter pilot, including me, long ago accepted the fact that risk, danger, and possibly a shortened life-span were all part of the price for all the thrills and joys of sitting in that

226

cockpit where so few would ever sit, enjoying a freedom of movement and maneuverability that bordered on ecstasy.

One factor that had to be considered was how tough the life was on the wives of fighter pilots. During our first 18 months there, the wing at RAF Lakenheath lost 18 F-100s. Luckily, many of the pilots bailed out safely, but it was extremely stressful on wives living right on the base, who on a few occasions hear a window-rattling boom as a plane crashed on the runway, a quarter-mile or so away.

Each day, when they bid their husbands goodbye as they headed off to work, they were never sure he would be coming home that night. Or whether, instead, there would be a dreaded visit from the Chaplain, whose unenviable task it was to deliver the bad news of another fatality.

The pilots themselves, and definitely in my case as well, responded to those accidents very differently. As I was told when I first learned to fly, they had the reputation of being very cocky, but that extreme confidence insulated them from any notions that they could ever die in an airplane. Indeed, such an attitude was a vitally necessary part of each pilot's makeup that allowed him to climb that ladder each time, start the engine, and roar off to another "death defying adventure" that he called "going to work."

Certainly, most of us had some close calls from time to time, indeed most likely more frequently in the unforgiving F-100 than in any plane in the inventory at that time.

But the very fact that we survived them simply reinforced the notion that we "would live to be 100," and that we were just simply too good to ever die in one of those beasts.

LATER ON: RECALLING SOME "CLOSE ONES" THAT ONLY GO AWAY SLOWLY

One of the closest calls I ever had occurred in those three years of peacetime flying in the Hun. The plane's wings were designed with long panels along the leading edge, called "slats," and those panels pushed back and changed the shape of the wing at 290 knots as air pressure mounted and we reached speeds where the "wing plan form" became streamlined, allowing normal or even supersonic flight. That wing shape stayed constant until we either pulled back on the stick and increased G forces or were first taking off or when we slowed to land. In those three circumstances, the slats rolled forward, and thus changed the shape to a "conventional" wing with the curve called "camber: so we could fly at slower speeds with a different wing design.

The only time trouble would come is if one of the rollers on one of those two slats got stuck, and didn't do what it was supposed to do at whatever speed it was supposed to do it. And there was no such thing as a good time for that to happen. Suddenly you were "flying" with asymmetric wings, and the plane tended to abruptly roll inverted. Only fast action and a lot of opposite rudder could prevent real disaster, because immediately, the plane began misbehaving dreadfully.

One day during my third year at RAF Lakenheath, I was flying on a routine flight to do rocket, bomb and gunnery practice at the range at Aviano, Italy, where we were on a 30-day TDY. I rolled in on a steep dive to fire the rockets that were in two sets of pods on the outboard "stations" of each wing. I reached the firing point, still screaming toward the ground, fired, and immediately pulled back on the stick to start a climbing recovery to higher altitude.

Instantly, the plane snap-rolled me upside-down, and all the back pressure on the stick was rapidly adding to the steepness of my thirty-degree dive, simultaneously decreasing rapidly the time left before my plane and I reached an appointment with the ground. Instinctively, I decreased stick pressure, pushed in hard on the rudder opposite the direction we had rolled, and moved the stick in the same direction as the rudder to roll back upright. It was like trying to control a runaway horse with the bit in its mouth, and as soon as I was able to get the plane rolled past the 90-degree point toward upside-right, I began pulling very hard on the stick to get the nose up, running the plane to the ragged edge of stalling, which would simply cause us to mush into the ground if I pulled the stick any harder to lift the nose.

Somehow, using a lot of rudder opposite the direction it wanted to roll, and pulling as hard as possible without stalling, I managed to recover to level flight. But I was told later by the range officer that recovery had come at between 10 and 15 feet above the ground, and in the process, I blew over one of the canvas strafe panels on the range. Those panels are only 20 feet off the ground. Strangely, it all happened so fast, I didn't have time to be scared.

Looking back, I haven't the vaguest idea how I managed to get the plane back to Aviano and on the ground, but recalling that "sporting event" and too many others from my time in the Hun, I tried to explain, at least to myself, why eventually, "enough was enough," and why I decided to move on to other adventures in my life. In doing so, in this poem, I blended a number of incidents, folding in the Aviano close-call with a different night in combat, where "recovery," for other reasons, was also problematic, and on the edge of disaster.

o-0-o

ADIEU SLEEK MISTRESS
Farewell, my Darling Mistress,
    I have loved you long and true
and we shared so many visions, you and I.
    But the price of all that loving's gone too high.

How we chased the edge of
        ecstasy
on far off golden hills
    and skimmed the peaks
        and treetops
to a thousand mind-blown thrills.

Was it you lost heart
        and strength
    that day
when we went up eight miles to play
    above the jaws of thunderhead?
Or did my artless hands
    lose touch and skill

229

at that most crucial moment
ere we plummeted
    like lead
    or screaming Icarus
    into those jaws of misty,
       churning power
         and dread.

No matter.
    It was just another "once again"
    when, pushed by mindless, fearless joy
       and passion,
(and a pride that "touch" like mine was rare in town)
       our dance along the
feather edge of Heaven
        ended
    in betrayal without warning,
        spun me down
in microseconds
    to the dark
       hot rim of hell
         and early coffin.
What a clown I was
to think that recovery and landing meant that everything was
mended.
    (Did I hear you sneer,
"I'll get you soon again -- and maybe often"?)

Then there were those blurry days
       and awful fights.
We had reasons then for flying on the edge

or just beyond
Those were hurry days and nights,
          when men died in the seconds we were gone,
     so staying close, and fighting hard and diving without heights
through blinding clouds and flying lead
was very much in fashion.
          Half flying in a mushy stall, enraged and full of passion
seemed very much the thing to do.
And you would play along.
          You'd join right in my deadly song
          and lure me in just right.
Behaving.
Until that ever-after night
          when low, and slow and hurting
for every extra inch of height
          and every knot of speed
we went into a too-steep dive
          to join that awful fight.
(It was about the dozenth pass, I die in half my dreams,
     just thinking how
I kept us far too long inside our own cocoon of lead;
     in nightmares now I see the bullets taking off my head.)
Why did you choose, at pull-up,
     to roll me upside down
     so pulling harder put us in the ground?
Technicians later told me, in all those fancy terms:
"Stuck slat, a change in wing-plan form,
     asymmetry." All that.
All I know is,
     for frozen parts of seconds I still dream of,

my every ounce of skill
                    and more
(there wasn't time for terror)
recovered flight and ended our brief thrill.
You'd taken us beyond the edge
            far further than we'd ever been in practice
                    and far further than I ever want to be or than we'd
ever been before.

Technicians have their fancy terms
            with which they tell the tale.
For me, it all comes down to this, My Dear:
            "Betrayal."

Ah, the things we did in practice!
The way we'd test each others' limits
            when no one else was looking
                    ...or thinking much of "regulations."
And so,
        by now I know the fate
                    of those who dream so far out
                            on the edge
                    of such forbidden love,
who push this blended Pair
        until
                    the Pair is One, a kind of love
    then risk disaster,
Flaunting–maybe breaking–
        all the rules of Man and Nature
                    out beyond what men call flight
                    and high above.

232

I know that only other
        gifted, daring crazies
                would ever understand
                (if they had lived).
But they are secret, silent lovers, too
        with smiling eyes and mistresses.
        Trapped by their awesome skills
                and love.
                Or else they're dead.
                Or nearly so, just one too many times.
They found, like me,
        the price of love
        too high, my cruel Mistress.

                I must land.

Farewell to all that love and other sorrows
        all that wonder, fear
                and ecstasy
        narcosis of the sky
                and flight
That always left me willing
                to sacrifice tomorrows
                        for tonight
                and one more thrill
                        or war
                or battle full of G's and fright
or journey to the ragged edge
where Flight is long forgotten
        and survival may not happen....
But the thrill, and the Knowing

of new limits now surpassed
Seemed somehow worth the terror
as this Hunk of Metal
you've became
and I
go screaming down the canyon
of the sky
to certain death
that didn't happen
Though every trace of flight,
love,
or delight
is long forgotten.
(With endless Luck we once again survived.)

Enough. (Or can that ever be, for me?)
Though the pain inside may never end,
the price of loving you
has gone too high.
And though my heart will never mend,
deep at its inner core
I can never fly again
(or I will die--because to fly now anywhere
except so far out on the edge
is such a Bore
as to be pointless).
And though the Parting
from you kills as well,
My Sleek and Deadly Mistress,
at least I'll die
more slowly than before.   *– Fairfax, VA, 26 May 1991*

THE PRICE OF ALL THOSE AIRBORNE THRILLS

When General MacArthur delivered his famous West Point farewell speech on May 12, 1962, he reminded the Cadet Corps of the significance of the words "Duty, Honor, Country."

I'm sure that as he spoke, he well understood the tremendous personal sacrifices entailed in living up to those words. Looking back over my own short military career now, I can say that I am equally sure that few, if any in his audience fully understood the sorrowful implications inherent in those words.

But with all the mounting separation from my wife and family, first with a year in Vietnam, then all the TDY in Europe, I realized, as I now look back, that I had a pretty good understanding of the full implication, and the full price, of those stirring words.

Even though "I walk with different sorrows now," my long periods away in those eight-plus Air Force years were only the beginning of a life where family separation for extended periods was the real down side of all those adventures in fighter planes and in later journalistic adventures and assignments.

A WARRIOR'S TEARS

I

Long e'er I tasted honeyed lips
Or learned of all your wondrous charms,
Before my heart, which bleeds and rips,
Was warmed within your loving arms,
Before I knew of woman's ways,
Or knew of life or love at all,
Before I learned its tortuous maze,
I was well-schooled in Duty's call.

II

Though I was young when first I felt
The wracking toll that Duty took

In bone and marrow, bruise and welt
Upon my body, still I shook
The sweat and blood away,
and learned Life's lesson:
That through sacrifice
Each goal and happy dream was earned,
If I would only pay the price.

III

For years I schooled my body's skills
And pondered words of wisdom taught,
Until I won each clash of wills—
Won honors for my "battles" fought.
But, oh, my teachers never knew:
Their lofty words drag men through hell,
Their hearts were never ripped in two.
They've never had to say "Farewell".

IV

"Responsibility," they'd say,
And "Truth," and "Duty" bind us all.
But now, oh, how I rue the day
I learned to answer Duty's call.
I didn't know its loud red phone
Would hurtle me through monsoon nights
Would wrack with terror every bone
As I dived into awful fights.

V

And now I've learned heart-rending strain
And loneliness and deep black sorrow,

For duties call to me again

And leave sharp pain that's worse tomorrow.

Why did not life e'er teach me true

The price for which those fine words sell,

As when, with tears I turn to you,

And hold you close, then say "Farewell."

o-0-o

LEAVING ENGLAND AND THE AIR FORCE BEHIND, 1971

In May, 1971, Linda and I and our small daughters, "Molly" and Ariel Ann, flew to Dover Air Force Base in Delaware, where I processed out of the Air Force after eight-and-a-half years of active duty, a mostly wonderful experience. But it was becoming repetitive.

A few days later, I reported in to the Voice of America news room, which seemed best among all the news organizations for me to fulfill another of my dreams: to be a foreign correspondent. On my first day, the boss asked me why I would ever leave the exciting life of flying jet fighters. I replied, "*Because the world of ideas is even more exciting than the world of speed.*" I must have been clairvoyant.

A year later, we moved to Hong Kong for a two-year stint, and when I was not home "China-Watching" and reporting on events there, I was away in Vietnam, Laos, Cambodia, the Philippines or elsewhere in East Asia 72 percent of the time.

Then, for the next three years, as VOA's bureau chief and correspondent in Tokyo, the stimulating challenge of China-watching continued (and became a lifelong pursuit). Time away from home was more limited those three years—only 70 percent of the time gone!

Over a total of 21 years at VOA, I was fortunate to also spend two years in graduate school in England, supervise the daily operations of over 200 employees as deputy director of the News Division, and attend, then teach two years at our National War College. I also lived two years in Islamabad, Pakistan, where my primary duty was to report on the Afghan-Soviet War, which concluded on my "watch," in 1989. To say VOA provided huge, wonderful learning opportunities, and many, varied challenges, would be an understatement.

CHAPTER X

GROUNDED AND GROWING
1971- Present

WISDOM

"He who learns must suffer. And even in our sleep, pain that cannot forget falls drop by drop upon our heart. And in our despair, against our will, comes wisdom to us by the awful grace of God."
—Aeschylus, quoting Agamemnon

o-0-o

"In a kingdom of blind men, the one-eyed man does not always become king; often, he goes mad.
--John J. Schulz
(Last lines in a final lecture to each class.
Boston University, 1996-2008)

A CHANCE TO LEARN AND GROW BY LEAPS AND BOUNDS:
FIVE YEARS REPORTING FROM EAST ASIA

In 1972, a year after being selected in a writing contest to join the Voice of America News Division, I found myself headed back to Saigon from my new base in Hong Kong, where Linda and our two girls lived permanently, and where I worked in my office there whenever I wasn't on the road covering major stories around Southeast Asia.

In selecting me, my boss at VOA asked, "We want you to be our second correspondent in Hong Kong. How do you feel about going back to Vietnam, that's going to be part of your 'beat' out there?" I laughed and said, "When I left Vietnam, I swore I would never go back." During those two years, before taking over the bureau in Tokyo from 1974-77, I was "away on assignments" to Vietnam, Laos, Cambodia (once) and the Philippines—a total of 72 percent time away from home. It wasn't so bad in Tokyo—I was only away 70 percent of the time.

The job was a good one; VOA in those years broadcast in 47 languages and globally had twice the listening audience of the BBC World Service, according to their surveys and ours. Importantly, we had "time and space" in our reports and broadcasts to headquarters to not only cover the stories that mattered, but to cover all the important details that gave critical added context to each story, and fully answered not only "what happened," but what it all meant. That typically meant we wrote and broadcast two-minute reports; my colleagues at the networks who were based in Saigon, Hong Kong and Tokyo had about 47 seconds to cover the same events.

It didn't take many trips to Saigon, and to many parts of South Vietnam where significant battles raged, to realize that the Vietnam War had changed in just about every way from the one I had participated in from April 1967 to April 1968. In a leisure moment, over coffee in a downtown Saigon restaurant frequented by many war correspondents from around the world, I wrote of my sense of disillusionment. Years later, I showed it to two or three dozen high ranking officers who were classmates at the National War College in 1985-86, concerned that the poem might somehow be seen as diminishing their efforts there. Rick Shinseki, for example, had lost a half of one foot fighting there, and had perhaps an even greater "stake" in the war effort as a result. He read it carefully, and said, "No, John, this gets it right, go ahead and put it in our yearbook." And that is where it was first published.

SAIGON REVISITED

Back when the World, the War, and I
Were young, and still believed,
There seemed a purpose to it all;
And because I was young, I grieved.

Grieved for a world out of kilter,
For a war that so few understood,
And for men I valued and trusted
Who did jobs that no one else could.

Now the world has gone mad; the war
Has no end…And I'm old.
And returned to the scene of my war
And the days I was bold.

The streets of Saigon may run bloody,
And my friends may have died there for naught.

240

And the death of my youth in a year here
May be pointless as all of our thought.

For we thought we were helping a people,
But all that we helped were the whores.
We thought someone might care if we won.
But the prostitutes win all the wars.

Now I'm too old for girls who are "pretty,"
And I'm tired of wars that don't end.
And I'm tired of Saigon, and all that's gone on
And this sickness that may never end.

The streets of Saigon may yet bloody,
And from what I have seen of the trends,
The world could shatter tomorrow...
But I've shed my last tears—for my friends.

I shed them back when the world and the war
And I were still young...and believed.
There seemed a purpose to all of it then.
And I was still young...so I grieved.
— *Saigon, September 1972*

o-0-o

FEELING OLD, TIRED, AND A BIT JADED

Those five years of extensive travel and too many visits to battle areas and war zones in Laos and Vietnam, and once to the Moro Uprising in the Philippines, left me tired, and sometimes exhausted.

But in trying to describe my job, I once said, "My task is to talk with Presidents, Prime Ministers, Kings and Killers. And usually, the killers are the most interesting."

241

It was also a time when the job called for expertise on China, and analytical reporting on many rather historic events that occurred there in those five years: the death of Chou En-lai, Mao Zedong, the rise and fall of the "Gang of Four" who plotted unsuccessfully to take power, and much more. And in each of several countries, knowing the impact of VOA and the BBC World Service, the national leaders made a special point of talking with both of us, and I found they were telling things that included their point of view, which in some cases included the reasons why they thought they had to suspend the national Constitution and take all the functions of government into their own hands.

They were very interesting, highly intelligent, extremely ambitious and sometimes exceptionally insightful individuals. Thus, simply stated, those five years required a very steep learning curve, much travel, and a huge amount of reading in scholarly and other books and articles to better understand context and report accurately on what was going on.

But it also made me feel very old beyond my years some of the time, and as I changed gears into a less physically active, but nonetheless intensive and highly demanding new environment, there were times when all the new insights gained from reading so much more than I had ever had time for on relevant and important subjects sometimes left me, late at night, feeling not just tired, but like I had lived 100 years already.

THE TRAVELER
I'm very old in minutes,
Though I'm not so old in years
For I have "triple timed it"
Both in Laughter and in Tears.

I've seen the World's capitals,
And all their shining places,
As well as all their teeming slums,
And all their staring faces.

I've "got" my man and shot my man
As Mister Kipling said,
The former is still growing,
And the latter is quite dead.

I've seen the World's loveliest,
And chased them for their beauties
And loved them for the whole night through–
Then tended to day's duties.

I've seen the lovely face of Gods
From Rome to far Cathay,
And talked with wise and holy men
And knelt with them to pray.

I've flown with many good men,
And chased them through the skies
And watched their supersonic jets
Blow up before my eyes....

Yes, I'm very old in minutes,
Though I'm not so old in years,
And the knowledge of it saddens me
More than the wisdom cheers.

−Oxford, England, 1978

A FEW WORDS ABOUT WHY "I Don't go Hunting Anymore"

This "Hunting" poem was written soon after a 1994 conversation in Washington, D.C. with a co-worker at the Arms Control Association, where I was then editor-in-chief of *Arms Control Today* magazine. He had asked me about hunting and combat flying, which is recounted in the opening lines below.

I want to stress that the poem was never intended to disparage hunters or fishermen. Rather, it is a brief explanation as to why I "don't go hunting anymore." I found it significant that among the images that came to me during and just after that brief conversation was that terrible afternoon at Bien Hoa Air Base when Clyde Carter of "Dice," and Airman First Class Victor Negron of the 510th TFS maintenance crew, died so suddenly. When the poem was published in *The Intake's* Spring, 2012 issue and sent to the 1,600 members who are former F-100 pilots, I received several e-mails from readers saying they also found that they no longer enjoyed hunting or fishing—and for the same reasons.

I DON'T GO HUNTING ANYMORE

"I saw this film about a guy
    who was a fighter pilot back in World War Two.
He said he's never hunted since.
        He used to love to hunt," he said.
        "What about you?"
My mountains in Montana,
    Golden fields where pheasants hid,
        is what I thought I'd see.
"I can see how that just might be true,
        me too," was all I said
before I walked away engulfed in different memory.

For I have hunted men
    each day
for what could seem
    a lifetime sentence, ever after
(had I not drowned it out
    in other kinds of living,
        other sorrows
           and in laughter).

Hunted, high blooded.
          Found. And killed
                    in quantities,
     armed men who hunted me
                    in even greater quantities
                              (and not just ten times ten).

I've seen men die
          here on the ground.
And in blinding, rapid motion
          freeze-framed forever...
                    dead forever....
          in some tiny
                    and now special
                              piece of sky
I've seen my brothers die.

I've seen bodies stacked
          like cordwood six feet high
                    in a time and place they still call Tet,
and watched a friend
whose head and helmet
          came away with bits of plane
                    disintegrating just above our heads
                              on his final "fly-by"
                                        his...last...mission.
I watched the Super Saber's wing
          become a scythe
                    swift in its knifing down
that cut a boy-man right in two
not eighty feet away.

Then I,
soon after that too-special final flight,
      went out again to fly
that sometimes coffin,
      widow maker, thunder bird
and killing instrument of mine
      that came along
      as I went hunting once again;
(with 'right' and 'wrong'
all certain in my mind
      and quite irrelevant
        in real war).
I've shot to kill
far more than just two hundred times,
      and at the core
enjoyed the knowing of my skill
enjoyed the thrill
      of hunting.
And the finding. Knew
that any moment
it could be my time to die.
The men I hunted
      found me, too,
      and shot to kill.
Long days and nights they tried to wrap me in
      their curtains of lead.
(I told myself that if I died,
at least I'd die while doing
what a fighter pilot does
and die the way a fighter pilot should,
and not in bed.)

246

And "sorry" isn't relevant
    I wouldn't change a thing,
except perhaps restore to life
    some friends who flew my wing.
No, I don't hunt
    or fish.
And anymore
        I have no wish to try.
    Nor do I wish
to be again
    a fighter from the sky.
There was a point to killing then
with me and other men "in season."
There is no point to killing
    stupid fish
    or helpless deer.
And as for flying
    or for killing,
Now there is no reason
    (and no nightmares...
        and no fear).
       – *Washington, D.C, October 1994*

ADMIRING THE WORLD'S "FINER THINGS," – BUT DON'T TOUCH!

By the time Linda and I had been married 25 years, we calculated that we had been apart for seven of those years, chiefly with me on the road or living alone in Vietnam or later, in Islamabad, when I was covering the Soviet-Afghan war from 1987-89. I began to realize that these travels and the time alone and encounters with many interesting men and women didn't really create "temptations" for me. Some of the on-the-road, or living-alone foreign correspondents made other choices about their social lives, and I could certainly enjoy and appreciate "attractive things and people," not least the ladies in Europe when I worked there from time to time. But I worked to avoid allowing situations to become "complicated." I recall encountering one lovely lady who made it more than obvious that she, to put it euphemistically, "found me attractive." Realizing, not for the first time, that I had not taken the bait or succumbed to temptation, I puzzled over the incident on a long plane ride home. And then I began to write what I had concluded. I never finished the poem then, but found it 15 years later in a file, and finally found all the right words.

GO AWAY, I'M BUSY, MISS

When I was younger
I was easily seduced
by speed, fine craftsmanship and ideas.

Now I've had enough of speed, and mine's reduced.
Fine craftsmanship costs much.
And I am of an age
when any beauty I might so appreciate
does not reciprocate.

But of Ideas:
there are many all around me,
in all kinds of places they have found me.
And while they don't all thrill
as once did races in a jet,
or special, crafted skill...
they have their various charms
                and can seduce me yet.
                        − Boston, 1997

o-0-o

248

NIGHTIME THOUGHTS THAT CHANGED MY LIFE FOREVER....

In the midnight hours of November, 1976, home in Tokyo from yet another intense week or two covering world events somewhere in East Asia, I began thinking about my future, what I wanted to do next, what goals I wanted to set, what high mountains I still needed to climb. After doing so, I began to scribble a summary of what I had concluded. The result was "The Call."

A week later, in November of 1976, at the age of 37, I began the process of applying to Oxford University to study International Relations, with concentrations on East Asia, and on strategic studies. That decision, and the subsequent two years of study there beginning in the Fall of 1977, later opened doors to unimagined opportunities and more honors and awards than I had ever aspired to in wildest dreams.

Degrees from that place of "dreaming spires" really *do* make a difference. And yet I've never met a "Yank" who studied there who wasn't humbled, rather than arrogant, about that utterly life-changing academic experience.

THE CALL

There's a spirit moving in me
That I do not understand.
For, as foam upon the wave crests
Or as winds upon the sand,
Its shape is ever-changing
And it holds no constant form.
Yet it wells and boils like water
When the kettle gets too warm.

Ah, how well I've learned to hide it,
As I smile throughout each day,
Being pleasant, warm and friendly...
And I've learned just what to say.

249

How it sears my very brain pan
When it wells too much inside;
How I pity those who see me
When it gets too much to hide!

Yet the spirit, too, is wondrous
And God's special gift to me,
For it stretches, drives and guides me
To the man I'll someday be.
How it lashes when I'm lazy,
Now it screams, "It's time to start."
And it gently then reminds me
That I'm not yet quite that smart.

For years the driving winds and waves
I thought had all subsided.
I thought the years had mellowed me
And serenity presided.
But the sea inside me's welling,
And some waves now have a crest,
And the winds, no longer gentle, call
"You soon must start the quest."

-- Tokyo, November, 1976

"THE CHOSEN FEW"

The National War College (NWC) is at Fort McNair in Washington, D.C. It was established in 1947 by Gen. Eisenhower, who recognized that his military training did not prepare him to deal with presidents, prime ministers and other heads of state--all of which were part and parcel of his job as Supreme Allied Commander in Europe in WW II. During the time I was there in this "most senior course in government (1985-6), the class consisted of 40 Lt. Colonels and Colonels from the Air Force and Army, 27 Navy, 11 Marine and two

Coast Guard officers from the "sea services." Jointly sponsored by the State Department, each class also included senior officials from the State Department, plus a sprinkling from the CIA, FBI, Defense and one from the Treasury Department. Ten more officers were there to write books of relevance to our armed forces.

These were truly the "handpicked few," earmarked to rise to the highest positions of command and management in their organizations. They were all given an added ego boost by being selected, and as they sized each other up, each realized that they were in rarified air for the next 10 months.

Sometimes, perhaps, the spouses felt that the ego boosts were slightly overdosed. My wife relayed to me one of the great one-liners of the year, contributed by one of the wives who had just arrived at an NWC social event.... She said she so enjoyed these gatherings, where she could "Watch them all put their egos in a bushel basket and park them outside the door" as they entered the house for the party.

That said, they were an amazing group of men and women, the most impressive collection of people I have ever been around. Later, that Class of 1986 became the "most ranked" and successful in their government careers since the NWC opened its doors in 1947.

UNEXPECTED VISIT TO ANOTHER TIME AND PLACE... AND WAR

Toward the end of the 10 months of studies and lecture at the National War College, we were divided into more than a dozen groups and dispatched to places all over the globe for two weeks of "on the ground" study of political and geopolitical issues and situations that might better inform our judgments, should we someday become senior government decision-makers. My research group visited Rome and the command center for U.S forces in the Mediterranean before going to Greece and Turkey to examine the issues that make relations tense between those two NATO allies. Our group, and all the others, met and talked with the highest level political and military leaders in the places we visited. Our group was also treated by the Turkish Air Force Commander to a demonstration of air-to-ground bombing and strafe practice at the gunnery range at Murted Air Base.

The Turkish pilots were flying F-100s.

I tried to explain to my dozen classmates what was going on, what they were trying to do, and what was going on in the cockpits of each of the four airplanes. As we climbed back into the bus to leave, I felt I had done a poor job of conveying the demonstration--one that had unexpected impact and a flood of memories for me.

I decided to take a second try at explaining what they had seen, and began to scribble in my notebook. I then read it to them on the bus as a "better explanation":

ROLLER COASTER

Falling down a wingtip
    And screaming down the sky,
Instruments unwinding fast
    And airspeed pushing high.

Earth is coming fast now
    And fireflies of lead
Dance and sparkle all around
    My pretty little head.

Hissing speed begins to roar
    The gunsight tracks along.
Cannon ports will open soon
    To start a deadly song.

Soaring soon from blackout grey
    To nose-high, sky-bright blue
On bended wings to dying speeds,
    Then fall, and fight anew.

Slipping past the ragged stall
    And falling down the wing,

Back into the teeth of war
   With more lead songs to sing.

Tumbledown, and up the loop,
   Twist, and dive and soar.
Another Roller Coaster ride,
   Another day at war.

(At the gunnery range, Murted AFB, Turkey,
With my National War College Classmates, April, 1986)

THIS IS PROBABLY NOT A GOOD IDEA....

In 1991, Linda and I began biweekly trips south from northern Virginia to the small town of Cape Charles, VA, to restore a nice old house. I thought, with Jack Nicklaus and Arnold Palmer golf courses scheduled to be built very nearby, the house would be a nice investment we could sell later. Linda had other ideas, and opted for us to retire there when I told her to "make the call on where we would live." Beginning about 1995, after it was fixed up, and with us then residing in Boston, we rented it out. On one occasion, I ended up in a somewhat unpleasant encounter with the husband of the couple then renting our place. Unexpectedly, that encounter occurred near Main Street, and at one point he raised his fists and prepared to get in a "boxing match" of sorts. He was 20 years or more younger, at least as tall, and in far better shape than I was, indeed in better shape than almost any 55-year-old, I'm sure.

What unfolded in that encounter provided me with some additional self-knowledge that I was not really aware of until then.

As he squared off to start a fight, I instantly recalled what I had learned in my "combative measures" training at Flight School, 25 or so years before. In a flash, I had analyzed all the weaknesses in his stance and posture, and could see at least four ways to hurt him rather badly in no more than two very quick and unexpected "moves."

What surprised me most was how calm I was as I said to him in a normal, but firm voice: "Before we begin, let me give you some advice once passed on to me. 'Never fight a guy who's been in combat

253

or in jail.' And I've been in both. Now, you are younger, stronger and slightly taller than me, and in far better shape. But I have to warn you, I will not be the only one going to the hospital, and this won't end, until medical help, probably for both of us, will be needed. My real problem is selecting between several options as to how to strike so that none of my moves accidentally kill you, because that is how I was trained to fight...and it wasn't boxing, either. You could likely 'win,' but you are very, very vulnerable, and unless you knock me unconscious or badly cripple me, this fight won't be over till you are in the same shape I am." He lowered his fists, and, in some form of civil discourse, we sorted things out about the "missing and tardy rent,"

I was more surprised than he was by my reaction, and I thought about it for some weeks before finding words that expressed properly the thoughts that emerged from that added contemplation. .

I also knew that this added self-knowledge about who and what I was, due to the life I had led, needed to be integrated or situations might continue to crop up as a surprise to me, and a somewhat unpleasant encounter for someone else in the future.

NEVER FIGHT A GUY WHO'S BEEN IN COMBAT OR IN JAIL

Wisdom
comes in floating snatches
mostly thoughts for here and now.
But sometimes phrases take me places
you have never been
    and cannot go
    where high above, my craft and I
put giant scratches on the sky
    or screaming low, just missed the trees and bullet traces
at speeds you'll never see in any races.

"Never fight a guy who's been
    in combat or in jail,"

a new friend said as we were chatting.
I laughed, about something relevant to this or that,
But in microseconds
   that sometimes used to
seem like centuries
I flashed away
to yesterday: I knew why:
         I used to fly
and kill with every ounce of
   malice
   and aforethought
         I could muster.
And did it with great skill.

   II
Short of killing me,
   even now,
in any milder fight
(in which I am now old,
   and slowed, and weak,
though never do I count among the meek)
It might be best not to begin
because there will be
   no such thing as "win"
until the ambulance
   is there
to start the very necessary
   repair
on he who is, by definition,
   "loser."
Those are the unshared expectations

going in
(which also means the fight
had better be for things worthwhile);
I already know how high
   the prices get.
In situations others fear,
        mostly I smile.
I've been too close to dead too many times to fear
a broken nose or bleeding ear.
        – Cape Charles, VA, and Boston, MA, May 1996

ANOTHER BAD IDEA, THIS TIME IN LONDON...

I thought the confrontation in Cape Charles some years before was a "one off thing," as the Brits would say. But several years later, on the subway–"the underground"–in London, where I taught two graduate school classes for six weeks each summer for nine years, I had another of those "What the heck did you just do?" moments that could have done me damage. I was not long in my compartment on the underground train when I observed three guys in their mid-twenties giving a very rough time to an attractive young lady of about the same age. They were making lewd suggestions and began to touch her, increasing her sense of terror by the moment. I looked around and saw that most of the people riding with me were watching the same very unpleasant scene unfold. But no one was saying or doing anything.

I was carrying a portable tape recorder that I'd used to play something in class that day. It was attached to a three-foot strap, and I realized this would have to be my only weapon. I moved up to within a couple of feet of the unshaven and rough-looking men and told them it was time to cease and desist. And I said that if they had any problem with that, we could all get out at the next subway stop and settle things there. I recall pointing out to them that there were three of them and only one of me, but that I would not be fighting fair, and that I could almost guarantee one or two of them would be injured pretty badly before they beat me up so badly I couldn't fight on.

256

To my amazement, they did back away, not in fear, but perhaps because they had been "called out," they were embarrassed or returned to their senses. They left the subway at the next station; I did not follow them off, nor was I expected to do so, from all I gathered. The young lady thanked me profusely, and I explained that I had two daughters about her age, and would hope someone would help them if they ever needed it.

Some days later, I tried to analyze what in heaven's name had prompted me to act, when all common sense warned to "stay out of this, you are badly outnumbered." This "Warrior Requiem" was about as close as I could come to an explanation about myself...to myself.

REQUIEM TO A WARRIOR
Ancient am I as a warrior
    Since long ere before I was grown.
Competition like war,
    and true battle's roar
Has been most of the life I have known.
Flannelled, or padded or flying
    Or seemingly resting for more,
With guns or ideas or a smile
    There never was peace at the core

My blood is from poets and warriors,
    And the price for my hungers I've known–
For I chose to climb high, and even to fly,
    But such hunger has made me alone.
Each who has chosen to love me,
    Ultimately senses or knows,
That deep in my core, I'm girded for war
    Off in places where no one else goes.

Resting is different from peaceful,
    And history won't mark my name

257

But often the fact of my passing
    Has changed the outcome of the game.

The rewards of such life are not many,
    But with star-driven men just like me,
A glance and a nod, or a friendship for life
    Lets each know there's another like he.

I'll take my good times where I find them,
    But a lifetime's desire to be best
Means I'll guard those I've chosen to love well,
    But my mind and my soul...never rest .– *London, , 2002*

o-0-o

LET'S THINK AGAIN ABOUT THAT NEW MEDAL...

Much of my life, at unexpected and uninvited moments, thoughts come to me and then transform into poems that I feel compelled to write down, just to get them out of my system. Over the years, these "unbidden Muses" have transported me back to far earlier times, and that relatively brief period when being a pilot was my full-time job. The timing was rather fortuitous on this poem below, which is a takeoff from Rudyard Kipling's famous "Gunga Din," one of the many poems we memorized in our senior English class in high school.

A few weeks later, there was considerable controversy and several news stories related to a decision by the Defense Department to award a new "Distinguished Warfare Medal" to those who guided the remote-control attack drones over the skies of Afghanistan from a trailer set up on a base in Las Vegas, Nevada.

At first, the plan was to rank this decoration above the Bronze Star and the Purple Heart awarded to men and women in combat for extraordinary bravery under fire, and in the latter case, for being wounded in combat.

That decision was changed after it stirred so much controversy, and the whole idea seems to have been shelved by current Secretary of Defense Chuck Hagel.

258

But I realized the poem, and especially the last four lines, expressed not only my views, but very likely, the views of soldiers and airmen who had flown in combat in any of our wars. .

In April, 2013, I was honored to be the Master of Ceremonies for the Super Sabre Society reunion in Las Vegas. The SSS gathers every other year for three days or so, topped off by a final banquet. There, I told some jokes, but took the chance that these crusty old veterans of the F-100 would at least tolerate several of the poems included in this book. I was a bit surprised, and very relieved to find that they listened to each with rapt attention, and applauded most loudly after hearing "Kipling Revisited."

KIPLING REVISITED
(A toast to Close Air Support fighter pilots)

You may talk of gin and tonic
When you're nearly supersonic
And you're forty thousand feet above the fray
But when it comes to flyin'
There'll be troops beneath you dyin'
As you dodge among the treetops night and day.

I remember way back when,
In a place called Four Corps then,
There were NVA about as thick as thieves.
They had guns of every kind,
Which weren't difficult to find
And, down there, our pilots dropped like falling leaves.

I remember well the night
Two of us got in a fight
With quad Fifties and far worse set up to blast
There were fireflies galore
As we dived down into war
Twenty times a'knowin' each dive was our last.

259

Both our planes were shot to hell,
How we lived, I cannot tell,
But some nights, even now, it's not "the past."
In my dreams up comes the lead
All around my pretty head
(And I hope this nightmare will now be the last).

All those bullets as they clattered
Somehow never really mattered
For we never took a hit where we were sittin'.
With our cannons roaring hot
We gave them all we brought
Without a single thought of ever quittin'.

A thousand guns were aimed our way
And the night seemed bright as day
And it seemed like fireworks were everywhere.
We kept diving in to fight
(It was terror-driven flight)
And remains like yesterday in each nightmare.

Looking back on those nights now
It is hard to recall how
We ever did such fearless things so often.
We both laughed and had a beer
As we told our tales with cheer,
But we're lucky we came home outside a coffin.

As I sit here, far away,
With my hair now all gone gray,
Some people ask me what it's like to fly.
I speak of all the wonder

Of a takeoff, roaring thunder,
But without the bullet holes, it's just a lie.

– Cape Charles, VA, Jan. 2013

o-0-o

"THE HOUSE I LIVED IN NOW SEEMS SMALLER...."

Having left Missoula, Montana, two days after university graduation, jobs in places home and abroad meant the chance to visit parents and my hometown were few and far between. The many adventures flying, as a foreign correspondent, Oxford scholar and National War College grad meant my hometown and classmates may not have changed all that much...but I had.

In 1987, back to deliver the commencement address at my high school, several old classmates and I decided to hook up for an afternoon picnic in the park. While it was a good time to reminisce and enjoy the good fellowship, one of the guys, well known back in the day for his barbed wit and "put down" one-liners, seemed to find me an especially choice target for the day. Some of it was pretty nasty, but I found my reaction was one of sorrow rather than anger. In reality, Missoula to this day is an utterly wonderful place, but I was seeing it, and him, and all of them, with rather tired eyes, and many new scratches on my mind. On the plane back to Washington, D.C., I tried to capture my thoughts. I began by recalling Thomas Wolfe's book, *You Can't Go Home Again.*

GOING HOME AGAIN

There's a bleakness in this town
and a vacuous tranquility
about the place
that presses all about,
and down, and in upon the
brains of this
wholesome
safe and happy crowd.

261

There's an empty
        longing
in the eyes of that former classmate
with the not-so-empty
waistline.
Once a slightly-less-than-mediocre
        pulling guard,
and now a slightly-less-than-mediocre

                                man
who counts the empty beer cans
to see if tonight was a good time.

-- Missoula, Montana, 1987

o-0-o

YOU WON'T BE TESTED ON WHAT I SAY NEXT, BUT TAKE IT WITH YOU ANYWAY

In my closing lecture to each of my classes for 13 years at Boston University, I tried to impart a bit of advice to guide my students in their journey through life. I said that surely they would like to lead a life that includes having friends all around them who are interesting, interested, well-travelled, sophisticated, thoughtful and informed, and perhaps, even wise. Just as you must therefore choose your friends wisely, choose your sources of information carefully as well, and being highly selective, choose those sources that are balanced, comprehensive, cover the truly important events and ideas the world has to offer, and recognize that too often we read things instead that are "interesting, but not important."

In reality, many things that are very important may not seem at first that entertaining or interesting, but that is where good journalists come in, figuring out ways to make the important things interesting to the listener or reader.

There are, I would warn them, only a few truly excellent sources for news and information that matters, but by using your limited time to focus your reading there, you will very likely become a person who is also interesting, interested, well-travelled, sophisticated,

262

thoughtful, informed, and perhaps, even wise. As happens, you will rapidly find that your search for the very kinds of friends that can be most valuable and simulating to your life is not that difficult, because you, too, will now be the kind of person they are seeking to include in their lives. And I would then warn them to be aware, that from my experience, *"In a kingdom of blind men, the one-eyed man does not always become king. Often, he goes mad!"*

Turning last to how to live life in general, I would urge them to live each moment, get the most out of each hour, and day and situation, and to live every moment to the fullest. Don't put off things of importance until tomorrow when the mundane work is all done. Tomorrow never comes, and your precious, precious hours are slipping away. And then I would close by reading this to them.

There was always a stunned silence as I left the room for the last time in their lives.

TIME AND THEE ... AND ME

Can't you hear the seconds ticking,
and the thud, thud, thud of heartbeats
that means we're that much older
and that Death is getting bolder
as we march in blind progression
in a sheep-like, robot fashion
to an end we can't believe in
and won't face...and never grieve in
Can't we Stop!!!!

Can't we take our precious little
of that time that we so squander
and buy only those few things
we know are truly worth the Price?

263

No...
we scurry, scurry, scurry
in a blind and trapped-rat frenzy
after junk of all description...
Paying out
our precious little
of what life we have to live yet,
thinking–knowing–that our lives will never end.
So we fuss and froth and blindly rush
and spend, and spend and spend.

Don't we know the cost of laughter
and that life has precious loveliness to sell?
We just put it off till "After"
and it's after all the wrong things:
After kids and after groceries,
after hate and war and rainstorms
after school and work and washing up
And we don't believe there's such a thing as Hell.

They've all said it, we don't listen...
we've ignored so many wise ones
and go on with blind concerns of
"right and wrong,"
And we're dying in the fields
and the bedrooms--on the highways
and we're dying, dying, dying
            all
                    day
                long.
– Read to about 1,700 students during 13 years at Boston University

264

AMBITION NEEDS OCCASIONAL "REALITY CHECKS"

Somewhere in the 1980s, with so many wonderful adventures and so much intellectual stimulation behind me, and more of both encountered each day as a student at our National War College (and later, for two years, as a professor), I realized my journey through life had taken me to many "far-away places with strange sounding names," and as well to conversations and friendship with rulers and beggars, brilliant thinkers, elegant writers, and intense experiences that could not match Air Force fighter flying, but were very challenging and stimulating nonetheless.

At some point, I had encountered a wonderful quote describing the "products" of Oxford University over the centuries, and one phrase in particular resonated as a perfect goal for me from then on:

> *"Without pomposity, they have skipped being*
> *famous...and became consequential."*

But life has a way of bringing the loftiest among us down to earth, and anyone who acquires wisdom--and such people are rare indeed--knows that regular visits to reality provide perspective and balance--and a proper dose of humility--as we go about our days. Even living the most glamorous life, the dishes still need washing.

THE EGOTIST

Encased in pain
and filled with warring germs...
Traveling endlessly between those
self-defeating peaks
(Overconfidence and Self-deprecation).

Now,
all my wars
are miniscule skirmishes
and all the victories are Dunkirks
plucked across the Sea of Rationalization
from the beaches of Defeat.

265

Hannibal
crossed the Alps....
Occasionally
I cross the street against the light.

Alexander
conquered all the known world
before the age of thirty-three.
I beat a running bout of flu
the week before my birthday.

Descartes
sat alone and decided that he thought,
therefore he was....
I sit alone
And decide the monthly budget.
I am,
therefore, the bills are due again
before the tenth.

*(Published as "The Chosen Few"
in the NWC Class of '86 Yearbook)*

###

GLOSSARY OF TERMS AND ABBREVIATIONS

This will be particularly useful to readers who did not serve in the U.S. Air Force. Each term is also explained the first time it appears in the book.

Afterburner—A large section after the main engine in modern fighter planes where more fuel and ram air is injected in a "burner basket" to provide additional propulsion and significant extra boost to the plane. In the F-100 it added 6,000 pounds of thrust (50% more) to the 10,000 pounds of thrust at normal full power on the J-57 engine.

Bail Out or **Eject**—Both refer to leaving the aircraft abruptly in a dire emergency, usually assisted by a rocket boost that fires the seat at least 50 feet above the airplane, then separates and, at low altitude, pulls the parachute cord automatically. In fighters, pilots wear parachutes and are strapped to the "rocket" seat at all times.

Cannons—In this book the cannons are the four internally mounted 20mm, rapid fire weapons in nose portion of the F-100. Together, all four cannons produced over 6,000 rounds per minute (100 rounds per second). A switch in the cockpit allowed the pilot to fire two, or all four cannons at once.

Command Post—At each Air Force Wing in the world, the Wing Command Post is manned 24 hours a day. From that central control area, radio messages can be transmitted to virtually every building in times of emergency, or when an Operational Readiness Inspection Team lands to begin a simulated "war" exercise. In Vietnam, the Wing Command Posts were in constant communication contact with 7th AF HQ near Saigon.

Chu Hoi—Turncoat Vietcong who, after surrendering, would elect to fight for South Vietnam's Army, sometimes called "the ARVN" or Army of the Republic of Vietnam.

FAC—**Forward Air Controller**—On every "ground attack" mission in Vietnam, every attack pass was controlled by the airborne FAC, who was flying a prop-driven single engine plane at low altitude. Using white phosphorous rockets to mark each intended target with smoke, and maintaining radio contact with the ground battle commander and the flights of attacking fighter planes, he controlled every "air portion" of the battlefield. After missions, FACs gave bomb/battle damage assessments (BDA) to the fighter Flight Leader, who reported the BDA at home base.

Fire or Overheat lights—Two lights on the dashboard in the cockpit of all jet planes, indicating a very serious problem with the aircraft that requires immediate action and full attention.

Going "home"—here means reassignment from Vietnam to an AF job at any base or post in the world.

Hun and Hun driver—Shorthand reference to the word "hundred" in its numerical designation in "F-100," whose "driver" was the pilot.

Lead vs. lead—Throughout, when the word is capitalized, it is pronounced "leed" and refers to the formation flight leader. Pilots flying formation on his wings are referred to as "Two, Three, and Four." While spelled the same, "lead" (in lower case, pronounced "led") means bullets, outbound from a fighter as "strafe" *(below)* in an attack, or anti-aircraft ground fire aimed at any aircraft.

"Mobile" or Mobile Control—Whenever an Air Force runway is "active," a Mobile Control Officer is assigned to sit in the shack beside the active runway landing area. He can and will call incoming pilots on the radio and may fire a flare as well to signal pilots they are on an unsafe landing approach...either a bad angle, no landing gear down, etc.

Nape—Shorthand for "napalm," a firebomb that was a mix of fuel and explosives delivered from close proximity in a shallow, low-level dive, which would spread burning naphtha and fuel up to 100 yards. In more recent years, napalm is no longer in use by U.S. forces.

NVA—North Vietnamese Army.

TDY—Temporary Duty. These assignments could last up to six months. Longer than that meant it was a permanent new assignment.

R&R—Rest and Relaxation, a formal status authorized for servicemen and women by written order.

Strafe—An air-to-ground or air-to-air attack by fighter planes firing bullets from their cannons, or, nowadays, their Gatling guns.

A Tour—refers to "serving" a previous "tour of duty" for months or years in other aircraft or other places. A combat tour in Vietnam for the Air Force was one year, which could be voluntarily extended.

VC—Viet Cong or Vietcong (alternate spelling). Usually referred to indigenous South Vietnamese Communists fighting to take over the country, or to reunite it with North Vietnam. Often they were irregular, part-time guerrillas and wore the black pajamas and shallow coned hat common to ordinary farmers, which helped them blend in after hit-and-run attacks.

About the Author

John J. Schulz is a retired news executive and former Voice of America foreign correspondent who also has been an Oxford scholar, National War College student (1985-86), editor of *Arms Control Today* magazine and Associate Director, The Arms Control Association (1992-95) and, in college, a prize-winning poet and varsity quarterback. In 1967-8 he flew 275 missions as an F-100 fighter pilot in Vietnam. His 22 combat decorations included the Silver Star, three Distinguished Flying Crosses, two Vietnamese Gallantry Crosses and several single-mission Air Medals.

His M-Phil (1979) and D-Phil. (1981) degrees in international relations are from Oxford University in England. From 1989-91. He was a Professor of National Security Studies at the National War College in Washington from 1989 to '91. In 1995, he was named a Distinguished Alumnus of the University of Montana.

In his 13 years at Boston University (1995-2009), he was a department chair for three years and later, Dean of the College of Communication for three more. In 2001 he was the first recipient of the "Professor of the Year" award given by the fraternities and sororities at B.U.

He retired in 2009 and resides in Cape Charles, Virginia, with his wife, Linda.

His 36-page booklet, *Please Don't Do That! A Pocket Guide to Good Writing* (2008), was the top-selling publication at Marquette Books in 2009.

o-0-o

(Order more books or send comments to jjschulz@bu.edu)

Made in the USA
Middletown, DE
27 March 2019